Sex Differences in Antisocial Behaviour
Conduct Disorder, Delinquency, and Violence in the Dunedin Longitudinal Study

Why are females antisocial so seldom and males antisocial so often? This key question is addressed in a fresh approach to sex differences in the causes, course, and consequences of antisocial behaviour. The book presents all-new findings from a landmark investigation of 1,000 males and females studied from ages 3 to 21 years. It shows that young people develop antisocial behaviour for two main reasons. One form of antisocial behaviour is a neuro-developmental disorder afflicting males, with low prevalence in the population, early childhood onset, and subsequent persistence. The other form of antisocial behaviour, afflicting females as well as males, is common, and emerges in the context of social relationships. The book offers insights about diagnosis and measurement, the importance of puberty, the problem of partner violence, and the nature of intergenerational transmission. It puts forward a new agenda for research about both neurodevelopmental and social influences on antisocial behaviour.

TERRIE E. MOFFITT is Professor of Social Behaviour and Development at the Institute of Psychiatry, King's College, London, Professor of Psychology at the University of Wisconsin-Madison, and Associate Director of the Dunedin Multidisciplinary Health and Development Research Unit.

AVSHALOM CASPI is Professor of Personality and Social Psychology at the Institute of Psychiatry, King's College, London, and at the University of Wisconsin-Madison.

SIR MICHAEL RUTTER is Professor of Developmental Psychopathology at the Institute of Psychiatry, King's College, London, and Deputy Chairman of the Wellcome Trust.

PHIL A. SILVA is Director Emeritus of the Dunedin Multidisciplinary Health and Development Research Unit at the University of Otago School of Medicine.

D0170494

Cambridge Studies in Criminology

Editors

Alfred Blumstein, *Carnegie Mellon University*
David Farrington, *University of Cambridge*

This series publishes high-quality research monographs of either theoretical or empirical emphasis in all areas of criminology, including measurement of offending, explanations of offending, police, courts, incapacitation, corrections, sentencing, deterrence, rehabilitation, and other related topics. It is intended to be both interdisciplinary and international in scope.

Also in the series:

Sex Differences in Antisocial Behaviour

Conduct Disorder, Delinquency, and Violence in the Dunedin Longitudinal Study

Terrie E. Moffitt, Avshalom Caspi

Institute of Psychiatry, King's College London and University of Wisconsin-Madison

Michael Rutter

Institute of Psychiatry, King's College London

Phil A. Silva

University of Otago

CAMBRIDGE
UNIVERSITY PRESS

PUBLISHED BY THE PRESS SYNDICATE OF THE UNIVERSITY OF CAMBRIDGE
The Pitt Building, Trumpington Street, Cambridge, United Kingdom

CAMBRIDGE UNIVERSITY PRESS
The Edinburgh Building, Cambridge CB2 2RU, UK
40 West 20th Street, New York, NY 10011–4211, USA
10 Stamford Road, Oakleigh, VIC 3166, Australia
Ruiz de Alarcón 13, 28014 Madrid, Spain
Dock House, The Waterfront, Cape Town 8001, South Africa

http://www.cambridge.org

First published 2001

Printed in the United Kingdom at the University Press, Cambridge

Typeface 10/13 pt ITC New Baskerville   *System* QuarkXPress™   [SE]

A catalogue record for this book is available from the British Library

Library of Congress Cataloguing in Publication data

ISBN 0 521 80445 0 hardback
ISBN 0 521 01066 7 paperback

This book is dedicated to three people we admire:

Professor Emeritus Eleanor Maccoby, who pioneered the psychological study of sex differences; Professor Emeritus Lee Robins, who pioneered the longitudinal study of antisocial behaviour; and police officer and community leader Mr Paul Stevenson, who helped to gather the data for this book.

Contents

Figures

Tables

Preface

This book presents all-new findings from the Dunedin Study, which has followed 1,000 males and females from ages 3 to 21. Unlike previous studies of sex differences, we incorporate information about how antisocial behaviour changes with age over the first two decades of life, a stage when it emerges, peaks, and consolidates into antisocial disorders and serious crime. Unlike previous studies of age effects on antisocial behaviour, we incorporate information about sex differences. This novel synthetic look at age and sex opens windows on the fundamental aetiology of antisocial behaviour, ruling out some old hypotheses and pointing to some new ones. The findings will interest students of antisocial behaviour, but the questions we frame – and the analytic approaches we use to answer them – demonstrate an approach that is applicable to any behavioural problem or mental disorder showing a sex difference.

The book incorporates approaches from three disciplines: developmental psychology, psychiatry, and criminology. Using dimensional measures of antisocial behaviour, diagnostic measures of psychiatric disorders, and measures of adjudicated delinquency and violent crime, chapters examine sex differences in the developmental course, causes, correlates, and sequelae of antisocial behaviour. We test the hypothesis that girls pass a higher threshold of risk to become as antisocial as boys, finding evidence counter to the hypothesis. We test the hypothesis that the diagnostic cut-offs defining conduct disorder should be set at a lower, milder, level for girls than for boys, finding that this is not justified.

Taken together, the new findings in the book's seventeen chapters show that young people develop antisocial behaviour for two main reasons. On the one hand, one form of antisocial behaviour may be understood as a disorder having neuro-developmental origins that, alongside autism, hyperactivity, and dyslexia, shows a strong male preponderance, early childhood onset, subsequent persistence, and low prevalence in the population. The book shows that extreme sex differences are linked with this form of antisocial behaviour. This form is a good candidate phenotype for molecular and quantitative genetic research. On the other hand, the book's findings show that the bulk of antisocial behaviour, especially by females, is best understood as a social phenomenon originating in the context of social relationships, with onset in adolescence, and high prevalence. The book shows that sex differences linked with this form are negligible; for example, the antisocial activities of males and females are especially alike when alcohol and drugs are involved, near the time of female puberty, and when females are yoked with males in intimate relationships. This form needs more basic research on processes of social influence.

The book's findings point to the overarching conclusion that females' antisocial behaviour obeys the same causal laws as males'. Females are unlikely to develop the neuro-developmental form because they are unlikely to have the risk factors for it, whereas they are as likely as males to develop the socially influenced form because they share with males the risk factors for it. The book's final chapter puts forward an agenda to stimulate future research into both neuro-developmental/genetic and social-influence origins of antisocial behaviour. These are the most promising directions for basic science work on individual differences in antisocial disorders and violence.

Acknowledgements

This book was made possible by more than two decades of collaboration among Study members, scientists, and funding agencies. For painstakingly constructing the twenty-year archive of data analyzed in this book we thank the Dunedin Study members and their parents, teachers, peer-informants, and partners, the Dunedin Unit research staff, the Unit's multidisciplinary team of principal investigators, Unit director Richie Poulton, the New Zealand Police, and officer Paul Stevenson. Hona Lee Harrington, Don Lynam, and Brad Wright assisted with statistical analyses. Jay Rodger and Matt Smart provided critical technical support. Five anonymous peer reviewers helped us to improve the book. The Dunedin Study and our work were supported by the New Zealand Health Research Council, the US National Institute of Mental Health (MH45070, MH49414, MH56344), the US National Institute of Justice (94-IJ-CX0041), the William T. Grant Foundation, the University of Wisconsin Alumni Research Foundation, the UK Department of Health, and the British Medical Research Council.

CHAPTER ONE

Introduction

It is widely understood that males are generally much more antisocial than females (Cook and Laub, 1998; Eme and Kavanaugh, 1995; Giordano and Cernkovich, 1997; Rutter, Giller, and Hagell, 1998; Steffensmeier and Allan, 1996). However, the implications of this sex difference for understanding the fundamental causes of antisocial behaviour have been virtually unexplored. We think that studying sex differences across the first decades of life offers an untapped resource for uncovering the causes of antisocial behaviour. Consider two fundamental facts about the distribution of antisocial behaviour across sex and age. It shows a male preponderance, and it shows a large increase in prevalence during adolescence. Other problem behaviours increase a lot during adolescence as does antisocial behaviour, but they show a female preponderance: depression and eating disorders, for example. Generally, social and psychological explanations have been put forward to explain the female preponderance, adolescent rise, and high prevalence of these emotional problems (Bebbington, 1996; Emslie, Hunt, and MacIntyre 1999). In contrast, some problem behaviours show a strong male preponderance as does antisocial behaviour, but they do not increase at all in adolescence, for example, attention-deficit hyperactivity, language delay, reading retardation, and autism. Generally, neuro-biological explanations have been put forward to explain the male preponderance, stability across age, and low prevalence of hyperactivity, dyslexia, and autism (Earls, 1987; Eme, 1979; Ounstead and Taylor, 1972).

Antisocial behaviour seems to be the sole anomaly in this otherwise orderly scheme. There has been much speculation about heterogeneous causes behind antisocial behaviour (Caspi and Moffitt, 1995; Rutter, Giller, and Hagell, 1998), and it is possible that some antisocial behaviour resembles emotional problems in having social origins, while other antisocial behaviour resembles the neuro-developmental problems. The primary aim of this book is to sort out this anomaly by systematically analyzing the antisocial behaviour of males and females across the first two decades of life. We reasoned that a study of sex differences and similarities might uncover insights that could help to resolve the anomaly, and indeed it did.

Along the way, the secondary aim of this book is to raise the visibility of the sex difference as a critical tool for the study of all problem behaviours that have an unequal sex distribution. The empirical findings presented in the book are the results of new analyses from the Dunedin Study, not previously published. They will be of particular interest to students of antisocial behaviour. However, the questions framed in this book, and the analytic approaches that we use to answer them, are broadly applicable to the many human problems that show a sex difference. Thus, the overarching goal of this book is to pose research questions and to demonstrate analytic approaches that will be applicable to a broad spectrum of problem behaviours.

A précis of aims and findings

This section briefly highlights the aims and findings of the chapters in this book. Each empirical chapter is organized somewhat like a traditional research report. Each chapter ends with bullet points listing 'take-home messages' and 'unanswered questions'. The 'take-home messages' are intended to articulate our findings with accountability and clarity, and to make them easily accessible to a broad and busy readership. The 'unanswered questions' are intended to acknowledge the many important issues that our own study was unable to address, and to stimulate future research by articulating testable research questions.

Description of the study design
Our empirical aim is to describe the developmental epidemiology of sex differences and antisocial behaviour during the first two decades of life, in the context of one long-term longitudinal study of a contemporary representative cohort of some thousand males and females born in 1972 to 1973 – the Dunedin Multidisciplinary Health and Development Study. Chapter 2 describes the Study, its research setting and its methods, and addresses how findings from this sample may be extended to other times and places. Throughout the book, we cite related studies from other times and places, and note whether or not Dunedin Study findings are consistent with theirs.

The Study's *longitudinal design* allowed us to examine sex differences in antisocial behaviour across nine assessments spanning the period from 3 to 21 years of age, and thereby covering the peak ages for the emergence of antisocial behaviour. Many of the analyses in this book focus on *antisocial behaviour during adolescence* both as the prime outcome of childhood risk and as an important predictor of subsequent adult outcomes. We emphasize adolescence because this is the developmental stage during which antisocial behaviour peaks in onset, prevalence, and incidence, and when antisocial behaviour tends to be consolidated into the diagnosable psychiatric disorders and patterns of criminal offending that are of great concern to mental health and criminal justice professionals.

The Dunedin Study's *multiple data sources* are diverse, and include parents' reports, teachers' reports and self-reports that are collected in most longitudinal studies of this kind. In addition, we also make use of observers' ratings, official police and court records, peer-informant reports, and partners' reports. Thus, the book contains comparisons of how findings about antisocial behaviour might vary depending on the source of the data. Chapters also address questions of gender bias in measurements: are courts lenient with females? Should diagnostic criteria be relaxed for females? Is female partner violence self-defence? We present results from *two methods of quantifying antisocial behaviour*: dimensional scales of such behaviour and categorical diagnoses of conduct disorder. By undertaking parallel analyses for both methods of measurement, we are able to shed light on whether findings about the population distribution of antisocial behaviour also apply to the extreme, presumably pathological, end of the distribution (Hinshaw, Lahey, and Hart, 1993). Analyzing multiple measures of antisocial behaviour is also intended to make the book's findings relevant to the concerns of multiple disciplines. Criminologists will find official police and court records and delinquency scales familiar, while child psychiatrists may be more familiar with conduct disorder diagnoses. To help readers interpret the measures that are less familiar to them, chapters describe the content of each measure, at the item level.

Sex differences in the amount of antisocial behaviour

Despite widespread consensus that males are more antisocial than females, the question of whether this is true throughout the whole course of development, in all circumstances, and in every kind of antisocial activity, is very far from settled. Accordingly, the first aim of this book is to query the generality of the sex difference. Chapters 3 to 5 present findings on overall sex differences in the amount of antisocial behaviour, measured with dimensional variables, diagnoses of disorder, and official offending records, for both non-violent and violent acts. To our knowledge, these chapters offer one of the most comprehensive developmental portraits of sex differences in the amount of antisocial behaviour across the first two decades of life. In these descriptive chapters, as elsewhere in the book, sex differences are presented with reference to statistical effect sizes.

On the whole, the data in these three chapters confirm the ubiquity of the sex difference, but they also reveal some interesting and important lawful exceptions to this rule. In particular, males and females are remarkably similar with respect to their illicit use of drugs and with respect to their involvement in domestic violence. (Extra analyses show that the sex similarity in domestic violence applies to clinical cases of serious abuse, and is not an artefact of women's self-defence.) It is also noteworthy that sex differences are minimal with respect to the common forms of antisocial behaviour which typify the adolescent age period and which are relatively unassociated with other forms of pathology. The data demonstrate that this peak of adolescence-limited antisocial behaviour is linked, among girls, with their personal pubertal timing.

Not surprisingly, the male excess of antisocial behaviour is especially evident with respect to violent behaviour and violent crimes, as might be anticipated by the greater muscular strength of males. What was not quite so self-evident, however, is the finding detailed in chapter 16 that the male preponderance is most evident with respect to early-onset life-course-persistent antisocial behaviour. We attempted to determine whether or not this might be an artefact of the differences of overall level of antisocial behaviour between the two sexes by defining life-course-persistence according to the norms within each sex. The marked preponderance of males still held. This is an important form of antisocial behaviour in males but it is quite uncommon in females. Moreover, although the risk factors that predict life-course-persistent antisocial behaviour were the same for females as for males, the rarity of this serious form of behaviour among young women arose as a natural consequence of the rarity among girls of the risk factors for it.

Sex differences in the developmental course of antisocial behaviour

The book also aims to venture beyond the routine test for sex differences in the amount of antisocial behaviour. In seeking to understand the 'how' of the sex difference, we explore possible ways in which being male or female might influence developmental features of antisocial behaviour such as its stability over time or its age of onset. Chapters 6 and 7 compare official and self-report data and reveal that although a first 'official' offence in adulthood is not unusual, among both sexes participation in antisocial behaviour seldom begins in adulthood and almost all people who will behave antisocially do so first during adolescence. As already noted, life-course persistence was the feature that most strikingly differentiated males and females. Thus, early-onset and persistent cases of antisocial disorder are rare and tend to be male, but among the majority of young people involved in antisocial behaviour the data revealed a surprising similarity across the two sexes with respect to both stability and onset age.

Testing for sex differences in developmental processes

In our reading of the literature, we found that sex differences in the *amount* of antisocial behaviour are frequently mistaken for evidence that males and females experience different antisocial developmental processes. In fact, the extant literature contains very few actual empirical demonstrations of sex differences in the aetiological factors involved with becoming antisocial, in the correlates of antisocial behaviour, or in its long-term consequences – the topics considered in chapters 8 through 16. Thus, the aim of these nine chapters is to address this gap in the empirical data base. In the past, three forms of error may have encouraged a too-hasty belief that there are differences in the causal processes affecting males and females: insufficient statistical testing, the use of single-sex samples, and publication bias. Here we explain how these errors come about.

All too often, it is assumed that if a risk factor significantly predicts antisocial outcomes in one sex but not in the other, this means that there is a significant difference between the sexes. Obviously, this is a faulty approach because comparing two *p* values is not the same as testing whether two coefficients differ significantly from each other. Comparing findings from separate analyses for each sex readily leads to false conclusions, and a study using Monte Carlo simulations has demonstrated that this danger is exacerbated when the sample sizes are modest (Cohen, Cohen and Brook, 1995). It is highly likely that many reports of sex differences in the literature are false because these are not properly tested.

The literature is replete with studies of just one sex, usually males. Often the researchers who study males caution that their findings *may not* apply to females, but this caution is sometimes misunderstood to mean that they *cannot* apply to females. Conversely, when females alone are sampled, the sampling decision has often been based on the assumption that findings will necessarily be unique to females. All too frequently, the findings from samples of females are discussed as being female-specific, but single-sex studies cannot address the sex-specificity of their findings. The effects of sex on antisocial behaviour can be deduced only from samples that contain both males and females in sufficient numbers for appropriate statistical testing. Such research designs have been distinctly unusual in the past.

When a sex difference is found in a study, this is often reflected in the paper's title. The practice is to be expected, given the keen interest in sex differences in predictors and outcomes. Nevertheless, many reports that include both sexes check for sex interactions and, not finding any that could justify separate presentations by sex, collapse the sample. An informal survey of the literature on antisocial behaviour suggests that these 'less interesting' no-sex-difference findings are quite common. Because no-difference findings are seldom announced in the titles of papers (or in the 'key words'), they escape attention, particularly from today's computerized searches. This imbalance in paper titles contributes to a cumulative impression that sex differences are more common that sex similarities. But without an exhaustive and systematic meta-analysis, we cannot know whether or not this impression is correct. Seeking to avoid the aforementioned problems of inference, we systematically tested the Dunedin Study data base for sex differences in developmental processes.

Possible causes of sex differences in antisocial behaviour

Findings about the risk processes leading up to antisocial behaviour are presented in chapters 8, 9 and 10. Knowledge about the relevant risk factors has been greatly enhanced by the accumulation of findings from longitudinal studies (Campbell, 1995; Loeber and Hay 1997; Rutter, Giller and Hagell, 1998). From the array of possible risk factors, we identified a roster of more than thirty-five risk factors measured in the Dunedin Study, representing the domains of family life, neuro-cognitive risk, childhood behaviour, peer relations, and personality traits.

The analyses start by examining whether or not the same risk factors operate in males and females, and then go on to determine whether or not the size of effect in the two sexes differs significantly. We were aware of the much weaker statistical power for detecting significant interaction effects, as compared with that for main effects (McClelland and Judd, 1993). We paid special attention to the possibility that there might be large differences between the two sexes in risk-factor effects, even though they failed to show any significant statistical interaction. In the event, the findings showed remarkable similarities between males and females with respect to risk factors for antisocial behaviour. Chapter 8 reports that we found little evidence to suggest that males were more vulnerable to any set of risk factors than were females. Not only were much the same factors important, but the size of effects was generally comparable across the sexes.

Chapters 9 and 10 address the 'differential exposure hypothesis', namely that males are more likely to be exposed to risk factors or that they tend to be exposed to more severe risk factors. The findings were striking in showing that males *were* more likely to experience neuro-cognitive deficits, undercontrolled temperamental features, weak constraint (poor impulse control), and hyperactivity. Moreover, taken together, these risk factors accounted for most of the sex difference found in antisocial behaviour. By contrast, there was no evidence of differential exposure to family risk factors. Family risk factors *are* important for antisocial behaviour, but this is so for both males and females in roughly similar degree, and therefore family risk and protective factors cannot account for sex differences in anti-social behaviour.

Disorders that are comorbid with antisocial behaviour

Chapter 11 aims to provide epidemiological information about which other psychopathologies are experienced by antisocial individuals. Comorbid psychiatric and social problems were an essential feature of antisocial behaviour in both sexes; almost all antisocial individuals in the Dunedin sample have comorbid disorders. Attention-deficit hyperactivity, cannabis dependence, and schizophreniform symptoms are all tightly linked to conduct disorder. One particular pattern did differ by sex: as they grew to adulthood, women with conduct problems suffered at high rates from serious depression.

Sex-typed adult developmental outcomes

Chapters 13 and 14 aim to compare the early-adult outcomes of males and females who had been antisocial as adolescents, examining a broad array of adult outcomes measured at age 21 in the Dunedin Study. At this age, the sequelae of conduct problems proved to be gender-typed. A conduct-problem history predicted women's adult adjustment in relation to home life, health, and depression. In contrast, conduct problems forecast men's adjustment in relation to work, substance abuse, and the judicial crime-control system. Both antisocial males and females were highly likely to become intimate with an antisocial mate, to produce babies while they were still in their teens, and to engage in domestic violence in their homes, thus setting the stage of risk for the next generation. One key finding was that young women's delinquency was strongly exacerbated when they partnered with an antisocial mate, whereas young men were not influenced in this way, a finding pointing to the importance of social influences within intimate relationships on females' antisocial behaviour.

Three diagnostic hypotheses regarding sex differences in antisocial behaviour

Chapters 12, 15, and 16 deal with three specific hypotheses that have been put forward in relation to sex differences in antisocial behaviour. Chapter 12 tests the hypothesis that girls must pass a higher threshold of risk to become as antisocial as boys (Eme, 1992), with findings that run counter to the hypothesis. Chapter 15 tests the hypothesis that the diagnostic cut-offs that define conduct disorder should be set at a lower, milder, level for girls than for boys (Zoccolillo, 1993), again with findings that indicate that this would not be justified. Chapter 16 tests the hypothesis that the taxonomy of life-course-persistent versus adolescence-limited antisocial behaviour describes the phenomena in girls as well as it does with boys (Moffitt, 1994). Although the taxonomy certainly applies in much the same way in both sexes, life-course-persistent antisocial behaviour is a distinctly uncommon phenomenon in females, most of whom fit the adolescence-limited pattern.

Synthesis and recommendations for future research

The final chapter aims to provide a synthesis of findings from earlier chapters, and lays out an agenda for future research into antisocial behaviour. In chapter 17, we conclude that the more severe, early-onset presentation of antisocial behaviour that is typical of some 5 per cent of males is associated with neuro-cognitive features and probably involves strong genetic and other biological influences. By contrast, females' antisocial involvement tends to fluctuate much more according to circumstances, suggesting that the variety of antisocial involvement that is more typical of females is particularly influenced by social factors. Indeed, in contrast to the assumption that socialization generates sex differences, we found evidence that socialization effects may generate sex similarities in antisocial behaviour. In particular, the findings point to the conclusion that, with regard to socialization influences, male peers play a prominent role in shaping the antisocial behaviour of females.

Chapter 17 derives five research priorities from the findings in this book: (1) investigating the origins of sex differences in individual-level neuro-developmental problems and the risk processes associated with them; (2) investigating the extent to which the same neuro-developmental risk factors operate in the same way across problem behaviours that show a male preponderance; (3) investigating social-contextual influences on anti-social behaviour, especially influences from peers and intimate partners; (4) comparing the effects of high-risk environments on brothers and sisters, with particular attention to person–environment correlations and interactions; and (5) investigating sex differences in other problem behaviours, using strategies similar to those employed here.

CHAPTER TWO

The Dunedin Multidisciplinary Health and Development Study

The 1,000 young people we describe in this book are members of an unselected birth cohort that represents a wide range of social origins. Since their births in 1972–3 they have been members of an ongoing longitudinal study called the Dunedin Multidisciplinary Health and Development Study. Their problem behaviour has been assessed repeatedly during their lives, as shown in table 2.1. Although in this book we examine data from all of the assessments, from age 3 to age 21, many of the analyses focus especially on the developmental period when participation in antisocial behaviour peaks, between ages 13 and 21. Thus, the data presented here describe the behaviour of the age cohort that contributed an extremely large proportion to their nation's crime rate between 1985 and 1995.

The Dunedin Multidisciplinary Health and Development Study is ideally designed for three types of research: (1) prediction studies of the childhood correlates of later health and behaviour outcomes, (2) developmental studies of continuity and change in health and behaviour, and (3) epidemiological studies of the prevalence and incidence of health problems and behaviour problems, and associations among problem types. This book presents all three types of analysis.

Description of the research sample and Study design

Sample

The history of the Study and its design features have been described in detail in a book prepared by the team of investigators (Silva and Stanton, 1996). Briefly, the Study is a longitudinal investigation of the health, development,

Table 2.1. *The Dunedin Multidisciplinary Health and Development Study: members of the sample assessed at each age*

Year	Phase	Assessment birthday	Reporting period	Number eligible	Number seen	% seen
1972–3	I	Birth	Birth	1,661	1,661	100
1975–6	III	3	2–3	1,139[a]	1,037	91
1977–8	V	5	4–5	1,037	991	96
1979–80	VII	7	6–7	1,035[b]	954	92
1981–2	IX	9	8–9	1,035[b]	955	92
1983–4	XI	11	10–11	1,033[b]	925	90
1985–6	XIII	13	12–13	1,031[b]	850	82
1987–8	XV	15	14–15	1,029[b]	976	95
1990–1	XVIII	18	17–18	1,027[b]	993	97
1993–4	XXI	21	20–21	1,020[b]	992	97

Notes:
[a] Number resident in Otago (province).
[b] Surviving Study members.

and behaviour of a complete cohort of births between 1 April 1972 and 31 March 1973, in Dunedin, a provincial capital city of 120,000 on New Zealand's South Island. Perinatal data were obtained at delivery, and when the children were later traced for follow-up at age three, 1,037 (91 per cent of the eligible births, of whom 52 per cent were boys and 48 per cent were girls) participated in the assessment, forming the base sample for the longitudinal study.

With regard to social origins, the children's fathers were representative of the social class distribution in the general population of similar age in New Zealand's South Island. With regard to racial distribution, the Study members are of predominantly white European ancestry, which matches the ethnic distribution of New Zealand's South Island. When the Study members were born, fewer than 2 per cent of their mothers identified their babies as Maori or Pacific Islander, while 18 years later fewer than 7 per cent of the Study members identified themselves as having Maori or Pacific Islander ancestry. About half of the Study members still live in or near their birth city, Dunedin. The rest have primarily emigrated as young adults to other cities in New Zealand and Australia, and a minority are now living in Great Britain, North America and Asia.

Assessment procedures

In the Dunedin Study, each assessment is called a 'phase', named for the cohort's birthday; for example, phase XV indicates that data were gathered at or near the Study members' fifteenth birthdays. Almost all Study members are assessed at the Unit within sixty days of their birthday. As table 2.1 shows, for measures that use a past-twelve-month reporting period, as do all of the measures of antisocial behaviour and mental health, the respondents describe the twelve months prior to the current birthday. For example, phase XV data describe the period between the fourteenth and fifteenth birthdays, while Study members were actually aged 14. When considering age-related findings, such as those about age of onset, it is helpful to keep in mind that the data describe an age one year earlier than is implied by the convention of naming the Dunedin Study phases. We will mention this again at relevant points in the book.

The procedure for assessing the Dunedin Study members differs from that of other studies. Other studies generally assess behaviour problems by administering questionnaires in the classroom or through the post, by conducting telephone interviews, or by sending interviewers to the home. In the Dunedin Study, members are invited to spend a day at the research Unit at each assessment phase for private interviews and examinations. The Unit assumes Study members' costs to remove all barriers to their participation, for example, travel, lost wages, child care. The Unit's location provides privacy away from teachers or family members. All assessments are conducted through oral interviews, and thus reading difficulties do not affect the quality of the data. Interviewers hold tertiary degrees, and generally they have experience in related fields such as psychology, social work, nursing, or teaching. Although the assessment instruments are standardized, the interviewers are skilled in matching the questions to each Study member's vocabulary to diminish the effects of poor comprehension on the quality of the data.

On average there are eight assessment modules in each phase; for example, modules within one phase might include delinquency, dental examination, mental health, injuries, partner relationships, physical examination, labour-force experiences, asthma and allergies. Passive interviews, active examinations, breaks for tea or lunch, and walks between buildings are interspersed to help Study members keep alert and engaged. Each of the various research modules is presented in a different room by different interviewers who are blind to the Study members' responses to other modules. This practice is designed to diminish the artefactual inflation of effect sizes by shared method variance that plagues studies using measures collected on the same questionnaire, or in the same interview. The modules are presented in counter-balanced order across Study members, to prevent precedence effects or fatigue effects. Study members know that the time for each module's session is pre-established and they plan to spend the full day at the Unit, so they experience little motivation to hasten the end of the assessment by giving answers of 'no'. We believe that these features of data collection at the research Unit contribute to inferential power. Field interviews are available for Study members who are unable or unwilling to visit the Unit, but at each phase only about 5 per cent request a field interview.

Study members give consent separately for each module, but usually fewer than ten Study members refuse any particular module. The Study members have a life-long history of reporting sensitive personal information to us repeatedly, with no past breach of confidentiality. In addition, Study members know that the Unit directors will not intervene in their lives unless there is an emergent life-threatening matter. Thus, we believe that by the time they reached adolescence the Study members became willing to provide frank reports about sensitive topics such as their antisocial behaviours.

Structure of the data set for measuring antisocial behaviours

Table 2.2 presents an overview of the Study's measures of antisocial behaviour that were used in this book. In this section we introduce the Dunedin Study's measurement strategy and the resulting overall structure of the set of measures. In later sections, each measure will be described as it is used for analysis.

Because individuals undergo remarkable developmental changes during the two decades of life covered by this study, so too must the measures used to capture behavioural differences among individuals. Accordingly, as table 2.2 shows, we examine somewhat different measures under the antisocial conceptual label at different ages. There are three reasons for this. First, some constructs change their behavioural expression with age. For example, 'antisocial behaviour' in adolescence may be expressed in criminal offending such as car theft, but in early childhood it may be expressed in rough, uncontrolled behaviour such as biting or teasing other children. Whereas biting peers may have disappeared by adolescence car theft has not yet emerged in childhood. However, developmental research indicates that these behaviours may be linked in a pattern of 'heterotypic' continuity, in

Table 2.2. *Antisocial behaviour measures across time[a] and circumstance[b] in the Dunedin Study*

	Difficult temperament	Antisocial behaviour problems	Symptoms of antisocial disorder	Self-reported offending	Official criminal and delinquent offending	'Delinquent reputation'	Violence against a partner
Age 3 1975	Psychometrist ratings						
Age 5 1977	Psychometrist ratings	Teacher ratings Parent ratings					
Age 7 1979		Teacher ratings Parent ratings					
Age 9 1981		Teacher ratings Parent ratings					
Age 11 1983		Teacher ratings Parent ratings	DISC-C conduct disorder symptom scale and DSM-IV diagnosis		Police arrests		
Age 13 1985		Teacher ratings Parent ratings	DISC-C conduct disorder symptom scale and DSM-IV diagnosis	Self-reported delinquency	Police arrests Court convictions		
Age 15 1987		Parent ratings	DISC-C conduct disorder symptom scale and DSM-IV diagnosis	Self-reported delinquency	Police arrests Court convictions		
Age 18 1990			DIS-IIIR conduct disorder symptom scale and DSM-IV diagnosis	Self-reported delinquency	Court convictions	Peer informant reports	
Age 21 1993			DIS-IIIR symptom scale and antisocial personality disorder diagnosis	Self-reported crimes	Court convictions	Peer informant reports	Self-report of physical abuse Partner's report of abuse

Notes:

[a] Time = 19 years.

[b] Circumstance = across lab, home, school, public and peer settings.

which different behaviours at different ages appear to belong to the same equivalence class (Kagan, 1969). Accordingly, we measure age-appropriate behaviours at successive phases of the Study.

Second, different data sources are often needed to assess similar constructs at different ages. For example, self-reports can be reliable and valid during adolescence, but they were not an option in the Study members' early childhood. Parents and teachers may be good reporters about Study members' behaviours when they are children, but in adolescence much antisocial behaviour is concealed from parents and teachers, and by adulthood peers and partners know Study members' behaviour best. Accordingly, we rely on age-appropriate data sources at different ages.

Third, some constructs are not developmentally appropriate – or cannot be measured at certain ages. For example, court convictions for criminal offences are not made before age 13 in New Zealand's justice system. As another example, teacher reports of antisocial behaviour at school were not collected at phase 15 or after because age 15 was the end of compulsory schooling for our cohort, and we expected that the most antisocial individuals would selectively leave school, leading to a truncated range of teacher reports thereafter. Similarly, we first measured partner abuse at phase 21 because this was the first phase in which the majority of Study members would have a serious relationship. Accordingly, we measure different constructs that are part of the antisocial syndrome at different phases of the Study.

As shown by table 2.2, an important advantage of the data set constructed for the Dunedin sample is that antisocial behaviour has been measured from a variety of different reporting sources (e.g., observers, parents, teachers, partners, peer informants, police, courts, and the Study members themselves) using a variety of different methods (observations in the Unit, behaviour problem checklists, diagnostic interviews, and official records). This multi-modal measurement strategy samples behaviours from different ecological settings to maximize accurate coverage of behaviour that is by nature undesirable, often illegal, and therefore concealed. Multi-modal measurement also counterbalances the weaknesses of any particular measure with the complementary strengths of another measure. This is particularly the case for gathering both conviction records (which establish that antisocial acts are consequential, but woefully undercount them) and self-reports of delinquency (which more accurately portray the amount of offences, but unavoidably mix trivial acts with consequential acts). Finally, multi-modal measurement allows findings to generalize to the theoretical construct of antisocial behaviour, transcending the bounds of any particular measurement approach.

Sample attrition and missing data

The validity and generalizability of conclusions about antisocial behaviour are compromised when individuals are lost from longitudinal study in a non-random way, and it is thus imperative for natural history studies of antisocial behaviour to maintain their samples intact for as long as possible (Magnusson and Bergman, 1990). Table 2.1 reveals two important points about sample attrition and missing data in the Dunedin Study. First, the table shows that more than 97 per cent of the original Study members continued to participate in the most recent assessment which was conducted in 1993–4, when the Study members were 21 years old. Participation dropped below 90 per cent only at phase 13. Second, the table shows that attrition in the Dunedin Study has not been cumulative; that is, Study members who did not participate at some earlier phases did participate again at later phases. For example, whereas the highest participation rates were obtained at phases 5 and 21, the lowest participation rate was obtained at phase 13. This fluctuation in participation rates has led to missing data for many Study members on one or two measures of antisocial behaviour at some point in their lives.

Data on 16 antisocial measures were especially important for this book: parent and teacher ratings at ages 5, 7, 9, 11, and 13, parent ratings at 15, and self-reports of antisocial behaviour at ages 11, 13, 15, 18, and 21. To test whether or not missing data for any of the 16 focal variables introduced systematic bias to the study we created a missing-case indicator for each measure, where $0 = $ not missing and $1 = $ missing. We then correlated each of these 16 indicators with the scores on antisocial behaviour for cases who had present data on each of the 16 focal measures, generating a 16 by 16 correlation matrix with 240 unique coefficients. Only 26 of the 240 coefficients were statistically significant, the number expected by chance. The 26 significant correlations were small, ranging in magnitude from 0.08 to 0.18. Moreover, the 26 significant coefficients appeared randomly throughout the matrix, and thus did not indicate replicated bias for any age or reporting source. For example, cases who had missing parent reports at age 11 were rated as significantly more antisocial by their teachers at age 13 ($r = 0.18$), but they were not rated as more antisocial by their parents at age 13 ($r = 0.03$), nor had they been rated as more antisocial by their teachers earlier in the study. On the whole, these results suggest that cases missing data from any one source at any one age were not systematically more antisocial than cohort members who had present data.

Fortunately, because most of the Study members with missing data on one of the sixteen focal measures did have present data on the other measures, it was possible to substitute missing scores so that those Study members who were missing data on only one or two of the sixteen antisocial measures could be retained for our analyses. We used a strategy for substitution of missing data points that has the important advantages of preserving the distributional characteristics of the original variables and preserving the original correlations among variables.

Where possible, missing scores were substituted for each of the variables in turn, as follows: first, variable X was regressed upon variable Y. In all cases X and Y were measured from the same source (i.e., teacher, parent, or self). In all cases Y was measured at an age adjacent to X. In virtually all cases the correlation between the original X and Y exceeded 0.50, suggesting that Y was a good statistical predictor of X. Next, the resulting regression equation was solved and the predicted scores for X were retained. Finally, for any Study member with missing data on X, the predicted score was substituted. The number of cases of missing-data substitutions made across the sixteen variables ranged from 2 per cent (for self-report delinquency at 15) to 25 per cent (for self-reported delinquency at 13), averaging 4 per cent of cases with substituted scores per variable. In no case were more than two substitutions made among the sixteen measures for any particular Study member who was studied for this book. For this book, we analyzed individual measures of antisocial behaviour one by one, but we also constructed two measures of antisocial behaviour using multiple measures across sources and ages: chapter 4 introduces a dichotomous lifetime diagnosis of conduct disorder constructed for 1,012 Study members, and chapter 8 introduces a continuously distributed composite measure of antisocial behaviour during adolescence constructed for 956 Study members. Throughout the book we address missing data concerns by reporting the sample size for each of the analyses, and by testing and reporting any effects of missing data on the correlates of antisocial behaviour.

The New Zealand research setting

Social context

New Zealand has experienced astonishing economic and social change in recent years. A country that once prompted visitors from the northern hemisphere to observe 'New Zealand is so charming, just like home in the 1950s', is now a vibrant, technologically advanced Pacific Rim nation, with all the social and economic malaise that attends modernity. In this section we have elected to describe New Zealand as it was during the period when the Dunedin Study members were between 13 and 19 years old, the time when the cohort became involved in delinquent offending. Information about New Zealand during this period was taken from the annual *New Zealand Yearbooks* (published by Statistics New Zealand) which provide information about the nation based on the 1986 and 1991 censuses. We also include some statistics from New Zealand's 1996 census, to describe the circumstances under which the cohort entered young adulthood.

Like the United States and Canada, New Zealand is a 'young' nation. It was first colonized by Europeans about 150 years ago and the Treaty of Waitangi between Great Britain and the indigenous Maori peoples was signed in 1840. New Zealand is a monarchy with a parliamentary government and 3.5 million citizens. New Zealand may be thought of as a 'social democracy'; approximately 60 per cent of the national budget is spent for health care, education, and social welfare services. Some statistics are available to allow comparison between New Zealand and other countries on demographic factors that are thought to be related to rates of antisocial behaviour.

ETHNIC DIVERSITY

The New Zealand population is ethnically homogeneous; 80 per cent of New Zealanders are born in New Zealand of European descent, 12.4 per cent identify themselves as Maori, and the remainder are immigrants from northern Europe, Great Britain, and Pacific Island nations such as Tonga or Samoa. The South Island, where the Dunedin Study members were born, is less ethnically diverse than the North Island.

URBANIZATION AND POPULATION DENSITY

New Zealand is one of the most urbanized countries in the world, with 84 per cent of New Zealanders living in towns and cities, and more than 50 per cent of the population living in one of the country's four largest cities; Dunedin was the fourth largest during the first two decades of the Study members lives. This urbanization has been described as 'suburbanization', because 69 per cent of New Zealanders live in single-family houses, and only 8 per cent live in buildings of three or more apartments. Accordingly, population density is 12 persons per square kilometer (km^2), as compared to 2 per km^2 in Australia, 26 per km^2 in the United States, 19 in Sweden, and 328 in Japan.

AGE DISTRIBUTION

Like many western nations, New Zealand's population is greying; the median age in 1986 was 31 years, and only 20 per cent of the population was in the 10–19 age group who are at risk for delinquency. Life expectancy for New Zealanders matches that for Americans and citizens of the United Kingdom, 78 years for women and 72 years for men.

STANDARD OF LIVING

New Zealanders enjoy a good standard of living. Yearly private consumption per capita in 1987 (in rounded American dollars) was $6,000 for New Zealanders, $7,000 for Australians, $12,000 for Americans, $7,000 for Swedes, and $7,000 for Japanese. Infant mortality in 1991 (in deaths per 1,000 live births) was 8 in New Zealand, 7 in Australia, 9 in the United States, 6 in Sweden, and 5 in Japan. New Zealand was historically an agricultural economy, but today, as the Dunedin Study members enter the labour force, the manufacturing sector employs 23.5 per cent of all workers in New Zealand, a figure comparable to other developed countries such as Australia (24 per cent), the United States (25 per cent), and the United Kingdom (28 per cent). The percentage employed in the New Zealand services sector (66 per cent) is only slightly less than in the aforementioned comparison countries (71 per cent, 72 per cent, and 69 per cent) whereas the percentage employed in agriculture is higher, but small (11 per cent, 5 per cent, 3 per cent, and 2 per cent). On the United Nations' 'Human Development Index' (a composite of life expectancy, adult literacy, mean years of schooling, and gross domestic product per capita), New Zealand ranked ninth in 1994 among the world's countries. For comparison, the USA ranked fourth, and the United Kingdom ranked fifteenth.

UNEMPLOYMENT

Unemployment has been a serious problem for the generation of New Zealand's young people that is represented by the Dunedin birth cohort (Prime Ministerial Task Force on Employment 1994; Statistics New Zealand 1994). Until 1977 the unemployment rate in New Zealand remained below 1 per cent, whereas in most countries in the Organisation for Economic Cooperation and Development (OECD) it was between 3 per cent and 6 per cent. The New Zealand unemployment rate climbed to 5 per cent in the period between 1977 and 1986, prompted in part by reductions in trade agreements between New Zealand and Europe. The period between 1986 and 1991, when the Study members expected to leave high school to enter the labour force, saw New Zealand struggle to enter new international markets. This struggle produced dramatic labour-market changes in terms of job loss, types of jobs available, and technological development. During this period, the Labour government exited and new deregulation and restructuring policies – combined with the crash in the share market in 1987 – conspired to raise the unemployment rate to 10.1 per cent by 1992–1993, more than 2 points above the OECD average. By the early 1990s, New Zealand had begun to succeed in reaching Asian markets. Exports to Asia had increased by more than one-third between 1983 and 1993, whereas exports to the United Kingdom had decreased by half. However, New Zealand's economy became closely tied to Asian economies just as they began to falter in the late 1990s, precipitating new economic problems for New Zealand and for the Dunedin Study members as young adults.

National unemployment rates conceal much higher rates among teenagers and young adults. In 1993–4, when the Study members were interviewed at age 21, although the national unemployment rate was 10 per cent, among 15- to 24-year-olds it was about 18 per cent and for young workers with no high-school qualifications the unemployment rate was near 50 per cent. In the Dunedin birth cohort, 30 per cent experienced six months or more of unemployment between ages 15 and 21 (defined as unoccupied and actively searching for work), and 17 per cent were unemployed for more than a year. The transition from school to work in New Zealand is not 'smoothed' for young adults – there are no large-scale fully subsidized work schemes, and New Zealand's expenditure on 'active' labour market programmes (e.g., training for the unemployed, subsidized employment programmes) falls slightly below the OECD median at around 0.7 per cent of GDP. In general, the process of labour-market entry in New Zealand is similar to that in developed nations such as the United States, where young adults must rely primarily on their own initiative to secure employment (Prime Ministerial Task Force on Employment 1994).

FAMILY COMPOSITION
New Zealand's family structure is rapidly changing. Fewer than 5 per cent of marriages ended in divorce in 1986. However, this low rate should be understood in the context of a corresponding low rate of marriage. Among young New Zealanders, the median age at first marriage in 1996 was 29 for men and 27 for women. The prevalence of *de facto* cohabitation outside marriage increased by 46 per cent between 1991 and 1996, 1 in 10 couples living together were unmarried, and 80 per cent of those New Zealanders reporting *de facto* status on the 1996 census were between 20 and 34 years old.

Marriage patterns have implications for children: 52 per cent of 1995 babies were born to single mothers or to unmarried couples, as compared with only 8 per cent 25 years earlier. These changes in family structure have been linked with changing social norms and the increasing availability of social welfare benefits for single parents.

Comparison of behavioural problems in New Zealand and other countries

Cross-national comparisons of social-problem indicators lend some confidence about the generalizability of findings from the Dunedin Study to other industrialized countries. Prevalence rates of psychiatric disorders such as major depression (17 per cent), antisocial personality (3 per cent), and alcohol dependence (10 per cent) in the Dunedin sample at age 21 (Newman *et al.*, 1996) match closely the rates at this age period from the two nationally representative US surveys (Kessler *et al.*, 1994; Robins and Regier, 1991). Problem drinking is a major public health issue in New Zealand. A 1986 epidemiological survey of one of New Zealand's four largest cities revealed that 19 per cent of adults met formal diagnostic criteria for a psychiatric disorder of alcohol abuse or dependence during that year. An *additional* 17 per cent had experienced problem drinking at some time in their lives (Wells *et al.*, 1991).

New Zealand also resembles other western nations in rates of crime and violence. Prevalence rates of women victimized by severe physical domestic violence in the Dunedin sample at age 21 (13 per cent) match closely rates for this age group from the two nationally representative US surveys (cf. Magdol *et al.*, 1997; Fagan and Browne, 1994). The annual prevalence rate of victim-reported crime victimization from a national survey in New Zealand (28 per cent) matches closely rates from national victimization surveys in the Netherlands, Canada, Australia, and the US (van Dijk and Mayhew, 1992). Although the US rate of homicide is higher, probably reflecting the lethality of readily available firearms, the rates of crimes such as assault, rape, robbery, burglary, and car theft are comparable across the five countries. Prevalence rates of self-reported delinquent property, violence, and drug offending in the Dunedin sample match closely rates from surveys in fourteen other developed countries, including the US (Junger-Tas, Terlouw and Klein, 1994). In addition to similarity in the prevalence rates of many social problems, our own replication analyses suggest that the predictors of problem behaviour outcomes are the same across the Dunedin sample and a comparison Pittsburgh sample of white and black youth (Moffitt *et al.*, 1995). Throughout this book we will provide more detailed comparisons of our findings to findings obtained in other studies conducted in other nations. Comparisons of similarities, and especially the detection of differences, may help to identify areas where further research is needed.

Comparison of this cohort versus other historical periods

A limitation of all longitudinal studies, including the Dunedin Study, is their historical specificity (Cohen, Slomkowski, and Robins, 1999). This is because simple longitudinal studies assess members of a single birth cohort. Even cohort-sequential designs enrol multiple cohorts separated by only a few years, and thus have limited capacity to reflect major socio-historical shifts. Accordingly, it is unknown to what extent knowledge about the developmental epidemiology of antisocial behaviour is historically specific. Comparisons of findings about antisocial behaviour across historical periods would be useful – as has been shown by analyses of crime trends (e.g., Cook and Laub, 1998; Rutter and Smith, 1995) – but developmental epidemiology is a new field and strong research designs for estimating epidemiological facts about child and adolescent antisocial behaviour have only become available *during* the life span of the Dunedin Study members. In fact, it is of historical interest that the Dunedin Study was one of the first epidemiological studies to use a diagnostic system (DSM-III) to estimate the prevalence and incidence of conduct disorder (Anderson *et al.*, 1987). The very first epidemiological study of childhood antisocial behaviour is generally acknowledged to have been the Isle of Wight Study, conducted as recently as the late 1960s (Rutter, Tizard, and Whitmore, 1970). We hope that this book about the developmental epidemiology of sex differences among children born in the early 1970s will stimulate further tests in samples from more recent birth cohorts, and thereby generate more sound information about the development of antisocial behaviour.

Sex differences in the amount of antisocial behaviour: dimensional measures

Do males and females differ in their antisocial behaviour? This question has been addressed by developmental psychologists, social psychologists, psychiatrists, and criminologists. The answers provided are not always exactly the same for several reasons. First, different disciplines measure different behaviours that may or may not measure the same latent variable. For example, whereas child psychologists often focus on behaviours in situ such as rough-and-tumble play, criminologists tend to index antisocial behaviour through official records of conviction for crime. Second, different disciplines focus on antisocial behaviour at different points in the life span. Developmental researchers tend to focus on the early years of life, psychiatrists focus on adolescents, social psychologists focus on college students in their late teens and early twenties, and criminologists focus on older juveniles and adults. Third, different disciplines often rely on different methods to measure antisocial behaviour. For example, developmentalists often rely on observational methods, social psychologists rely on standardized experimental paradigms to elicit analogue responses, psychiatrists use diagnostic data gathered via parental and self-reports, and criminologists favor still different types of data, such as self-report interviews and police and court records.

These methodological factors tend to covary within discipline. For example, observational studies of naturalistic behaviours are primarily restricted to younger populations, whereas criminological studies of court records are generally restricted to older populations. What is remarkable is that despite such wide divergence in definition, sampling, and measurement, males consistently emerge as more antisocial than females (see, e.g., reviews by Bettencourt and Miller, 1996; Eagly and Steffen, 1986; Elliott,

Huizinga, and Menard, 1989; Hyde, 1984; Junger-Tas, Terlouw, and Klein, 1994; Knight, Fabes, and Higgins, 1996; Kruttschnitt, 1994; Maccoby and Jacklin, 1980; Rutter, Giller, and Hagell, 1998; Smith and Visher, 1980). Even national surveys of victimization experiences reveal that more victims identify their perpetrators as having been male (Sampson and Lauritsen, 1994).

In this chapter we undertake a systematic examination of sex differences in antisocial behaviour. In the first section of this chapter, we examine sex differences in reports of antisocial behaviour obtained via parent-, teacher-, self-, and informant-reports. In the second section, we examine sex differences in official records of antisocial behaviour. In the final section, we examine sex differences in the frequency of different types of offences. Sex differences in diagnosed conduct disorder will be examined in chapter 4 and sex differences in physical violence will be examined in chapter 5.

A. SEX DIFFERENCES IN MEAN LEVELS OF ANTISOCIAL BEHAVIOUR

We begin our examination of sex differences in antisocial behaviour by surveying reports of antisocial behaviour, from age 5 to age 21, obtained from four independent data sources: parents, teachers, the Study members themselves, and informants nominated by them.

Method

Measures
Each of the measures described in this section has been published earlier in the course of the longitudinal study. All have reliabilities >0.70. For each measure, we cite a methodological paper from the Dunedin Study that may be consulted for further details.

PARENT REPORTS OF ANTISOCIAL BEHAVIOUR
At ages 5, 7, 9, and 11 parents completed the Rutter Child Scale (RCS; Rutter, Tizard, and Whitmore, 1970; see also Elander and Rutter 1996 for review), a questionnaire that enquires about the major areas of a child's behavioural and emotional functioning during the past year. Parents rate each behaviour on the RCS as does not apply (0), applies somewhat (1), or certainly applies (2). As a measure of antisocial behaviour we used scores

from the 11-item 'antisocial' scale. Items describe children who frequently fight, bully other children, lie, disobey, steal, truant, destroy property, and have irritable tempers. Details about the reliability and validity of this scale in the Dunedin Study are available in McGee, Williams, and Silva (1985a). At ages 13 and 15, parents filled out the Revised Behaviour Problem Checklist (RBPC; Quay and Peterson, 1987), which contains more extensive and age-appropriate items than the RCS. Items were scored 0, 1, or 2, as they were for the RCS. The Social Aggression and Conduct Problems subscales of the RBPC were averaged to create a single measure of parent-reported antisocial behaviour at ages 13 and 15. Details about the reliability and validity of this scale are available in Caspi *et al.* (1995).

TEACHER REPORTS OF ANTISOCIAL BEHAVIOUR

At ages 5, 7, 9, 11, and 13 teachers completed the teacher version of the Rutter Child Scale (Rutter *et al.*, 1970), scored in the same way as its parent counterpart. Details about the reliability and validity of this scale are available in McGee, Williams and Bradshaw (1985).

SELF-REPORTS OF ANTISOCIAL BEHAVIOUR

At age 11, we constructed a self-reported measure of antisocial behaviour by summing items ('symptoms') endorsed by the child in the course of the conduct-disorder section of the Diagnostic Interview Schedule for Children (DISC-C), described in greater detail in chapter 4. The seven items include self-reports of physical fights, destroying property, telling lies, truanting, and stealing. At age 13, the Self-Reported Early Delinquency interview (SRED) was administered to the Study members. Details about the validity and reliability of this instrument in the Dunedin Study are available in Moffitt and Silva (1988). The SRED contains twenty-nine items tapping 'norm violating' behaviours and twenty-nine items tapping more serious illegal behaviours. Here we use only the illegal behaviour scale, which includes vandalism, shoplifting, alcohol and drug use, carrying a weapon, car theft, and physical assaults. At age 15, the 29-item illegal scale was re-administered to all Study members. At ages 18 and 21, the Self-Reported Delinquency interview was administered to the Study members. This standardized instrument was developed by Elliott and Huizinga (1989) for the National Youth Survey (Elliott *et al.*, 1983) and enquires about forty-eight different illegal acts that the Study members committed during the past twelve months, including self-reported violence, theft, and drug- and alcohol-related offences (see Section C of this chapter). Details about the reliability and validity of this instrument in the Dunedin study are available in Moffitt *et al.* (1994).

The reporting period for each of the self-report interviews from ages 11 to 21 was the past twelve months. At each age the Study members were interviewed about their participation in antisocial behaviour by examiners who were blind to their scores on other variables. For each age, we created a variety scale to index how many different antisocial acts the Study member committed at least once during the past twelve months. Variety scores are useful for individual-differences research for several reasons. First, they show the extent of involvement in different types of crimes, a variable that has been found to be a highly reliable predictor of future antisocial outcomes (Robins, 1978). Second, they are less skewed than frequency scores, although they are highly correlated with them (e.g., 0.70 in this sample). Third, they give equal weight to all delinquent acts, unlike frequency scores, which give more weight to minor crimes that are committed frequently (e.g., underage drinking) and less weight to serious, less frequent crimes (e.g., rape). Indeed, the use of variety scores to index individual differences in antisocial behaviour is endorsed by criminologists: 'It appears that the best available operational measure of the propensity to offend is a count of the number of distinct problem behaviours engaged in by a youth (that is a variety scale)' (Hirschi and Gottfedson, 1995, p. 134).

INFORMANT REPORTS OF ANTISOCIAL BEHAVIOUR

At ages 18 and 21, Study members were asked to nominate a friend, partner, or family member who knew them well, and to give us informed consent to send those informants a mail questionnaire. At each age, informants responded to four items that enquired about the Study members' antisocial behaviour during the last twelve months: 'problems with aggression, such as fighting or controlling anger', 'doing things against the law, such as stealing or vandalism', 'problems related to the use of alcohol', and 'problems related to the use of marijuana or other drugs'. These items were coded as: (0) doesn't apply, (1) applies somewhat, and (2) certainly applies. Details about the reliability and validity of this measure in the Dunedin Study are available in Krueger *et al.* (1994).

Data analysis approach

Because different measures of antisocial behaviour were administered to different reporting sources at different ages, we standardized each of the measures within age using the z-score transformation; each measure of antisocial behaviour thus had a mean of 0 and a standard deviation of 1. This procedure allowed us to compare the magnitude of sex differences observed at different ages and using different sources. We performed t-tests on each of the measures to test for mean-level differences between males and females.

In addition to indicating which differences are statistically significant, it is possible, using the z-scores reported to calculate the effect sizes of the obtained sex differences, using the formula,

$$d = (M_m - M_f)/sd,$$

where M_m is the male mean, M_f is the female mean, and sd is the standard deviation taken over the whole sample. Operationally defined, $d = 0.2$ is a small effect size, $d = 0.5$ is a medium effect size, and $d = 0.8$ is a large effect size (Cohen, 1992).

Results

Table 3.1 shows the mean z-scores, standardized for the whole sample (males and females) within each age period, from age 5 to age 21. As table 3.1 shows, the data sources covaried with age. During the first decade of life, only parents and teachers provided information about the children's anti-social behaviour. Moving into the third decade of life, parents and teachers were no longer considered to be sufficiently well-informed about the activities of the Study members and so we turned to self- and informant-reports of antisocial behaviour. What was remarkable was the consistency of the results across age and data sources. At almost every age and with almost every data source, males and females differed in their antisocial behaviour by around a 0.25 standard deviation unit difference, a small effect size.

There were two deviations from this general pattern. The first was that an especially large sex difference emerged between ages 17 and 21. However, this increased sex difference was confined to self-reports of anti-social behaviour and was not paralleled by a larger than expected difference in informant reports of antisocial behaviour. It could be that the larger sex difference in self-reported delinquency observed at phases 18 and 21 is a methodological artefact. The self-reported delinquency interview at phases 18 and 21 contained a greater variety of offences than the interview at phases 13 and 15 and, to some extent, the wording of the questions in the version of the instrument used at the older ages highlighted the severity of the acts to a greater extent (e.g., 'going around with a group

Table 3.1. *Mean z-scores for males and females on measures of antisocial behaviours, standardized for the whole sample within age, for boys and girls*

	Age 5	Age 7	Age 9	Age 11	Age 13	Age 15	Age 18	Age 21
Parent reports[a]								
male mean	0.11	0.12	0.13	0.08	0.10	0.05		
female mean	−0.11	−0.12	−0.13	−0.09	−0.11	−0.05		
Teacher reports								
male mean	0.13	0.09	0.16	0.16	0.18			
female mean	−0.14	−0.10	−0.17	−0.17	−0.19			
Self-reports[b]								
male mean				0.16	0.15	0.10	0.28	0.31
female mean				−0.17	−0.16	−0.10	−0.30	−0.33
Informant reports								
male mean							0.13	0.16
female mean							−0.13	−0.15
Mean effect size of the sex difference in antisocial behaviours								
SD units	0.25	0.21	0.30	0.28	0.30	0.15	0.42	0.48

Notes:
all means are significantly different at $p < 0.01$ except parent report at age 15.
Group Ns range from 453–519 for boys and 459–488 for girls.
[a] At phases 5–11 parent reports were obtained from the Rutter Child Scale; at phases 13–15 from the Revised Behaviour Problem Checklist.
[b] At phase 11 self-reports were obtained from the DISC-C; at phases 13–15 from the SRED, and at phases 18–21 from the SRD.

of 3 or more getting into fights' at phases 13 and 15 vs 'gang fighting' at phases 18 and 21).

The second deviation from the overall pattern of sex differences is that the narrowest sex difference emerged in middle adolescence. Whether we examine the pattern of sex differences across age using parental reports (the first row of table 3.1) or self-reports (the third row of table 3.1), males and females were least likely to differ in their antisocial behaviour between 14 and 15 years of age. The size of the parent-reported phase-15 sex difference was less than half (45 per cent) of the parent-reported sex differences at the other ages and the size of the self-reported phase-15 sex difference was likewise only 43 per cent of the self-reported sex differences at the other ages. We shall return to discuss this finding in chapter 4, where we will see that the period between ages 13 to 15 also brings with it the smallest sex difference in the prevalence of diagnoses of conduct disorder.

Comment: cross-national replication

An important limitation of our analysis is that it is based on a single birth cohort growing up in one nation. However, cross-national comparisons lend support to our conclusions. A comparison of parent-reported externalizing problems showed that boys obtained higher externalizing scores in all twelve cultures studied (Australia, Belgium, China, Germany, Greece, Israel, Jamaica, the Netherlands, Puerto Rico, Sweden, Thailand, and the United States; Crijnen, Achenbach, and Verhulst, 1997). This 12-culture comparison was conducted using the most psychometrically tested dimensional measure of antisocial behaviour (Stanger, Achenbach, and Verhulst, 1997). Likewise, a comparison of self-reports of juvenile delinquency showed that boys committed more offences than girls in every country studied (Belgium, England and Wales, Finland, Germany, Greece, Italy, the Netherlands, Northern Ireland, Portugal, Switzerland, Spain, and the United States; Junger-Tas, Terlouw, and Klein, 1994). In combination, data from multiple nations and multiple informants suggest that boys are indeed more antisocial than girls from an early age onwards. The developmental Dunedin data suggest that this pattern of sex differences is robust across age, but the sex difference may be narrowest in mid-adolescence.

B. SEX DIFFERENCES IN OFFICIAL RECORDS OF OFFENDING

So far we have looked at measures of females' and males' antisocial behaviour taken from individual reporters who know the subject: parents, teachers, informants, and the self. It is useful to look also at data taken from public crime-control agencies. Official records are flawed because they overlook many antisocial acts and because they measure partially the behaviour of victims, police officers, lawyers, and judges, as well as the behaviour of our Study members. Nevertheless, they do provide valuable evidence that behaviour was consequential enough to attract official attention and intervention. If many disparate data sources produce comparable sex differences, this convergence would warrant stronger inferences about the nature of sex differences in antisocial behaviour.

Method

Measures

YOUTH AID POLICE RECORDS

'Police contacts' included all police actions that resulted in the filing of a standard incident form on which a New Zealand constable reports offences known to be committed by a juvenile between age 10 and 16 years, inclusive. In New Zealand, 'juvenile' status ends when offenders enter the adult justice system at the seventeenth birthday. At police departments throughout New Zealand, juvenile records were searched for 97 per cent of the Study members. These records were not available for deceased Study members and a small number of Study members who moved outside New Zealand before age 17. The sample was representative of New Zealand juveniles as a whole in the rate of police contacts they experienced (Moffitt, 1989).

COURT RECORDS

Records of convictions at all courts in New Zealand and Australia were searched, with the informed consent of the Study members, using the computer system of the New Zealand Police. Records included convictions in Children's and Young Persons' Court from age 13 to age 16 years, inclusive, and convictions in adult Criminal Court from age 17 years until the time of the phase 21 interview. Study members had been convicted of non-violent offences (e.g., possession or sale of illegal substances, theft, burglary, shoplifting, vandalism) and violent offences (e.g., disorderly behaviour likely to cause violence, using an attack dog on a person, assault with intent to injure, rape, aggravated robbery, manslaughter).

COSTS OF CRIME

In addition to consulting official data sources we also sought to quantify the costs of crime. To obtain estimates of the cost of crime, we relied on the work of economists who have quantified in dollar terms the cost of each type of crime committed. These estimates take into account the social costs of crime (e.g., costs to the criminal justice system, costs of replacing stolen property) as well as costs to victims (e.g., reduced productivity, health care, out-of-pocket expenses to prevent re-victimisation). Because such a comprehensive analysis of the costs and consequences of crimes is not available for New Zealand *per se*, we used estimates calculated for the United States (Cohen, Miller, and Rossman, 1994, especially tables 16 and 17, p. 128; Miller, Cohen, and Wiersema, 1996, especially table 2, p. 9) to assign a dollar value to crimes for which Dunedin Study members have been convicted, on a per crime basis (e.g., assault, drink driving, burglary, motor vehicle theft).

MINISTRY OF TRANSPORT RECORDS

At the time when Dunedin cohort members were under age 21, traffic convictions for motor vehicle offences were under the surveillance, control, and record-keeping of a separate enforcement agency, the Ministry of Transport. Records from this agency were searched for Study members whose adult criminal records were also searched.

Data analysis approach

To examine sex differences in official measures of offending, we cross-tabulated the various official indices of antisocial behaviour by sex, and report the resulting odds ratios. To obtain effect sizes that would be comparable to the standardized mean difference measures (d) reported in section A of this chapter, we estimated a standardized mean difference statistic by taking the product of the log odds ratio and $\sqrt{3}/\pi$ (Haddock, Rindskopf, and Shadish, 1998).

Results

Table 3.2 shows that males were significantly more likely to have had contact with police as juveniles. From their tenth to their seventeenth birthdays, the males in the study had between zero to 18 contacts with the police. They were more likely than females to have been contacted by the police by an odds ratio of 2 (d = 0.43) and were more likely to have been contacted by the police multiple times by an odds ratio of 4 (d = 0.78). Not surprisingly, males were significantly more likely to have been convicted for a criminal offence in a court of law by an odds ratio of 3 (d = 0.62). The greatest sex difference was in relation to violent offences, for which males were more likely to be convicted by an odds ratio of 4.8 (d = 0.86). The smallest sex difference was for drug and alcohol related offences (d = 0.57).

Not only were males more likely to be convicted, they were also significantly more likely to have been sentenced to gaol by an odds ratio of nearly 12 (d = 1.34). This finding conforms to the average daily prison census in New Zealand, which is approximately 4,000 men but only 150 women (Statistics New Zealand, 1994). Table 3.2 also shows that the costs attributable to the crimes of male Study members were far higher than the costs attributable to female Study members. To a certain extent, more frequent imprisonment and

Table 3.2. *Comparison of males' and females' official records of contact with police and of court convictions*

Measure of offending	Males	Females	M:F odds ratio	Sex difference p < 0.05
Youth Aid Police Records, age 10–16 inclusive	*N = 473*	*N = 458*		
Range of contacts per person	0–18	0–12	—	—
Ever contacted by police?	20%	10%	2.1	yes
Contacted more than once?	9%	2%	4.1	yes
Court Records, age 13–21 inclusive	*N = 510*	*N = 487*		
Range of convictions per person	0–81	0–22	—	—
Ever convicted of a crime?	20%	8%	3.1	yes
Convicted more than once?	13%	4%	3.1	yes
Drug/alcohol conviction	5%	2%	2.8	yes
Theft conviction	12%	4%	3.4	yes
Violent conviction	8%	2%	4.8	yes
Ever sentenced to jail or prison?	2.4%	0.2%	11.7	yes
Mean cost of all convictions per Study member	$6,987	$464	—	yes
Mean cost of all convictions per convicted Study member	$33,322	$5,886	—	yes
Ministry of Transport Record, age 15–20 inclusive	*N = 490*	*N = 469*		
Range of convictions per person	0–50	0–5	—	—
Traffic conviction	33%	10%	4.4	yes

Note: all male:female odds ratios on this table are statistically significant, as conveyed by a 95 per cent confidence interval that did not include 1.

higher costs for males were a function of their higher rates of violent crimes. The mean cost of $33,000 per male offender sounds impressive enough, yet it should be kept in mind that we calculated costs for only those offences resulting in a *conviction* before age 21. For many Study members, there were hundreds of undetected self-reported crimes for every crime that had resulted in a conviction. For example, for the year prior to the age-21 assessment Dunedin Study members self-reported twenty-two violent offences for every one violent conviction won against them by courts (Arseneault *et al.*, 2000). Records from a third agency, the Ministry of Transport, confirmed that males' transgressions exceed females' by an odds ratio greater than 4 (d = 0.82).

Comment: bias in official statistics?

When group differences are observed in official statistics of crime, we are obliged to ask whether the groups really *commit* more or fewer crimes, or whether one group is being systematically discriminated against by police and judges. This question is most commonly raised about race differences in official crime, but there has been a fair amount of research into this question in relation to sex differences too. Police officers and judges may generate the appearance of low crime rates for women by being lenient with them, motivated towards leniency perhaps by chivalry or paternalism. Reviews of this research conclude that there is no good evidence that a defendant's sex affects prosecution or conviction decisions, but women do sometimes receive lenient treatment at the point of sentencing, unless their crime is very serious (Johnson and Scheuble, 1991; Nagel and Hagan, 1983). It appears that judges tend pragmatically to avoid prison sentences for women who are mothers, unless the severity of the crime requires a prison sentence (Steffensmeier, Kramer, and Streifel, 1993). For our analysis, any such bias effect is negligible, because only 10 per cent of Study women were mothers, and sex differences in conviction rates were corroborated by measures such as self-reports that were immune from official bias.

C. SEX DIFFERENCES IN THE FREQUENCY OF DIFFERENT TYPES OF OFFENCES

So far we have looked at sex differences in antisocial behaviour by using the individual as the unit of analysis. Another way to look at sex differences is to use the incident of crime as the unit of analysis, and to ask: of all the crimes committed by a population in total, what proportion were committed by male offenders versus female offenders? Our self-reported measures of delinquency had asked and recorded the frequency of incidents of each offence that a Study member recalled having committed in the prior twelve months, for example, three robberies, eighteen automobile thefts, three hundred drug sales. In this section, we report the proportion of total crime burden in the birth cohort that was committed by males and females.

Method

Measures
TYPES OF OFFENCES
For each of the four ages at which we administered the self-reported delinquency interviews (ages 13, 15, 18, and 21), we divided the illegal items into

three subscales representing violence, theft, and controlled-substance offences. The self-reported violence offences included: aggravated assault (attacking with a weapon or intent to injure), simple assault, robbery, rape, arson, and gang fighting. The self-reported theft offences included: stealing from school, stealing something from a parked car, breaking and entering, and shoplifting, among others. The self-reported drug and alcohol related offences included: selling cannabis, using hard drugs, selling hard drugs, and being drunk and disorderly in a public place. We summed across items and individuals to attain a measure of total offence frequency for each sex. Court convictions were summed in the same way.

Data analysis approach

To examine sex differences in offence frequency, we calculated the percentage of the sample's total offences (for each offence category) that was accounted for by males vs. females and calculated the sex ratio of offences (set against 1 for females).

Results

Findings are presented in table 3.3. It is immediately apparent that the male Study members accounted for more of every type of offence, at virtually every age. Generally, males accounted for between two-thirds and four-fifths of total offences. The sex difference was slightly larger in official conviction data than in self-report data. This effect has been observed in previous research and is generally attributed to the relatively greater severity of crimes that are officially recorded (Hindelang, Hirschi and Weis, 1979). If females' crimes are less serious and violent they naturally appear less often in the records of agencies whose mission is to control serious and violent crime. Interestingly, the average male proportion we obtained for self-reported data was very similar to the proportion obtained by Sickmund *et al.* (1998) for US nationwide juvenile court statistics. Males were involved in 78 per cent of the delinquency cases handled by US juvenile courts in 1995, and in approximately 71 per cent of the offences reported by the Dunedin sample between ages 13 and 21.

Comment: sex similarity on drug and alcohol offences

Table 3.3 shows that the sex difference was largest for violent crimes and smallest for drug- and alcohol-related crimes. This contrasting pattern of a sex difference for violence and a sex resemblance for substance-related offences has been observed before. A meta-analysis of forty-four studies

Table 3.3. *Percentage of the sample's total offences in a given year (12-month period) committed by males versus females. Percentages are shown for violence, theft, and drug/alcohol offences, as measured via self-reports and court records*

% of the sample's . . .	Males	Females	Sex ratio of offences
Violent offences			
Self-report at 13	78%	22%	3.5:1
Self-report at 15	79%	21%	3.7:1
Self-report at 18	79%	21%	3.7:1
Self-report at 21	67%	33%	2:1
Convictions to age 21	97%	3%	32:1
Theft offences			
Self-report at 13	66%	34%	1.9:1
Self-report at 15	62%	38%	1.6:1
Self-report at 18	87%	13%	6.6:1
Self-report at 21	63%	37%	1.7:1
Convictions to age 21	81%	19%	4.2:1
Drug and alcohol offences			
Self-report at 13	61%	39%	1.5:1
Self-report at 15	51%	49%	1:1[a]
Self-report at 18	71%	29%	2.4:1
Self-report at 21	73%	27%	2.7:1
Convictions to age 21	71%	29%	2.4:1

Notes: Group Ns range from 376 to 510 for boys and 348 to 487 for girls.
[a] This ratio is not a significant sex difference. All other ratios are significant, $p < 0.01$.

(Smith and Visher, 1980) found that the sex difference was widest for violence and narrowest for drug- and alcohol-related offences. The US National Longitudinal Survey of Youth also found that males exceeded females on violent offences, but males and females were well matched on the prevalence of using alcohol, marijuana, and hard drugs (Windle, 1990). A cross-national comparison of self-reported delinquency revealed that around the world, more males than females are violent, but in seven of the fourteen countries surveyed, females and males were similar in their levels of drug-related offences (Junger-Tas, Terlouw and Klein, 1994). One report from the US National Youth Survey yielded a 1:1 sex ratio for hard drug use (Canter, 1982), and other reports from this survey noted that sex differences for drug abuse were weaker and less consistent than sex differences for other types of offences (Elliott, Huizinga and Menard, 1989). Sex similarity for drug use has also been found by the Rochester Youth Study (Huizinga, Loeber, and Thornberry, 1993) and in large multi-nation surveys reported by the World Health Organisation (King *et al.* 1996) and by the European School Project on Alcohol and Drugs (CAN and the Council of Europe, 1997).

In the Dunedin Study, females and males showed a 1:1 sex ratio on drug and alcohol offences particularly at age 15, but a sex difference appeared at later ages. This pattern was also reported in two American epidemiological studies. In the New York sample studied by Cohen *et al.* (1993), females' and males' rates of substance-abuse disorders were almost identical between ages 14 and 16, but boys' substance abuse exceeded girls' by two to one between ages 17 and 20. In the Denver Youth Study (Huizinga, Loeber, and Thornberry, 1993) very similar percentages of 15-year-old boys and girls reported using alcohol (about 40 per cent), marijuana (about 20 per cent), and other drugs (about 5 per cent). In comparison, both at ages 7–9 and at age 17, Denver boys reported much more substance abuse than girls, suggesting that sex similarity in substance abuse during the peri-pubertal period may be a temporary exception to the more general rule of more male substance abuse across the rest of the life course.

Comment: the concentration of crime

Studies of juvenile offenders show that although most juveniles have broken the law, only a small number of juveniles are responsible for the majority of offending. The Dunedin findings replicate this well-established observation about males and, in addition, reveal two interesting findings about sex and the concentration of crime. The first finding is that crimes were concentrated among a small number of individuals, for both males and females. For example, 50 per cent of the 64,062 offences reported by males at age 21 were reported by only 41 men (8 per cent). Similarly, 50 per cent of the 23,613 offences self-reported by females at age 21 were reported by only 27 women (6 per cent). (To put the Dunedin sample's total number of self-reported offences in perspective, consider that if every Study member had committed each of the self-report items once a day in the past year, the potential number of offences could have approached 15,000,000.) This concentration of self-reported crime among Dunedin females is consistent with the concentration first observed by Wolfgang, Figlio, and Sellin (1972) and subsequently reported for official data from many male samples (Blumstein *et al.* 1986). To our knowledge, this is the first observation that females' crime is similarly concentrated within females as males' crime is concentrated within males.

A second finding, and an important corollary of the first, is that even the most active Dunedin female offenders had not kept pace with their male counterparts. For example, at age 21 the most active 5 per cent of males accounted for 28 per cent of the sample's total 87,675 self-reported offences, whereas the most active 5 per cent of females accounted for 12 per cent of the total. A similar sex difference in the proportion of high-frequency offenders has been reported in the US National Youth Survey (Canter, 1982). These parallel findings suggest that the frequency of crime is equally concentrated within each sex, but even the most frequent female offenders account for a relatively small proportion of the total crime burden.

Take-home messages

- High-rate offending is concentrated among a few members of the female population (just as it is concentrated among a few members of the male population), but even the most active females offend at a rate much lower than the most active males.
- Males' antisocial behaviour is more often serious, and is thus more often officially sanctioned.
- Throughout the first two decades of life, and measured via multiple sources of data, males consistently emerge as more antisocial than females, with two exceptions . . .
- Males and females are most similar in their antisocial behaviour during middle adolescence, at around age 15.
- Males and females are most similar in their drug- and alcohol-related offences.

Unanswered questions

- Why do girls take up antisocial activities between ages 13 and 15?
- Why do girls show a preference for alcohol- and drug-related activities over other types of offending?

CHAPTER FOUR

Sex differences in the prevalence of antisocial behaviour: categorical diagnostic measures

Chapter 3 revealed that more males than females engage in antisocial behaviours, and males engage in more antisocial behaviours than females. It also revealed that males' antisocial behaviours relative to females' were more likely to be serious and committed persistently at a high rate. The possible exception was drug- and alcohol-related activities, on which girls resembled boys, especially near age 15. In contrast to the continuously distributed measures of antisocial behaviour examined in the previous chapter, this chapter compares the sexes on categorical measures: *diagnoses* of antisocial disorder. The criteria for a diagnosis of conduct disorder are intended to capture behaviours that are serious and committed persistently at a high rate. Behaviours related to drugs and alcohol are excluded from the criterion list. Therefore, we would expect to find sex differences in diagnoses that are as large as, if not larger than, the sex differences we saw in chapter 3's continuous measures of antisocial behaviours.

A review of the five epidemiological studies that reported DSM-III (American Psychiatric Association, 1980) diagnoses of childhood disorders concluded that across all five studies more boys than girls had conduct disorder, despite marked differences between studies in the age range of children studied, nationality, reporting sources, and procedures followed to convert the symptoms assessed into diagnostic categories (Costello, 1989). Epidemiological studies conducted using DSM-III-R (American Psychiatric Association, 1987) and ICD-10 definitions in the 1990s agree (Lahey *et al.*, 2000; Lewinsohn *et al.*, 1993; Offord *et al.*, 1996; Simonoff *et al.*, 1997; Verhulst *et al.*, 1997). A national survey of children and adolescents in Great Britain reported a ratio of 2 boys per girl for conduct disorder, averaged over ages 5 to 15 (Meltzer *et al.* 2000). A New York study reported a ratio of about 2 boys per girl for conduct disorder, averaged over ages 10 to 20 (Cohen et al., 1993). A study from the Great Smoky Mountains of the south-eastern United States reported a ratio of 4 boys per girl, averaged over ages 9, 11, and 13 (Costello et al., 1996). Here, we report sex ratios for DSM-IV (American Psychiatric Association, 1994) diagnoses in the Dunedin cohort at ages 11, 13, 15, 18, and 21.

Chapter 3 showed that males and females were similar in their amounts of antisocial behaviour at about age 15, and this chapter explores the observation further. Specifically, we will show that the peri-pubertal risk period for girls applies to diagnoses of conduct disorder, and we examine two reasons why this is true: sex differences in the mean age of puberty in the population, and individual differences among girls in their own pubertal timing.

Methods

Measures

Conduct symptoms were assessed in private standardised interviews, at age 11 during the Diagnostic Interview Schedule for Children-Child version (DISC-C, Costello et al., 1982) and at older ages during the Self-reported Delinquency Interview (Moffitt and Silva, 1988a; Moffitt et al., 1994), with a reporting period of twelve months at each age. Numbers of Study members with present data for diagnoses were 921 at 11, 843 at 13, 972 at 15, 934 at 18 and 961 at 21.[1]

Diagnoses for conduct disorder were reported in the literature following each data-collection phase of the Dunedin Study (Anderson et al., 1987; Frost, Moffitt, and McGee, 1989; McGee, Feehan, Williams et al., 1990; Feehan et al., 1994). Diagnoses for antisocial personality disorder were reported following phase 21 (Newman et al., 1996). These previous publications reported the reliability and validity of the diagnostic procedures. However, the previously published diagnoses of conduct disorder could not be used for this book for several reasons. First, to make comparisons across ages, we needed diagnoses made according to the same criteria, but the existing diagnoses had been made according to the then-current versions of the Diagnostic and Statistical Manual of Mental Disorders (American Psychiatric Association, 1980; 1987), which changed during the course of

[1] Oppositional disorder has not been routinely diagnosed in the Dunedin Study, because there is some question about the validity of self-reports for assessing oppositional symptoms (Bird, Goult, and Staghezza, 1992; Hart et al., 1994). Dunedin parent and teacher checklists included items assessing oppositional behaviour problems but these are insufficient for making diagnoses.

the longitudinal study. Second, the extant diagnoses also differed because at certain ages supplementary data from sources other than the child interview had been incorporated into the diagnostic algorithms for conduct disorder, and unfortunately this practice varied with the philosophy and strategy of the research team's members at the time.

For this book, we returned to the item-level data base to make diagnoses of conduct disorder according to the now-current criteria of DSM-IV. We drew on all of the information available to us in the archives, using items from interviews of the Study members, and from checklists completed by their parents and teachers. We counted a symptom as present if there was evidence for it from any source, following evidence that this approach enhances diagnostic validity (Bird, Gould, and Staghezza, 1992; Piacentini, Cohen, and Cohen, 1992).

Table 4.1 shows that our item-level data base contains information relevant to current diagnostic criteria, despite having been gathered before DSM-IV was published. The table shows two features of the data we used for diagnosis. (1) Of the 15 DSM-IV criteria, 8 were assessed at phase 11, 13 were assessed at phase 13, 12 at phase 15, and 10 at phase 18. However, the symptoms assessed at every phase (e.g. fighting) are among the most prevalent symptoms of conduct disorder, and those not assessed are found relatively rarely in the population, as evaluated in the Epidemiological Catchment Area Study (L.N. Robins, 1986) and in the DSM-IV field trials (Frick *et al.*, 1994). Thus, the items not available to us (e.g., cruelty, forced sex) would have contributed to diagnosis for only a small minority of conduct disorder cases and as a result the prevalence rates we report here are probably only slight underestimates. (2) Parent and teacher items were available to supplement child interviews only at the younger phases of the study. Although adult reports became less available at the older phases of the Study, by those phases adults are less knowledgeable reporters because much of teens' antisocial behaviour becomes hidden from adults' view. Moreover, the validity of the Study members' interview responses had probably improved because their cognitive maturity had grown, as had their confidence in our guarantee of confidentiality. Thus, this shift in reporting source was unavoidable but should not be consequential for our prevalence estimates. Certainly, missing diagnostic criteria and missing data from adult reports were shared equally by males and females in the Dunedin birth cohort. We can think of no reason why missing information needed for DSM-IV diagnoses should bias our study towards or away from finding sex differences.

Each criterion could be met by more than one item available from the self-, parent-, and teacher-report instruments. For example, 'tells lies' at

Table 4.1. *Diagnostic criteria for DSM-IV diagnosis of conduct disorder that were available in the Dunedin data archives at each assessment age, as reported by self, parent, or teacher*

DSM-IV symptom criterion	Age 10–11	Age 12–13	Age 14–15	Age 17–18
Physical fights	S,P,T	S,P,T	S,P	S
Destroys property	S,P,T	S,T	S	S
Tells lies	S,P,T	P,T	S,P	S
Runs away	S	S	S	S
Truants	S,P,T	S,P,T	S,P	S
Steals without confrontation	S,P,T	S,P,T	S,P	S
Bullies	P,T	P,T	P	
Carries or uses weapon		S	S	S
Steals with confrontation		S	S	S
Sets fires		S	S	S
Breaks and enters		S	S	S
Cruel to people		P	P	
Cruel to animals		S		
Stays out late at night despite parents' prohibition	S			
Forces sex				
Number of the 15 criteria available	8	13	12	10

Notes:
Most of the diagnostic criteria could be met by a response to more than one item.
S = from self-report interview, P = from parent checklist, T = from teacher checklist.

Phase 11 could be met by any of three different self-report questions from the DISC-C or by one item each from the parent and teacher checklists. (The list of items that constituted each diagnostic criterion at each phase is available from the authors.) The response formats for the various instruments differed (i.e, teacher questionnaires used 'no–does not apply' 'applies somewhat' 'yes–definitely applies' whereas self-report interviewers asked about act frequencies). To equate across instruments, we counted a symptom if it had been reported as 'yes-definitely applies' by a parent or teacher, or '1 or more times' by the Study member.

Table 4.2. *Prevalence rates of DSM-IV diagnoses of conduct disorder for males and females at ages 11, 13, 15, 18, and for their lifetime to age 21, estimated using different symptom-count criteria*

DSM-IV Disorder	3+ CD criteria		4+ CD criteria		5+ CD criteria		6+ CD criteria	
	Prevalence rate	M/F odds ratio	Prevalence rate	M/F odds ratio	Prevalence rate	M/F odds ratio	Prevalence rate	M/F odds ratio
CD at 11, total	23%	*1.8*	14%	*2.2*	6%	*3.5*	2%	*NA*
boys	28%		18%		10%		3%	
girls	18%		9%		3%		0%	
CD at 13, total	24%	*2.2*	13%	*2.6*	9%	*3*	6%	*3.1*
boys	31%		19%		13%		9%	
girls	16%		8%		5%		3%	
CD at 15, total	26%	*1.4*	18%	*1.7*	11%	*1.9*	7%	*1.7*
boys	30%		22%		14%		9%	
girls	22%		14%		8%		6%	
CD at 18, total	34%	*2*	17%	*3.4*	8%	*5.3*	5%	*8*
boys	42%		24%		14%		8%	
girls	26%		9%		3%		1%	
ASPD at 21, total	3%	*9.4*						
men	6%							
women	1%							
Lifetime total prevalence	55%	*1.9*	37%	*2.3*	22%	*2.4*	13%	*2.6*
boys	63%		46%		29%		19%	
girls	46%		27%		14%		8%	

Notes: N's with present data for diagnosis were 921 at 11, 843 at 13, 972 at 15, 934 at 18, 961 at 21, and 1,012 for lifetime diagnoses.
NA: the odds ratio could not be computed as no girls met 6 criteria at age 11.
All of the M:F odds ratios on this table are statistically significant as conveyed by a 95 per cent confidence interval that did not include 1.

Data analysis approach

We cross-tabulated diagnostic categories (yes, no) by sex, and report the resulting odds ratios.

Results

Table 4.2 shows the percentages of Dunedin males and females who met diagnostic criteria for conduct disorder. The columns of the table compare different cut-offs for making a diagnosis: 3, 4, 5, or 6 or more symptoms. The rows of the table compare boys and girls at five phases of the study, 11, 13, 15, 18, and 21. The final row presents percentages of males and females with a conduct disorder diagnosis at any of the assessment phases, that is, lifetime prevalence.

Prevalence rates of conduct disorder at each study phase

The DSM-IV specifies that three or more symptoms are needed for 'mild conduct disorder'. However, at that cut-off two-thirds of the boys and half of the girls in the Dunedin sample could have been diagnosed with conduct disorder at some time during the period of the Study. This is shown in the bottom line of table 4.2. We can think of two reasons why a criterion of three or more symptoms might over-diagnose members of the Dunedin Study. (1) We speculate that three symptoms may be more difficult to attain in the clinical or forensic settings for which DSM-IV was designed than in our longitudinal research design, and therefore three symptoms may be more indicative of psychopathology in those settings. In clinical or forensic settings, sources of information are often limited to patient self-report and/or official police records. Evidence of symptoms from those sources is sparse because the patient is usually motivated to conceal antisocial behaviours and official crime records capture only a tiny fraction of offences committed. In contrast, in a longitudinal study of a birth cohort such as ours, we enquire systematically about thirty or more specific antisocial behaviours, Study members have confidence that their self-reports will be kept confidential, and we have access to reports of symptom checklists from parents and teachers as well. In the Dunedin Study, we simply have access to much more symptom information than does the typical clinician. (2) In addition to the differences between longitudinal research and clinical/forensic methods, we might expect inflated numbers of Dunedin Study members to meet the three-symptom cut-off for another methodological reason. Our archival data did not include information to document specifically that every symptom had been repeated persistently across six months as stipulated by DSM-IV; for example, the parent and teacher reports of lying established only that this symptom 'definitely applies' for a reporting period of the past twelve months. Because of these two methodological reasons, three or more symptoms appeared to over-diagnose conduct disorder in this study, and we opted for a more strict criterion cut-off.

Following from our observation that three criteria are probably too few to signal true disorder in a study design such as ours, table 4.2 presents the prevalence rates and sex ratios obtained using cut-offs of 3, 4, 5, or 6 criteria. Reading from left to right across the table, it appears that each of the criterion cut-offs is an arbitrary point along a continuum of severity. Indeed, the linear nature of the criterion continuum would become even more strikingly apparent if we added to the left of table 4.2 the percentages of children who might be 'diagnosed' by virtue of one-plus or two-plus criterion cut-offs.

For the remainder of the research reported in this book, we elected to define a research diagnosis of conduct disorder as the presence of five or more diagnostic criteria. DSM-IV specifies that whereas only three criteria are required for mild conduct disorder, moderate to severe conduct disorder may be diagnosed if there are more than three criteria present. Five or more symptoms seemed a good research definition in this study, because the above-mentioned methodological considerations made lower cut-offs too inclusive. Moreover, this cut-off of five symptoms yielded prevalence rates and sex-ratios that came very close to those from the other epidemiological study that has covered a similar age span (age 11–20, Cohen *et al.*, 1993).

Comment: the consequences of diagnostic cut-offs for the sex ratio
Table 4.2 illustrates three findings about sex differences.

First, reading from left to right across the table, the sex gap grew somewhat wider as more symptom criteria were required for diagnosis. In the most striking example of this pattern, at phase 18 the male:female odds ratio for a conduct disorder diagnosis changed as the criterion for diagnosis became more strict, from an odds ratio of 2.0 (3+ symptoms) to 3.4 (4+ symptoms), to 5.3 (5+ symptoms), to 8.0 (6+ symptoms).

Second, reading from top to bottom down the table, the sex gap grew somewhat wider as the Study members aged. In the most striking example of this pattern, using 4-plus criteria for diagnosis, the male:female odds ratio for conduct disorder diagnosis changed from 2.2 at phase 11 to 2.6 at phase 13, to 1.7 at phase 15, to 3.4 at phase 18, and then to 9.4 for antisocial personality at age 21.

Third, the sex gap temporarily narrowed at age 15. The sex gap was wider before and after phase 15. The male:female odds ratio was on average 2.7 at age 13, then narrowed to 1.7 at 15, then again widened further to 4.6 at age 18. Interestingly, the New York epidemiological study also found a sex ratio of 1.7 for 14–16 year olds (Cohen *et al.*, 1993). Note that at Dunedin's phase 15, the sex gap did not widen as more and more criteria were required for diagnosis, suggesting that at phase 15 girls were not merely getting the diagnosis by meeting the minimum criteria. We return to explore this exceptionally small gender gap at phase 15 in the last section of this chapter.

Comment: lifetime diagnoses of conduct disorder

After settling on five symptoms as the definition of diagnosis for this research, we counted a Study member as having a lifetime diagnosis of conduct disorder if he or she had ever been diagnosed at any age. Of the 1,020 Study members living at phase 21, 1,012 had participated in at least one of the phases from 11 to 21, and were eligible for a lifetime diagnosis. This sum-up yielded 29 per cent of males and 14 per cent of females who received a lifetime diagnosis of conduct disorder. It should be noted that data with sufficient detail to make diagnoses were available only beginning at phase 11. Cases of conduct disorder do emerge prior to that age, but their prevalence is low and in any case their problems would tend to continue to age 11 (Campbell, 1995), suggesting that most of them would be captured in our lifetime group.

At the other end of the age-period covered by the study was antisocial personality disorder (ASPD), diagnosed for 3 women and 28 men at age 21. Details about the reliability, validity, and correlates of the ASPD diagnoses are available in Newman *et al.* (1996). Dunedin Study women's and men's rates of ASPD, 1 per cent and 6 per cent, are similar to the lifetime rates reported for the Epidemiological Catchment Area Study, 0.7 per cent and 4.3 per cent (Robins and Regier, 1991), and the US National Comorbidity Survey, 1.2 per cent and 5.8 per cent (Kessler *et al.*, 1994). Of the ASPD cases in the sample, 80 per cent were inside the lifetime conduct disorder group because they had met our cut-off of five or more symptoms of conduct disorder at some earlier phase of the study. We decided to include the other ASPD cases (six boys and one girl) in the lifetime group as well, because they had met the onset criterion for ASPD by having *three* or more conduct symptoms before age 15 (Newman *et al.*, 1996) which is the conventional definition of conduct disorder.

Our lifetime odds ratio between the sexes from phase 11 to 21 was 2.4, which corresponds to a moderate effect size (d = 0.49). This matched closely

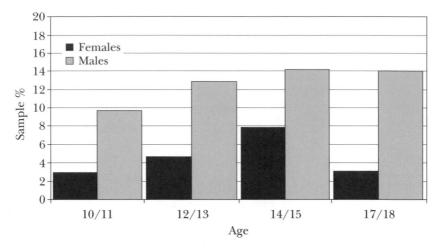

4.1A The prevalence of DSM-IV conduct disorder

the ratio for the New York sample of 10–20 year olds, 2.3, reported by Cohen *et al.* (1993). In addition, our lifetime prevalence of 29 per cent of males and 14 per cent of females compares favourably to the 34 per cent of males and 16 per cent of females, as recorded for respondents under age 29 in the Epidemiological Catchment Area Study (ECA; Robins and Regier, 1991). On the one hand, we might have expected the lifetime rate to be lower in the ECA than in Dunedin because adult ECA respondents were asked to report conduct disorder symptoms that occurred prior to age 15 retrospectively, a period of 3–15 years before the interview, and thus ECA respondents may have forgotten some symptoms. In contrast to the ECA, the Dunedin study ascertained symptoms from three reporters at four repeated assessments within the adolescent age period, resulting in fewer forgotten symptom criteria. On the other hand, we might have expected the lifetime rate to be higher in the ECA than in Dunedin because the ECA used a cut-off of three symptoms versus our cut-off of five. In the final analysis, less forgetting and less telescoping in the Dunedin study were perhaps balanced by our stricter criterion cut-off.

Comment: the peri-pubertal period is a special risk period for girls' conduct disorder
Using the five-plus diagnostic criterion, panel A of figure 4.1 shows the prevalence rates (panel A) and new-case incidence rates (panel B) of conduct disorder by age and sex. Taken together, the two panels suggest that the period around phase 15 was the peak period of both prevalence and new

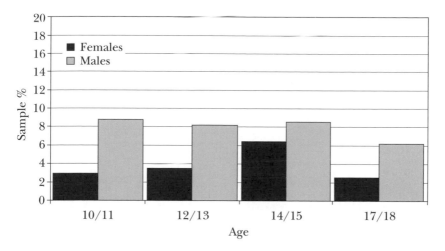

4.1B New case incidence of DSM-IV conduct disorder

onset for girls' conduct disorder. By contrast, boys' conduct disorder seemed relatively less age-dependent than girls'. Recall that in chapter 3, phase 15 also yielded the narrowest sex difference in continuously distributed delinquency measured from parent reports and self reports (see table 3.1). This pattern of a peri-pubertal peak in conduct disorder for girls, bringing with it the smallest sex difference in the life course, was also reported by the New York epidemiological study (see figure 5 in Cohen *et al.*, 1993) and the MECA study (Lahey *et al.*, 2000). This age pattern has been remarked on by Zoccolillo (1993; see table 7, p. 68) who reviewed the prevalence rates of diagnosed conduct disorder from eight studies in five countries. In those studies, the sex ratio was between 2:1 and 4:1 when the participants were under 13 years old or over 16 years old, but when the participants were between 13 and 16 years old, the sex ratio was approximately 1:1. Note that the narrowed sex gap in conduct disorder diagnoses emerges at the same age as the narrowed sex gap in drug and alcohol-related delinquency that we observed in chapter 3 (table 3.3 reported a 1:1 sex ratio for the frequency of substance offending at 15). However, drugs and alcohol are not included among DSM-IV criteria for conduct disorder. This tells us that the peak in diagnosis shown in figure 4.1 represents an increase in girls' participation in other kinds of antisocial activities, not solely drugs and alcohol.

Phase 15 conduct disorder symptoms covered the period between the fourteenth and fifteenth birthdays. By their thirteenth birthdays 53 per cent of Dunedin girls had experienced menarche and by their fifteenth birthdays 95 per cent had experienced menarche (Caspi and Moffitt, 1991).

Menarche is the last stage of female pubertal development (Tanner, 1978). According to Tanner (1978), our phase 15 data refer to a chronological age when most of the Dunedin girls were both biologically and socially older than most of the boys in the same birth cohort. This observation suggests that although phase 15 data ostensibly compare boys and girls of the same age, in terms of bio-social maturity phase 15 data actually compare boys who are still children to girls who are young women. Thus it should come as no surprise that the sex difference observed at ages 11 and 13 narrows at age 15.

Yet the sex difference widens again by phase 18, indicating that the phase-15 peak in female conduct problems is probably a short-lived peri-pubertal effect that lasts less than a few years for most girls. Using cross-sectional comparisons, the MECA study reported a virtually identical age pattern to the Dunedin pattern, in which the male:female ratio was 2.4 for 9–11 year olds, then narrowed to 1.7 for 12–14 year olds, and widened again to 3.7 among 15–17 year olds (Lahey *et al.*, 2000). This mid-adolescent peak followed by declining prevalence for girls was also observed in the Denver youth survey of 1,528 youth. There, boys engaged in significantly more delinquency than girls at ages 8–12 and later at ages 16–19, but at ages 13–15 there were no significant sex differences in offending (Espiritu, 1998). A similar pattern has been observed in the 1.7 million cases handled nationwide in 1995 by US juvenile courts (Sickmund *et al.*, 1998).

Moffitt (1994) suggested that most antisocial girls' behaviour fits what she termed the 'adolescence-limited' developmental pattern. This pattern arises from a teenager's attempt to escape the *maturity gap*, ambiguous and psychically uncomfortable years when biological maturity has outpaced social maturity. One way to cope in the maturity gap is by adopting the behavioural styles of antisocial peers, who seem older (or are older). Moffitt (1993a) added that adolescence-limited antisocial behaviour is promoted when teens trapped in the maturity gap have ready access to antisocial peers whose antisocial behaviour they may admire, observe, and mimic. In support of this notion, a longitudinal study that repeatedly assessed children's sociometric nominations of peers found that, as young people matured from elementary to middle school, both boys and girls grew more attracted to boys who were aggressive, and less attracted to peers who had good classroom behaviour (Bukowski, Sippola, and Newcomb, 2000). Also consistent with this explanation for the female peri-pubertal peak in conduct problems, earlier analyses of Dunedin data up to phase 15 showed that the onset of individual girls' antisocial behaviours was tied temporally to their personal pubertal age and that girls who experienced puberty ahead of their age-cohort were most at risk (Caspi and Moffitt, 1991; Caspi, Lynam,

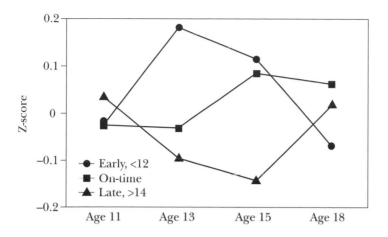

4.2 Girls' conduct disorder symptoms as a function of pubertal maturation

Moffitt and Silva, 1993). In figure 4.2 this pattern of findings is shown for symptoms of conduct disorder, and extended to age 18. (Unfortunately figure 4.2 cannot be constructed for boys because the Dunedin Study archive does not contain measures of male pubertal timing, but the relatively stable incidence rates for boys across the ages shown in figure 4.1 suggest that the precise timing of puberty is less important for conduct problems among boys than girls.)

Figure 4.2 shows the scale of conduct disorder symptoms, standardized to z-scores at each assessment age (11, 13, 15, and 18), comparing girls whose first menstrual period occurred early relative to the cohort (before their twelfth birthday), on-time for the cohort, or late (after their fourteenth birthday). We conducted planned contrasts between menarche groups as per procedures outlined in Caspi and Moffitt (1991) and Ge, Conger, and Elder (1996).[2] At age 11, the early, on-time, and late groups did not differ significantly from each other. At age 13, the early group had more conduct problems than the on-time group, $t(377) = 1.7$, $p < 0.10$, and the late group, $t(377) = 2.1$, $p < 0.05$, but the on-time and late groups did not differ significantly. At age 15, the early group and the on-time group no longer differed, but both the early group, $t(411) = 2.0$, $p < 0.05$, and the on-time group, $t(411) = 1.9$, $p < 0.05$, had more conduct problems than the late menarche group. At age 18, the late group caught up with the early and on-time groups

[2] We performed the analyses using a scale of conduct-disorder symptoms because the number of diagnosed girls at each age was small, and dividing them further into three menarche groups resulted in many cells too small for reliable significance testing.

and, just as at age 11, the three groups did not differ significantly in their mean levels of conduct disorder symptoms. The figure thus illustrates two points. First, girls' level of conduct disorder symptomatology is tied to their personal level of physical maturation, with relative increases in conduct problems occurring in the years immediately after puberty. Second, the earlier that girls mature relative to their peers the more likely they are to exhibit higher levels of conduct problems; the standardized scores show that, relative to their same-age peers who had not attained puberty, early-maturing girls exhibited the most problems after puberty (at age 13) followed by on-time girls (at age 15) and then by late-maturing girls (at age 18). Indeed, the prevalence of conduct disorder rose to 9 per cent in the years following menarche among early-menarche girls (at age 13), and in turn two years later (at age 15), it rose to 9 per cent among on-time-menarche girls as well. But although late-menarche girls showed a post-menarche rise in conduct disorder too (at age 18), conduct disorder afflicted only 5 per cent of them.

Comment: precocious puberty and adolescent girls' antisocial behaviour

The Dunedin findings show that pubertal development is a critical transitional period in girls' behavioural development and that early pubertal timing, in particular, is an important aetiological factor in the development of girls' adjustment problems. In addition to these findings, the link between early puberty and various problem behaviours and adjustment difficulties has been documented in several studies throughout North America and Europe (e.g., Dick *et al.*, 2000; Graber *et al.*, 1997; Simmons and Blyth, 1987; Stattin and Magnusson, 1991a; Wilson *et al.*, 1994). A good deal of evidence also suggests that the link between pubertal timing and conduct problems is mediated via relationships with peers. In Dunedin, we discovered that early puberty was followed by onset of antisocial behaviour mainly among girls who affiliated on a daily basis with male peers and who reported, relative to other girls, knowing more young people who were engaging in delinquency (Caspi *et al.*, 1993). Consistent with this notion, early-menarche Dunedin girls were more likely than other girls to have initiated sexual intercourse at a younger chronological age (Mantel-Haenszel test of linear association = 6.53 (df = 1), $p < 0.01$ (cf. Paul *et al.*, 2000). An American study (Ge, Conger, and Elder, 1996) and a Swedish study (Magnusson, 1988) reported the same developmental process, with the addition that the peers who were important influences on the girls' delinquency were of a specific type: they were *older* friends. Taken together, these findings suggest that the peak prevalence of antisocial behaviour among girls occurs near the female peri-pubertal period because pubescent girls are likely to affiliate with peers who are older and male, among whom delinquency is more widely prevalent, encouraged, and reinforced.

How and why early-puberty girls gain access to older and mixed-sex peer groups is not known. One possibility is that early-puberty girls seek out older friends because, during this age-period of heightened self-consciousnsess, they are more comfortable with peers who look like them. Another possibility is that early-puberty girls are rejected by their same-age and same-sex peers and thus gravitate toward older peers for companionship. A third possibility is that older males prey on early-puberty girls. Indeed, this third possibility suggests why early-puberty girls are influenced by older peers who model antisocial behaviour rather than by those who could model prosocial behaviour: it is likely that older males who seek a liaison exploiting the vulnerability of a girl whose physical development has outstripped her social and cognitive maturity are likely to have antisocial characteristics, including callous, predatory, and sensation-seeking tendencies. Future research, both qualitative and quantitative, needs to examine the nature of mixed-sex adolescent groups with special reference to antisocial behaviour. One promising way to explore the influence of males on females' antisocial behaviour is to examine intra-individual change among girls who move in and out of membership in gangs (e.g., Esbensen, Deschenes, and Winfree, 1999).

In sum, the data about pubertal timing and conduct problems suggest that it is not merely pubertal development that is associated with girls' conduct problems, but what matters most is a girl's particular experience of having a biologically mature appearance before she attains social and cognitive maturity. Future research needs to evaluate the pathways and processes by which these developmental asynchronies shape adolescent problem behaviours (Compas, Hinden, and Gerhardt, 1995).

Take-home messages

- The picture of sex differences and similarities remains unaltered, whether antisocial behaviour is measured with categorical diagnoses or continuous dimensions.
- DSM criteria cut-offs for a diagnosis of conduct disorder appear to be somewhat arbitrary points along a continuum of severity.
- The best number of symptoms for making a diagnosis may vary by setting. It is useful to take into account features of clinical or research settings that make it easy or difficult to ascertain symptoms.

- The sex ratio for the lifetime prevalence of antisocial disorder appears to be about 2.4 males to one female, across studies using different methods and different samples.
- More boys than girls have diagnosed conduct disorder at every age, with one exception . . .
- During the peri-pubertal period for girls – when almost all girls are more physically developed than same-aged boys – their prevalence and incidence of conduct disorder rises to produce the narrowest gap between the sexes (and smallest sex ratio) seen at any time in the life course.
- The social-stimulus value of girls' older appearance may exert pressure towards antisocial behaviour by signalling to older peers and to the girl herself that she looks old enough to join in the 'prohibited' activities indulged in by her older peers.

Unanswered questions
- Research is needed on the etiological validity and predictive validity of diagnostic cut-off points for separating youth with disorder from those without.
- What is the nature of the role played by older male peers in initiating conduct problems among peri-pubertal girls?

CHAPTER FIVE

Sex differences in physical violence and sex similarities in partner abuse

In the last two chapters we have seen evidence that males are uniformly more antisocial than females. In this chapter we turn our attention more specifically to sex differences in physical violence and aggression. We examine physical violence at different ages and in different settings as measured via multiple data sources: parent and teacher reports of fighting during childhood, informant reports of fighting, self-reports of violent delinquent offending, and official records of convictions for violent offences in adolescence and young adulthood.

Females have long been demonstrated to be less violent than males at every age and in every setting. This is true in research conducted by criminologists studying violent crime (Greenfield and Snell, 1999; Kruttschnitt, 1994) and by psychologists studying aggression (Bettencourt and Miller, 1996). This sex difference implicitly has been interpreted to mean that women differ fundamentally from men by lacking the underlying motivation or capacity for violence that men have. Following from this interpretation is the deduction that uncovering the source of the sex difference in antisocial behaviour is the key that will also unlock the secret of what causes male violence. This deduction has directed much scientific attention toward explanatory variables on which men and women differ in fundamental ways, primarily physical strength (Felson, 1996), or hormones such as testosterone (Dabbs and Morris, 1990; Mazur and Booth, 1998).

However, findings accumulating in a specialist area, partner-violence research, have drawn attention to a surprising and puzzling possible exception to the rule of female non-violence; several studies suggest that women are as likely to hit their intimate partners as are men (for reviews see Archer, 2000; Fagan and Browne, 1994; Fiebert, 1997). Because women lack physical strength they usually do less injury than men to their partners, at least when they do not have a weapon. Nonetheless, the fact that when angry or distressed, women can exhibit the same physically aggressive behaviours that men exhibit could call into question the assumption that women lack the motivation and capacity for aggression. Moreover, sex equality for relationship violence would direct research attention away from *biological features* that make the sexes behave differently, and towards the question of what it is about the *situational features* of an intimate relationship that makes them behave similarly. Current interest in comparisons between the sexes on partner violence prompted us to include in this chapter measures of self- and partner-reported violence toward a partner.

Methods

Measures

PARENT REPORTS OF FIGHTING
As part of the Rutter Child Scale (RCS; Rutter *et al.*, 1970), at ages 5, 7, 9, and 11 parents rated whether the item 'Frequently fights with other children' did not apply (0), applied somewhat (1), or certainly applied (2) to the Dunedin Study member. We created a 'fighting' scale by combining these four parent ratings (alpha = 0.70).

TEACHER REPORTS OF FIGHTING
As part of the teacher version of the Rutter Child Scale, at ages 5, 7, 9, and 11 teachers rated the same item. We created a 'fighting' scale by combining these four teacher ratings (alpha = 0.63).

SELF-REPORTS OF VIOLENT DELINQUENT OFFENDING
At each of the four ages at which we administered the self-reported delinquency interviews (ages 13, 15, 18, and 21), we created a scale indexing the number of different violent offences committed by the Study member. The violent offences include simple assault, aggravated assault, rape, strongarm robbery, and gang-fighting.

INFORMANT REPORTS OF FIGHTING
At ages 18 and 21, each Study member nominated an informant who knew him or her well, and in a postal questionnaire the informants were asked whether the item 'Problem controlling anger, gets into fights' did not apply (0), applied somewhat (1), or certainly applied (2) to the Study member. We created a 'fighting' scale by combining these two informant ratings.

COURT CONVICTIONS FOR VIOLENT OFFENCES

From the conviction data described in chapter 3, we identified those Study members who had been convicted for a violent offence. A total of 46 Study members had been convicted of a total of 115 violent offences by age 21, including the following offences: inciting or threatening violence, using an attack dog on a person, presenting an offensive weapon, threatening a police officer, rape, manual assault, assault on a police officer, assault with a deadly weapon, aggravated robbery, and homicide.

VIOLENCE AGAINST A PARTNER

At age 21, Study members reported about partner violence during the past year in an intimate relationship (83 per cent) or as part of their dating experience (8 per cent). Study members who had not dated at all during the past 12 months (8 per cent) could not be asked questions about partner abuse. Moffitt *et al.* (1997) describe in detail the interview procedures, item content, response format, and psychometric properties of the Dunedin Study measure of physical abuse. Briefly, an interviewer read aloud a question for each abusive behaviour in turn, and participants circled 'yes' or 'no' on a private answer sheet, first reporting if they had ever practised abusive behaviour towards their partner (perpetration), and later reporting their partner's behaviour towards them (victimization).

Because sex comparisons on partner abuse measures can be controversial, we will go into some detail here to document the reliability and validity of the Dunedin Study's measure. The physical abuse scale was comprised of thirteen items describing physical acts of violence: physically twisted your partner's arm; pushed, grabbed, or shoved your partner; slapped your partner; physically forced sex on your partner; shaken your partner; thrown or tried to throw your partner bodily; thrown an object at your partner; choked or strangled your partner; kicked, bit, or hit your partner with a fist; hit or tried to hit your partner with something; beaten your partner up; threatened your partner with a knife or gun; used a knife or gun on your partner. 'Yes' responses were summed up to generate a scale counting the variety of abusive behaviours performed. We chose a variety scale for several reasons (for a review see Moffitt *et al.*, 2000). First, variety scores are less-skewed measures of antisocial behaviour than frequency scores. Second, they give equal weight to all acts, unlike frequency scores, which give more weight to non-serious acts that are committed frequently (e.g. slapping a partner) and give less weight to serious but infrequent acts (e.g., using a knife on a partner). Third, variety scales are more reliable than frequency reports because 'Has X happened?' delivers a more accurate response format than 'How many times has X happened?', especially among the most aggressive respondents whose violent acts have lost their salience because they happen frequently. Fourth, variety measures have been shown to be highly correlated with frequency scores and with scores weighted for act seriousness, and are known to be the strongest predictors of future violence. Our tests of models of the items in the physical violence scale have shown that all of the items are strong indicators of a unifying construct of abuse, all of the items are equally valid as indicators of the construct, both the perpetration and victimization scales have strong internal consistency (alphas = 0.76 and 0.82, respectively), and these estimates of the reliability of the scale did not differ by sex (Moffitt et al., 1997; Moffitt et al., 2000). We assessed the construct validity of the scale by ascertaining that the high end of the variety scale represented the clinically severe abuse cases in the sample. The mean perpetration score among Study participants investigated by the police for abuse was 1.4 SD higher than the mean for the remainder of the sample, and the mean perpetration score for Study participants reporting injury was 1.3 SD higher than the remainder (both $p<$ 0.001).

In addition to interviewing the Study members about their abuse experiences, we conducted identical interviews with the partners of the Study members to ascertain whether or not a couple corroborated each other's independent reports. Partners were interviewed if the Study member had been dating them for at least six months, living with them, or married to them; 360 partners met this criteria and participated in the study. (Further details about our study of couples are provided in chapter 14, as well as in Krueger et al., 1998; Moffitt et al., 1997; Robins et al., 2000.) The partners were interviewed separately and privately, with confidentiality guaranteed, by different interviewers who were blind to the responses provided by the other member of the couple. Couple members did not know in advance the content of their partners' interview schedule. This eliminated the possibility that couples would confer about their responses prior to the interview. When interviews turned to the topic of partner abuse, participants were given the opportunity to decline participation in that part of the interview. No participant refused. As reported by Moffitt et al. (1997), perpetrators' reports of their own abusive behaviour correlated closely with their partners' (victims') independent reports about the perpetrators' behaviour. A correlation between self- and other-reports of a person's behaviour is a coefficient of determination which is interpreted without squaring as the variance in one reporter's score that is explained or corroborated by the other reporter's score (Kenny, 1998). The resulting latent correlation was 0.83

between reports of violence in the relationship by male perpetrators and their female victims, and 0.71 between reports for female perpetrators and their male victims. These various methodological studies indicate that the reports of perpetration and victimization that we obtained were reliable and valid.

Data analysis approach

We standardized each of the measures of physical violence, using the z-score transformation on the whole sample, to facilitate a comparison of mean-level differences across sources and ages. We performed t-tests on each of the measures to test for mean-level differences between males and females. Effect sizes for comparisons between the sexes in table 5.1 may be operationally defined as 0.2 SD = a small effect, 0.5 SD = a medium effect, and 0.8 SD = a large effect.

Results

General violence

Table 5.1 shows the z-scores on each of the measures of physical violence. Males scored significantly higher than females on almost every measure of physically aggressive or violent behaviour. According to parent-, teacher-, and informant-reports, males were significantly more likely than females to fight with others and had more problems controlling their anger. According to self-reports of delinquency, males were significantly more likely to commit violent offences at every age from early adolescence to young adulthood. These reports were corroborated by court conviction records. By age 21, males were significantly more likely to have been convicted of a violent offence by an odds ratio of 4.8 (95 per cent CI: 2.2–10.4). In sum, there was impressive convergence across five data sources throughout the first two decades of life that males behave more aggressively at every age and in multiple settings.

Partner violence

There was one deviation from the general pattern. According to their self-reports, as well as their partners' reports, women reported as much physical violence towards their partners as men did (or slightly more). The partner-violence panel of table 5.1 shows four rows. The first row presents self-reports of physical abuse as reported by the full sample of Study members themselves. The results show that the female Study members were significantly more likely to report having perpetrated violence against their partners than

Table 5.1. *A comparison of males' and females' mean scores on measures of physically aggressive or violent behaviours, standardized for the whole sample*

Measure of physical violence	N of males/females	Age	Males' mean z-score	Females' mean z-score	Which sex is more violent p<0.01
Parent/Teacher reports of . . .					
Teacher Rutter 'fights' items	512/479	5, 7, 9, 11	0.15	−0.16	males
Parent Rutter 'fights' items	534/502	5, 7, 9, 11	0.09	−0.10	males
Self-reports of . . .					
Violent delinquent offending	501/473	13	0.21	−0.22	males
Violent delinquent offending	494/466	15	0.18	−0.19	males
Violent delinquent offending	476/456	18	0.15	−0.16	males
Violent delinquent offending	488/468	21	0.14	−0.14	males
Informant reports of . . .					
Problem controlling anger, gets into fights	452/459	18–21	0.09	−0.09	males
Court convictions . . .					
Per cent with violent crimes	510/487	to 21	8%	2%	males

Violence against partner . . .

Self-reports of physical abuse, whole sample	478/461	21	−0.12	0.13	females
Self-reports of physical abuse, couple members[a]	351 couples	21	−0.12	0.13	females
Partner's (i.e., victim's) reports of physical abuse, couple members[a]	349 couples	21	0.07	−0.09	females
Joint reports of physical abuse, averaged from self and victim[b]	30 clinical abusive couples	21	0.84	0.72	no significant difference

Notes:

[a] Sample consists of original study members who brought a partner to the Unit to participate in the study at age 21, and their partners; 360 couples (720 individuals) participated. Significance tests shown here were based on paired t-tests comparing males versus females within heterosexual couples with present data.

[b] Sample consists of the 30 couples (60 individuals) comprising 9 per cent of the Dunedin couples sample, whose abuse had lead to injury, medical treatment, law enforcement intervention, or help-seeking from shelters, counsellors, or courts. Significance test was a paired t-test comparing males versus females within heterosexual couples with present data.

were the male Study members. The second row of the panel presents data about partner-violence perpetration as assessed only among members of the 360 couples who participated in the study. The results show that female members of the couples reported perpetrating significantly more physical violence that male members of the couples. The third row presents data about partner-violence *victimization,* in which the Study members and their partners were asked to report about their partners' abusive behaviour toward them. The results show that male members of the couple reported being victimized by an abusive partner more than female members of the couple, again implicating substantial violence committed by women.

The fourth row of table 5.1 presents data about partner-violence perpetration among the 30 couples within the couples sample who experienced clinically significant abuse (9 per cent). This group comprises couples whose abuse resulted in injury (cuts, sprains, bruises, knocked-out loss of consciousness, broken bones, loose teeth; 80 per cent of this clinical group), precipitated medical treatment (first aid, emergency room, overnight hospitalization; 17 per cent), attracted police intervention or a court conviction (for charges including 'male assaults female, with weapon', 'common manual assault, domestic' and 'breaches non-molestation order'; 40 per cent), and/or prompted help-seeking for abuse (from a women's shelter, a marriage therapist, a lawyer, or the courts via restraining orders; 40 per cent). More details about correlates of abuse in this clinical sub-sample are reported by Moffitt, Robins and Caspi (forthcoming). The last row of table 5.1 compares perpetration scores for men and women in these clinical abuse couples. The measure of abuse perpetration is a highly reliable composite average score from each person's self-report of perpetration and the partner's report of victimization by that person. Scores were standardized as z-scores using the whole couples sample. The mean perpetration z-score for the 30 women in the clinical abusive couples was 0.72 (SD = 1.3). The mean perpetration z-score for the 30 men in the clinical abusive couples was 0.84 (SD = 1.6). Relative to couples in which neither partner was abusive (25 per cent of the 360 couples), men and women in clinical abusive couples scored respectively 1.48 and 1.51 SD higher on abuse, but men and women in clinical abusive relationships did not differ from each other.

Comment: the study of partner violence is critical to understanding antisocial behaviour in both sexes

The findings in table 5.1 confirmed expectations and offered surprises. With regard to the expected, the Dunedin Study shows, along with other studies, that there is a clear and consistent association between sex and violence that obtains across all data sources: males are over-represented in physically aggressive behaviours and in crimes of violence (Kruttschnidt, 1994). These sex differentials have been present in almost every society studied (Archer and McDaniel, 1995). The effect size for this sex difference is small to moderate (see table 3.3 as well as table 5.1).

With regard to the surprising, the Dunedin Study shows, along with other studies, that women's overall rates of partner-violence perpetration are similar to those of men. This is not an isolated finding. Many studies have found that substantial numbers of women self-report abusive behaviours toward male partners (for a meta-analysis see Archer, 2000; for a bibliography, see Fiebert 1997) and epidemiological studies show that although males are more likely than females to engage in almost every type of violence, the single exception is family violence (Ellickson, Saner, and McGuigan, 1997; Fagan and Browne, 1994). For example, the American National Family Violence Survey (Straus and Gelles, 1986) and the American National Youth Survey (Morse, 1995), as well as the Dunedin Study (Magdol *et al.*, 1997) all show that women in the 18–24 age group commit as much physical violence towards their partners as men. In these three large-scale studies, the finding about sex similarity obtains whether one examines reports of perpetration or reports of victimization. This finding continues to be hotly contested, and therefore we next address the challenges to it.

CHALLENGE ONE: ARE THE DATA ON FEMALE PARTNER VIOLENCE REALLY VALID?

There has been much controversy about whether or not survey data showing that women commit partner abuse should be considered valid. Contributing to the controversy is the fact that two kinds of epidemiological studies have sometimes generated wildly discrepant estimates of female perpetration. However, the discrepant findings appear to emerge for an obvious methodological reason. Rates of female perpetration depend on whether the data-collection method emphasizes to the respondents one of two contexts: the context of crime victimization versus the context of the partner relationship (Mihalic and Elliott, 1997). When victimization-survey respondents are instructed to think about their *assault victimization experiences* and then asked to report the identity of their assailants, victims of both sexes report very low overall rates of partner abuse, and, specifically, male victims report relatively low rates of perpetration by women (e.g., Bachman and Saltzman, 1995; Langley, Martin, and Nada-Raja, 1997; Tjaden and Thoennes, 1998). In contrast, when respondents are instructed to think about their *relationships with partners* and then asked about the occurrence of abusive acts, they report much higher overall rates of partner abuse and the rates and types of partner-abuse perpetration reported for women are similar to (or slightly greater than) those of men. This effect of the way the questions are introduced has been demonstrated within a single interview conducted with the same respondents (Mihalic and Elliott, 1997). When the Dunedin men were interviewed by us about their relationships, they reported high rates of victimization by partners (Magdol *et al.*, 1997), whereas when the same men were interviewed on the same day by another researcher about their experiences as criminal assault victims, they reported low rates of victimization by partners (Langley *et al.*, 1997). The aforementioned discrepant findings about men's reports of female perpetration can be resolved if we assume that most men, when asked to describe a time they were assaulted, are triggered to recall assault by another man.

Reporting periods also affect the validity of men's reports of women's perpetration. In the American National Violence Against Women victimization survey, the sex difference in partner assault was found to be wide for lifetime reports but narrow for past-year reports (Tjaden and Thoennes, 1998). This discrepancy is consistent with the hypothesis that men's memories of assaults by women decay and are not easily retrieved unless the interview format specifically probes for them (no other explanation for the discrepancy in this survey suggests itself). Thus, although life-time statistics from national victimization surveys are often put forward as evidence that there is a wide sex difference in partner violence, the past-year statistics from these surveys point to the conclusion that men and women have similar rates of partner violence in Britain (Mirlees-Black, 1999) and America (Tjaden and Thoennes, 1998). Curiously, the lifetime data from victim surveys are cited more often than the past-year data, despite widespread consensus among scientists that past-year data are better measures.

The epidemiological surveys yielding the lowest rates of female perpetration share three methodological features: they used a lifetime reporting period, they primed respondents to recall criminal assault, and the researchers interviewed only victims and therefore their estimates of female abuse depended solely on men's recall. In contrast, the epidemiological surveys yielding similar rates of male and female perpetration have incorporated one or more of the following design features: they use a past-year reporting period, they prime respondents to recall conflicts with their partner, and they interview women about their perpetration as well as interviewing men about victimization. In such surveys the finding that women commit abuse has been corroborated by reports from both male victims and women perpetrators (Fiebert, 1997; Magdol *et al.*, 1997; O'Leary *et al.*, 1989; Straus and Gelles, 1986). In addition, our Dunedin findings suggest that sex similarities in partner violence are unlikely to be the product of biased reporting by men or women; as we reported earlier, the high agreement levels between members of a couple about violence in their relationship leaves little reason to doubt the trustworthiness of the data (Moffitt *et al.*, 1997). Moreover, as shown in table 5.1, the results point to sex similarities in partner violence regardless of whether the man or woman *within the same couple* is the source of the data.

CHALLENGE TWO: IS WOMEN'S PARTNER VIOLENCE MOTIVATED BY SELF-DEFENCE?

The interpretation of the finding that women participate in partner abuse is often challenged with the observation that any acts attributed to women must have been motivated by self-defence. If women's self-reports of perpetration represent nothing more than self-defence, then men's perpetration becomes once again the primary variable of concern, and a woman's perpetration is merely another outcome measure of male perpetration, alongside her injury. Early on, researchers attempted to uncover whether women's perpetration is self-defence or not by asking respondents who hit first; surveys showed that women say they hit first about half the time (Henton, Cate, Koval, Lloyd, and Christopher, 1993; Morse, 1995; Stets and Straus, 1990). The National Youth Survey was used for an in-depth analysis of this question, and findings revealed that about half of male and female respondents described their most serious fight in the past year as including mutual violence. When their most serious fight had involved one-sided violence that was not reciprocated, both men and women were twice as likely to report that the perpetrator was the female (Morse, 1995). Nonetheless, hitting first in an incident may still reflect pre-emptive self-defence if the woman has been subjected to attacks by the man in the past. The self-defence question is unlikely to be resolved in the near future, because it is inherently difficult to conduct a definitive empirical test of the motives behind private acts. However, four contemporary findings indicate the possibility that a self-defence account of women's perpetration is incomplete.

First, longitudinal-prospective research shows that a history of early delinquency predicts women's subsequent violence against their partners (Giordano, Millhollin, Cernkovich, Pugh, and Rudolph, 1999). This finding also obtains in the Dunedin Study, where we have shown that violent delinquency before age 15 predicts abuse perpetration at age 21 equally well for women and for men (Magdol *et al.*, 1998a). This shows that a pre-existing

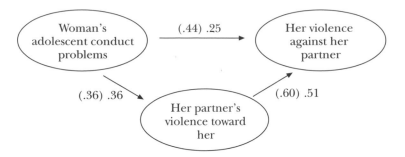

5.1 Testing the self-defence hypothesis: women with prior conduct problems abuse their partner in excess of any provoking effects of his abuse. N = 212 study women and their partners. Zero-order correlations are in parentheses next to standardised regression coefficients. All are significant at p < .05.

longstanding tendency to behave antisocially in interpersonal encounters predisposes both men and women to abuse their partners.

Second, in the Dunedin Study, we can go one step further and use our sub-sample of 360 couples (see chapter 14) to provide a direct test of the self-defence hypothesis. Specifically, we examined whether women with a history of conduct problems engaged in violence against their partners, after we controlled for the amount of violence that they said their partners committed against them. If women's abuse perpetration is a defensive reaction to male attack, women's history of conduct problems should fail to predict their abuse perpetration after controlling for their partners' abuse against them. To test this hypothesis, we performed the path analysis shown in figure 5.1. For this analysis, we assessed Study members' history of antisocial conduct problems by summing the DSM-IV symptoms listed in table 4.1. We used this conduct disorder score to predict Study womens' own self-reports of physical abuse at age 21 (against their partner), after controlling for their reports of victimization by him. The results in figure 5.1 show two noteworthy findings. First, women with a history of conduct problems were more likely to become involved in a relationship with an abusive man (beta = 0.36, p < 0.01), and being involved in a relationship with a physically abusive man contributed significantly to women's own perpetration of violence against their partners (beta = 0.51, p < 0.01). This significant pathway (or indirect effect) could be consistent with the self-defence hypothesis. It suggests that one reason women with a history of conduct problems hit their partners is because they become involved in relationships with men who abuse them. (This tendency of antisocial youth to form intimate relationships with antisocial partners who abuse them is discussed in greater depth in chapter 14.) Second, even after controlling for their partners' physical

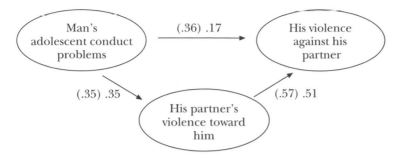

5.2 Men with prior conduct problems abuse their partner in excess of any provoking effects of her abuse. N = 129 study men and their partners. Zero-order correlations are in parentheses next to standardised regression coefficients. All are significant at p < .05.

abuse, women with a juvenile history of conduct problems were still likely to commit violence against their partners (beta = 0.25, p<0.01). That is, women with a history of antisocial behaviour hit their partners regardless of whether or not their partners hit them; apparently, women's perpetration was not simply a defensive reaction to male attack. The results in figure 5.2 show that the same findings also applied to Dunedin men. In tandem, the results in the two figures suggest that, among both men *and* women, the perpetration of partner violence in the context of adult intimate relationships is but another expression of an earlier-emerging antisocial propensity; it is not only a self-defensive response to violence committed against them by their partners.

Third, research from the Dunedin Study on the personality characteristics of abusers is pertinent to the self-defence hypothesis. If all women are uniformly vulnerable to male abuse and women's apparent perpetration represents solely a reasonable defensive reaction to male attack, we would not expect individual differences in personality to predict abuse perpetration among Dunedin women as well they do in Dunedin men. Yet the findings revealed that pre-existing characteristics such as approval of the use of aggression, excessive jealousy and suspiciousness, a tendency to experience intense and rapid negative emotions, and poor self-control, predicted which Dunedin women were to engage in violent behaviour towards their partners (and toward non-intimates too) three years later (Moffitt *et al.*, 2000). These extreme personality traits best predicted the behaviour of men and women in the Dunedin sample's clinically abusive couples, who had experienced injury, treatment, and/or law enforcement intervention (Moffitt, Robins, and Caspi, forthcoming). Taken together with an earlier finding that aggressivity is related to women's perpetration (O'Leary, Malone and Tyree, 1994), these personality findings weigh in on the side of women's perpetration being more than self-defence alone, at least in a substantial proportion of young couples.

Fourth, whereas self-defence may account for women's behaviour toward their intimate partners, self-defence is less intuitive as an account of their general crime toward non-intimate strangers; yet the pattern of concurrent overlap between partner abuse and general crime is approximately the same for Dunedin women as for Dunedin men (Moffitt *et al.*, 2000); in Dunedin, at age 21, women who hit their partners were 4.4 (95 per cent confidence interval: 2.1–9.1) times as likely to have committed a violent crime against someone other than an intimate partner. More evidence suggesting that women's capacity for violence extends beyond what can be accounted for by self-defence provoked by male battery comes from justice-system statistics which show that just under one-fifth of all American violent offenders are women and three-quarters of their victims are also women (according to nationwide victimization surveys, arrest data, convicted felonies, and census of correctional inmates; Greenfield and Snell, 1999). Undeniably, some women's perpetration is self-defence but the data suggest that many women's perpetration is motivated by the same intra-personal psychological factors that motivate men's perpetration of violence against their partners.

CHALLENGE THREE: IS WOMEN'S VIOLENCE AGAINST MEN CONSEQUENTIAL, OR TRIVIAL?

Although women's self-reports are increasingly accepted as valid, many writers argue that women's perpetration may exist but does not warrant study because women's inferior strength precludes them from inflicting injury (for cogent analysis of these arguments, see Straus, 1993, 1997, 1998). Male perpetrators are more likely to cause bodily injury, implying that male perpetrators therefore constitute the social problem that warrants research (e.g., Kurz, 1993). Despite this widespread perception that women do not injure, inflicting injury in domestic disputes is not the exclusive prerogative of men, as surveys reveal that one-third of domestic injuries are inflicted by women (Archer, 2000; Morse, 1995; Tjaden and Thoennes, 1998), although more injured women do obtain medical care (Morse, 1995). Moreover, lethal injury is not the prerogative of the strong, because weapons available to women can nullify any advantages that men may have in physical strength (Felson, 1996). This fact is made clear by large-scale studies of the most consequential of injurious incidents, domestic homicide, showing that lethal female-to-male violence is not rare; approximately one-quarter of domestic homicide offenders are women (Archer, 2000; Dugan, Nagin, and Rosenfeld, in press; Greenfield and Snell, 1999). Nonetheless, women's perpetration behaviour continues to be trivialized by assertions that only injury by men, and not aggressive behaviour by women, is important enough to warrant scientific focus.

Such assertions have gained currency with the recent claim that data on consequential injurious violence, that is, *real* violence, is best obtained by researching shelter samples or adjudicated samples. Shelter samples do yield the widest sex difference (Archer, 2000), but as a matter of pragmatics, shelter samples are ill suited for comparisons of men's and women's rates of violence because shelters do not admit male victims, shelter staff often coach women to minimize their role in domestic violence in preparation for prosecution against the partner, and shelters tend to refuse admission to women who are aggressive (Loseke, 1992). Nonetheless, the broader concern is that community surveys may generate data on high rates of female perpetration, but such data are misleading because they cannot be generalized to clinically significant cases of serious abuse (Johnson, 1995). Researchers have been cautioned against accepting the sex similarity in partner violence without an empirical test in a clinical sample (Straus, 1998). As such, we tested the assumption that sex differences would widen, and men's levels of abuse would exceed women's, if clinically significant abuse cases were studied. We isolated from the Dunedin birth cohort for special focus the thirty cases who were involved in a relationship having abuse that involved them in therapeutic or justice systems for the treatment and control of domestic violence. In 80 per cent of these couples abuse had lead to injury. As the last line of table 5.1 showed, both men and women in these couples had similar, and highly elevated, levels of abuse perpetration. This finding indicates that the sex-similarity in partner violence in the Dunedin Study is not an artefact of studying only mild levels of abuse.

Not surprisingly, partner violence in the population is arrayed along a continuum from none to mild to severe, and when the most severe end of the continuum is studied, stronger associations between partner violence and its correlates are found (e.g. MacMillan and Gartner, 1999; Pan, Neidig, and O'Leary, 1994). Is there evidence that the sex difference depends on severity? Some evidence suggests that a male excess of partner violence increases as the severity of the violence increases. The male:female sex ratio for past-year self- and victim-reports of partner violence is about 1:1. This male:female ratio widens to about 2:1 for measures of injury, and widens further to about 3:1 for domestic homicide. However, this pattern is open to alternate interpretation because official indicators of injury and homicide are influenced by selection biases that could result in under-estimates of female perpetration. Some researchers have argued that the specific violent behaviours used by women in domestic incidents are less serious than men's. Comparisons of the sexes on specific behaviours show that women are more likely to slap, whereas men are more likely to throw their partners bodily. However, the same comparisons reveal that women are more likely than men to use knives (Greenfield and Snell, 1999; Moffitt et al., 1997; Tjaden and Thoennes, 1998). Thus, both men's and women's choice of behaviour may be a matter of ease and efficacy, rather than severity. In our assessment, the evidence is not yet conclusive as to whether the sex difference varies with severity. In this chapter, we have shown that in the Dunedin sample, the sex similarity in abuse perpetration is as strong at the severest clinical end of the abuse continuum as it is at milder levels, though the finding we report here awaits replication.

In response to the claim that women's abuse is unimportant because it seldom injures men, researchers of family dynamics have cautioned that although women's abuse may not injure men, it may well lead to injury of the women themselves. Women's perpetration reported in community surveys may seem benign, but it could be promoted to the list of risk factors for women's injury because a woman's abusive behaviour may increase the probability that her partner will retaliate and escalate his own violence to injurious levels (Straus, 1990, 1993, 1997, 1998). Following this model, the argument that women's abuse perpetration in the community is too trivial to research could prove to be tantamount to arguing that smoking in the community is too trivial to research and scientists should focus on cases of lung cancer, or that condom use in the community is too trivial to research and scientists should focus on cases of HIV infection. It is now recognized that behaviours in the community that were previously thought to be benign can be risk factors for outcomes in the clinic and the courts. More research is needed to determine if women's abuse does indeed increase their own injury risk.

Finally, the assumption that physical injuries are the only consequential sequelae of partner abuse has been challenged by developmentalists, who provide ample evidence that a mother's abusive behaviour towards her male partner harms the mental health of young children who observe it (Grych and Fincham, 1990). Because mothers are such influential role models for their children, women's perpetration has been hypothesized to promote the next generation's aggression (Moffitt and Caspi, 1998). One study has demonstrated that marital violence initiated by mothers later predicted depression, substance dependence and crime among children who were grown to young adulthood, over and above the effects of other forms of family adversity (Fergusson and Horwood, 1998).

CONCLUSION

Our Dunedin analyses suggest that the sexes are similar on partner violence perpetration even at the most severe end of the violence continuum among couples suffering injury and official intervention, and we showed that self-defence is not a good explanation for this mutuality. But whether the sexes are *precisely* matched in their perpetration matters little in the face of other evidence that women inflict one-third of domestic injuries and one-quarter of domestic deaths. Our view is that female perpetration of violence inside intimate relationships is a valid phenomenon that is very common, very consequential, and very poorly understood, and warrants more research focus, not less.

Violence researchers from the fields of criminology and abnormal psychology have been impressed by the difference between the sexes in measures of general violence. This impression has directed researchers toward a search for individual characteristics (often biological) that differentiate males from females and that might explain why they behave so differently. We suggest that it is time for violence researchers to take on board the extremely robust finding that inside intimate relationships and the privacy of home, females are just as physically aggressive as males. Once acknowledged, this epidemiological fact should direct researchers toward a search for situational influences shared by males and females that might explain why they behave so similarly. (We will return to this question of social influence within intimate relationships in chapter 14.) A complete theory of violence must account for both the sex differences in general violence and the sex convergence in family violence. Anything less tells only half the story.

Take-home messages

- Males score higher than females on measures of physical aggression and violence at every age and in every setting, except . . . .
- On measures of partner violence, the violent behaviour of males is matched or exceeded by that of females.
- The sex similarity on partner violence appears to be robust, applies to clinically significant couples whose abuse is injurious, treated, and/or adjudicated, and cannot be explained by the hypothesis that women's aggression is self-defence.

Unanswered questions

- There is currently no compelling explanation for the well-documented finding that women commit as much physical violence toward their partners as men do. Theoretical accounts of sex differences in anti-social behaviour must grapple with this exception to an otherwise general rule that men are more aggressive.
- More research is needed on the consequences of women's domestic violence, for the mental and physical health of male partners, of children, and of the women themselves.

CHAPTER SIX

Sex and the developmental stability of antisocial behaviour

How stable is antisocial behaviour? Even in the 1970s, during the heyday of 'situationism' in psychology, behavioural scientists acknowledged that individual differences in aggressive behaviour are stable (Olweus, 1979). Longitudinal studies completed both before and after Olweus' review showed that antisocial behaviour was predictable from one point in time to another (e.g., Huesmann *et al.*, 1982; Farrington, 1986; Macfarlane, Allen, and Honzik, 1954; Stattin and Magnusson, 1991b; Pulkinnen and Pitkanen, 1993; Patterson, Reid, and Dishion, 1992; Stanger, Achenbach, and Verhulst, 1997). However, most of the studies of the stability of antisocial behaviour have examined only males because historically few longitudinal studies of antisocial behaviour have sampled girls; in fact, the two most oft-cited authoritative reviews on the topic of the stability of antisocial behaviour reviewed studies of males only (Loeber, 1982; Olweus, 1979). Some authors state that antisocial behaviour is less stable and predictable among females than among males (e.g., Cairns and Cairns, 1984; Moss and Susman, 1980), while other authors state that there is no reliable sex difference in the stability of antisocial behaviour (Cairns and Cairns, 1994; Tremblay *et al.*, 1992). In our reading of the literature, we were impressed at how often each view was stated with confidence. Both cannot be correct.

The goal of this chapter is to test whether antisocial behaviour is equally stable from childhood to adolescence to adulthood in both males and females. To examine this question we compared the stability of individual differences across time using different types of measures of antisocial behaviour, to test if estimates of stability depend on the source of data about antisocial behaviour.

A. CONTINUITY AND CHANGE IN CONDUCT DISORDER

We began our examination of sex differences in the stability of antisocial behaviour by evaluating the extent of continuity and change in diagnoses of conduct disorder during adolescence. According to one hypothesis, 'children who display extremely high rates of antisocial behaviour early in life are more likely to continue to show high rates of antisocial behaviour than those with lower rates of antisocial behaviour' (Loeber, 1982, p. 1433). In other words, the children whose antisocial behaviour is rated the most severe are likely to defy regression to the mean and remain in the severe range over time (Patterson, 1982). Because males are more likely than females to show extreme levels of antisocial behaviour, those males who do so may also be more likely to show continuity of their extreme state over time. Sex differences in continuity would be consistent with the results in chapter 4, which showed that among males during the second decade of life, age was only weakly associated with the prevalence of conduct disorder. In contrast, chapter 4 revealed that few females met diagnostic criteria in early adolescence, quite a few showed onset of disorder following puberty, and a majority showed apparent remission of their disorder by late adolescence. This observation suggests that if diagnoses of conduct disorder were made repeatedly for the same sample, the boys would show higher stability of disorder than the girls.

Methods

Measures
DSM-IV diagnoses of conduct disorder. Diagnoses of conduct disorder at ages 11, 13, 15 and 18 are described in chapter 4.

Data analysis approach
At each age Study members were classified into those who met (vs. those who did not meet) diagnostic criteria for conduct disorder. For a series of four observation periods, there are 2^4 possible response patterns that describe the history of conduct disorder over the four time periods. These patterns range from Study members who are consistently classified as conduct-disordered to those who are consistently classified as non-conduct-disordered. The pattern of stability and change in conduct disorder over time may be described by the state-to-state transition matrices linking the child's diagnostic status at one time to his or her status at some future time. An example of the state-to-state transition matrix is given below. In this

matrix, the child's status at some Time t is related to his or her status at some later Time t + 1, and the cells of the matrix show the conditional probabilities that a child who was in a given state at some Time t will be observed in a given state at some Time t + 1.

		t + 1	
		Conduct Disorder	No Conduct Disorder
t	Conduct Disorder	a	1 − a
	No Conduct Disorder	1 − b	b

The parameters of this transition matrix have ready interpretations as an account of the process of change over the interval t, t + 1. Specifically:

1. The parameter 'a' shows the probability that a child who met diagnostic criteria for conduct disorder at Time t would continue to meet diagnostic criteria at Time t + 1. This parameter measures the stability of conduct disorder. Accordingly, the parameter (1 − a) provides an estimate of the rate at which remission of conduct disorder occurred with the interval t, t + 1.

2. Similarly, parameter 'b' estimates the rate at which children who do not meet criteria for conduct disorder remain undiagnosed during the interval t, t + 1, and the parameter (1 − b) represents the rate at which children without conduct disorder develop conduct disorder over this interval.

Results

Table 6.1 reports on the state-to-state transitions in conduct disorder during the four assessment intervals from phase 11 to phase 18 of the Dunedin Study. The transition probabilities are presented separately for males and females averaged across assessment intervals of one phase (phase 11–13, phase 13–15, phase 15–18), assessment intervals of two phases (phase 11–15, phase 13–18) and an assessment interval of three phases (phase 11–18). The important differences between the sexes are indexed by the stability and remission transitions. About half (49 per cent) of the males who were diagnosed with conduct disorder at any one phase between phases 11 and 18 showed stability of the disorder and were likely to be diagnosed with conduct disorder at the next phase whereas the other half (51 per cent) showed apparent remission of their status and were classified as non-disordered at the next phase. In contrast, only 16 per cent of the females showed stability of the disorder across an interval of one phase and fully 83 per cent showed

Table 6.1. *Continuity and change in conduct disorder: observed transition probabilities between conduct disorder (CD) diagnoses*

Time interval	Stability of CD		Remission of CD		Stability of non-CD		New onset of CD	
	Males	Females	Males	Females	Males	Females	Males	Females
1 phase[a]	0.49	0.16	0.51	0.83	0.92	0.96	0.08	0.04
2 phases[b]	0.36	0.11	0.64	0.89	0.89	0.95	0.11	0.05
3 phases[c]	0.30	0.00	0.70	1.00	0.89	0.98	0.11	0.01

Notes:

[a] Includes intervals between 11–13 years, 13–15 years, and 15–18 years. Analysis was based on 2,573 transitions.

[b] Includes intervals between 11–15 years and 13–18 years. Analysis was based on 1,791 transitions.

[c] Includes interval between 11–18 years. Analysis was based on 859 transitions.

apparent remission of their status. Across assessment intervals of two as well as three phases, about one-third of the males (36 per cent and 30 per cent, respectively) showed stability of conduct disorder whereas nearly two-thirds (64 per cent and 70 per cent, respectively) showed remission. In contrast, only 11 per cent of the females showed stability across two assessment intervals and none of the females showed stability from phase 11 to phase 18.

B. THE STABILITY OF INDIVIDUAL DIFFERENCES IN ANTISOCIAL BEHAVIOUR

The results in the previous section showed that there were sex differences in the stability of antisocial behaviour when stability was defined in terms of passing the threshold for diagnosis. That is, when we applied the same diagnostic criteria for defining conduct disorder to the whole sample, males show much more continuity of disorder than females. In this section, we now examine whether there are sex differences in the stability of antisocial behaviour when stability is defined in terms of retaining one's placement in a distribution of scores relative to other persons. Whereas in the previous section we examined the stability of more extreme forms of antisocial behaviour by calculating the probability that a person will meet the criteria for conduct disorder given that he or she met the criteria at earlier ages, in this section we assess the stability of antisocial behaviour by correlating parent-, teacher-, self-, and informant-reports of antisocial behaviour across time for males and females relative to their same-sex peers.

Methods

Measures

Parent reports of antisocial behaviour, when the Study members were aged 5, 7, 9, 11, 13, and 15, were described in chapter 3.

Teacher reports of antisocial behaviour, when the Study members were aged 5, 7, 9, 11, and 13, were described in chapter 3.

Self-reports of antisocial behaviour, at ages 11, 13, 15, 18, and 21, were described in chapter 3.

Informant reports of Study members' antisocial behaviour, at ages 18 and 21, were described in chapter 3.

Data analysis approach

To assess the stability of individual differences we calculated Pearson product-moment correlations between ratings of antisocial behaviour across time.

Results

The results are presented in four tables, each corresponding to its data source: table 6.2 shows the cross-age correlations for parent reports of antisocial behaviour; table 6.3 shows the cross-age correlations for teacher-reports; table 6.4 shows the cross-age correlations for self-reports; table 6.5 shows the cross-age correlations for informant reports. In each table, the cross-age correlations for boys appear above the diagonal and the comparable correlations for girls appear below the diagonal. The pairwise N for the tabled correlations ranged from 457 to 478 for females and from 482 to 507 for males.

The first three tables provide support for the 'twin laws of longitudinal research' (Caspi and Roberts, 1999): first, the stability of individual differences increases as the age of study participants increases. Second, the stability of individual differences decreases as the time interval between observations increases. The Dunedin findings replicated this law with specific reference to antisocial behaviour, and extended this conclusion in two ways: by showing that this empirical generalization applied to both males

Table 6.2. *The cross-age stability of individual differences in parent reports of antisocial behaviour for boys and girls. Girls' stability coefficients are below the diagonal*

Age	5	7	9	11	13	15
5	1	0.57*	0.52*	0.45*	0.38*	0.36*
7	0.54*	1	0.71*	0.56*	0.43*	0.34*
9	0.47*	0.63*	1	0.61*	0.50*	0.43*
11	0.47*	0.54*	0.66*	1	0.56*	0.50*
13	0.41*	0.51*	0.55*	0.63*	1	0.74*
15	0.34*	0.40*	0.45*	0.55*	0.70*	1

Notes: Measures were the Rutter Antisocial Scale at ages 5–11, and the Peterson-Quay Conduct + Aggression Scale at ages 13–15. All data were collected via self-completed questionnaire.
* Significant at $p < 0.01$.

Table 6.3. *The cross-age stability of individual differences in teacher reports of antisocial behaviour for boys and girls. Girls' stability coefficients are below the diagonal*

Age	5	7	9	11	13
5	1	0.51*	0.43*	0.39*	0.32*
7	0.33*	1	0.56*	0.49*	0.36*
9	0.35*	0.51*	1	0.52*	0.31*
11	0.20*	0.30*	0.36*	1	0.39*
13	0.17*	0.32*	0.32*	0.30*	1

Notes: Measures were the Rutter Antisocial Scale at ages 5–13. All data were collected via postal checklist.
* Significant at $p < 0.01$.

and females and by showing that it obtained when using different data sources.

Estimates of the stability of antisocial behaviour differed somewhat depending on the data source. Parental ratings of both male and female Study members yielded the highest stability coefficients, followed by teacher- and self-ratings. It could be that continuity introduced by the same rater over time (i.e., the parent) accounted for the higher all-around esti-

Table 6.4. *The cross-age stability of individual differences in self-reports of antisocial behaviour for boys and girls. Girls' stability coefficients are below the diagonal*

Age	11	13	15	18	21
11	1	0.32*	0.23*	0.20*	0.12*
13	0.15*	1	0.55*	0.35*	0.23*
15	0.08	0.52*	1	0.59*	0.42*
18	−0.02	0.23*	0.33*	1	0.68*
21	−0.02	0.32*	0.43*	0.63*	1

Notes: Measures were the DISC-C CD Scale at age 11, Self-Reported Early Delinquency Scale at ages 13–15, and the Self-Reported Delinquency Variety Scale at ages 18–21. All data were collected via interview.
* Significant at $p < 0.01$.

Table 6.5. *The cross-age stability of individual differences in informants' reports of antisocial behaviour for boys and girls. Girls' stability coefficients are below the diagonal*

Age	18	21
18	1	0.50*
21	0.29*	1

Notes: Data were collected via postal checklist.
* Significant at $p < 0.01$.

mates of stability relative to teacher ratings (different teachers reported at different phases). This is because parental ratings capture not only the 'true' stability of children's behaviour but also the stability of parental perceptions and reporting styles. What may be less obvious is the reason for the differences between tables 6.2 and 6.4, because the correlations in each of these two tables are made up from observations provided by the same rater over time (the parent and the self, respectively). However, it is important to note that whereas the parents were adults when they made the ratings at every phase, the children were still maturing and thus were not necessarily the 'same' rater at every assessment phase. Developmental changes between ages 11 and 21 may mean that at different assessment phases the Study members had a different cognitive view of the reporting instrument as well as of their own behaviour. Another methodological confound, which may have served to lower the all-around stability estimates in table 6.3, is that the age-11 instrument was different from the instrument used at the subsequent ages. When the age-11 self-ratings are removed from table 6.3, the stability estimates approximate those obtained from parental ratings.

There were a few indications of sex differences in the stability of anti-social behaviour. Across the four tables, twenty-four of the thirty-six stability coefficients were higher for males than for females, but the differences were very small and statistically negligible. The fewest sex differences emerged in the stability estimates obtained from parent ratings of antisocial behaviour (table 6.2). More sex differences emerged in the stability estimates obtained from teacher ratings (table 6.3), self-ratings (table 6.4), and informant ratings (table 6.5). It should be noted that the sex differences in table 6.4 were primarily attributable to the longitudinal decay associated with girls' age-11 self-reports of antisocial behaviour. The lower stability associated with these ratings may be due to restriction of range; girls' scores on this age-11 measure were severely skewed toward zero. When ratings from this age period were removed from table 6.4, there was little evidence of sex differences in the stability of self-reports of antisocial behaviour.

Comment: the stability of antisocial behaviour is stronger than it looks here

Just how big should a 'stability coefficient' be to be impressive? The meaning of effect sizes has been clarified elsewhere (e.g., Rosenthal and Rubin, 1982), and the stability coefficients reported here deserve but only a few additional comments. First, Pearson stability correlations should be interpreted without squaring as the variance in one measure at one point in time that is explained by a measure at another point in time. This is because if one is interested in the percentage of variance common to two variables purported to measure the same construct (that is, if the variables are indi-cators of the same latent construct), the unsquared correlation is the appro-priate index (Ozer, 1985). Understood in these terms, the results in tables 6.2–5 point to moderate and at times even strong effect sizes for the stabil-ity of antisocial behaviour across the first two decades of life (Cohen, 1992).

Second, measures that are aggregated across multiple sources of data and across multiple settings (e.g., parents and teachers) are likely to yield higher estimates of stability than reported here because different sources of data about antisocial behaviour yield complementary information about individ-ual differences (Loeber *et al.*, 1990) and thus multi-source composites yield a more reliable indication of an individual's stable, cross-situational tendencies (Bank *et al.*, 1990). We did not aggregate measures in this chapter, because our goal was to compare stabilities across different data sources.

Third, our correlations are uncorrected for measurement error. Such correlations provide a misleading impression because they conflate any true change with artefactual change arising from errors in measurement. This conflation produces overestimates of change and underestimates of stability. Corrections for measurement unreliability point to even greater stability of individual differences in antisocial behaviour than shown by the simple correlations we report here (Fergusson and Horwood, 1993). Understood in these terms, the correlations in tables 6.2–5 under-represent the stability of antisocial behaviour. Reports in which longitudinal antisocial measures were corrected for measurement error have revealed stability coefficients greater than 0.70 across periods of 5–10 years from childhood to adolescence (Olweus, 1979). In the Dunedin Study, we have reported corrected estimates in the range of 0.60 (Jeglum-Bartusch *et al.*, 1997). (Note: we did not include multi-source, multi-method structural equation models in this chapter to avoid the length of such a presentation in a data set of this complexity; moreover, the reliability of the measures of antisocial behaviour is the same for both sexes, and measurement error attenuation, being constant across the sexes, is thus immaterial to the question of whether or not there are sex differences in the stability of individual differences. However, Jeglum-Bartusch *et al.* (1997) present detailed structural models of stability for parent-, teacher-, and self-reports from ages 5 to 18 in the Dunedin Study.)

On the whole, then, the coefficients reported in this section provide a conservative underestimate of the stability of individual differences. Nonetheless, the findings illustrate that in all probability antisocial males and females will remain more antisocial than their same-sex age-peers across time and in diverse circumstances. When it comes to antisocial behaviour, knowledge about an individual's placement in a distribution is psychometrically informative and clinically meaningful. This is equally true for males and females.

Take-home messages

- Different data sources – including parent-, teacher-, and self-ratings – suggest that the antisocial behaviour of males and females is predictable across time.
- Over the first two decades of life, *relative to their same-sex peers*, antisocial boys and girls are equally likely to retain their standing in the distribution of antisocial behaviour. Both sexes show at least moderate stability.

- Although antisocial girls retain their rank across time relative to their sex, girls are less likely than boys to sustain over time behaviour that is extreme enough to warrant a diagnosis.
- Males and females are not equally likely to retain a diagnosis of conduct disorder over time; when the same diagnostic criteria defining disorder are applied to both males and females, males show much more continuity of disorder than females.

Unanswered question

- What explains the instability of diagnosable conduct disorder among girls?

CHAPTER SEVEN

Sex and the age of onset of delinquency and conduct disorder

Of all the developmental parameters of antisocial behaviour, perhaps the most extensively studied has been the age at which it begins (LeBlanc and Loeber, 1998). An exhaustive review by Farrington and eight expert colleagues (Farrington, Loeber, Elliott, *et al.*, 1990) precludes the need for us to review this large literature here. It can be summarised by the well-documented observation that early onset of antisocial behaviour problems is the single best predictor of serious adult criminal outcomes. Despite the importance of age of onset for theory and prevention planning, we found no published systematic comparisons of sex differences in this important variable. Unpublished sex comparisons of onset are cited by Elliott (1994) who mentioned that fewer girls than boys initiated self-reported serious offending at every age, and by Weiner and Wolfgang (1989) who mentioned that more girls than boys were first registered by police before age 14. Because these reports are unpublished, and seem to conflict, this chapter compares the sexes on age of onset.

Sex comparisons of onset age are interesting because it is possible to make opposing predictions about what the results might be. On the one hand, if, as we have seen, girls compared to boys have less extreme antisocial behaviour, or less aetiological press toward antisocial behaviour, we might expect girls would show onset at *older* ages on average. On the other hand, if, as we have also seen, the onset of antisocial behaviour for girls is closely tied to pubertal timing, we might expect girls would show onset at *younger* ages on average because girls tend to complete puberty a year or two before boys. In this chapter, we compare Dunedin boys and girls on age of onset of antisocial behaviour, using official crime, diagnosis of conduct disorder, and self-reported delinquency.

Method

Measures

Court convictions for crimes and *police arrest* contacts for juvenile offences were measured using the official record sources described earlier in chapter 3. *DSM-IV diagnoses of conduct disorder* were measured using the procedures described earlier in chapter 4. *Self-reports of delinquent behaviours* were measured using the assessments described earlier in chapter 3.

Data analysis approach

To determine the age of onset of antisocial behaviour we prepared cumulative onset graphs which show the ages at which males and females began different behaviours. In these graphs the variable of interest is the length of time that elapses before an event (such as a conviction, an arrest, a diagnosis, or a self-reported act) occurs. Survival analysis was used to take into account the fact that there are some individuals for whom the event has not occurred. To evaluate differences between males and females, we used a non-parametric test, which is approximately a χ^2 (1 df), to compare survival times for the two groups.

Results

The cumulative-onset graphs show that at every age for each of the four measures, more boys than girls had begun antisocial behaviour. The probability of remaining non-antisocial across time was significantly higher for girls than for boys whether measured by conviction (figure 7.1, $\chi^2 = 32.2$, $p < 0.001$), arrest (figure 7.2, $\chi^2 = 17.2$, $p < 0.001$), diagnosis (figure 7.3, $\chi^2 = 30.9$, $p < 0.001$) or self-report (figure 7.4, $\chi^2 = 22.8$, $p < 0.001$).

Comment: estimates of age of onset depend on the source of data

Estimates of the age at which antisocial behaviour begins were strongly dependent on the source of the data. Consider age 15, which appeared to be a watershed for Dunedin Study members. By their fifteenth birthdays, only 1 per cent of girls had onset antisocial behaviour as measured by conviction, but 8 per cent had onset as measured by arrest, 12 per cent had onset as measured by diagnosis, and fully 72 per cent had onset as measured by their own self-reports of illegal behaviours. The effect of data source was similar for males. By age 15, only 4 per cent of boys had been convicted, but 15 per cent had been arrested, 23 per cent had been diagnosed, and 80 per cent had self-reported the onset of illegal behaviours.

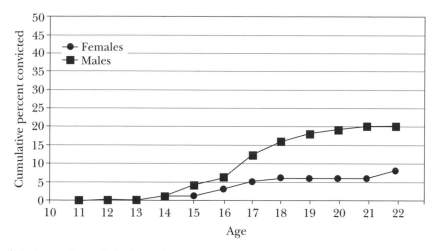

7.1 Age at first criminal conviction

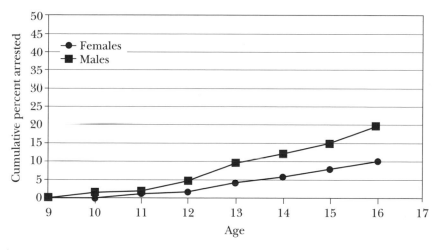

7.2 Age at first criminal arrest

This comparison of different data sources suggests that investigations that rely on official data to study crime careers will ascertain age of onset approximately 3 to 5 years after it has happened. Similar findings have emerged from other studies in other countries. For example, a Canadian survey showed that self-reported onset antedated conviction by about 3.5 years (Loeber and LeBlanc, 1990), and a US survey showed that onset of 'serious' delinquency antedated the first court contact by 2.5 years and self-

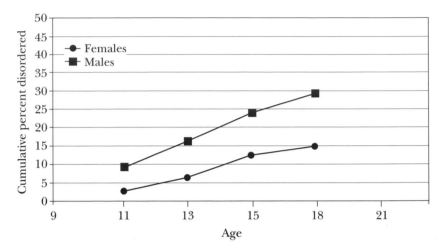

7.3 Age at first DSM-IV conduct disorder diagnosis

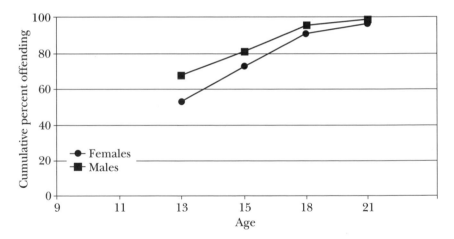

7.4 Age at first self-reported delinquency

reported onset of 'moderate' delinquency antedated the first court contact by 5 years (US Office of Juvenile Justice and Delinquency Prevention, 1998).

Comment: adult-onset antisocial behaviour is extremely rare
Some investigators have suggested, on the basis of examining official data sources, that significant numbers of offenders are adult-onset (Farrington, Ohlin, and Wilson, 1986), but this conclusion appears to be based on an

artefact of official measurement as self-report studies show that only 1 per cent to 4 per cent of males commit their first criminal offence after age 17 (Elliott, Huizinga and Menard, 1989). Indeed, by phase 18 virtually all of the Dunedin Study members had already engaged in some form of illegal behaviour at some time, according to their self-reports shown on figure 7.4. Only 9 per cent of males and 14 per cent of females remained naive to all delinquency by age 18, and only 3 per cent of males and 5 per cent of females first offended as an adult between phases 18 and 21. These findings carry an important lesson for methodology in developmental research into crime careers. 'Adult-onset' offenders cannot be defined for study with any certainty unless self-reported data are available to rule out juvenile onset prior to subjects' first official contact with the judicial system. When self-report data are consulted, they reveal that onset of antisocial behaviour after adolescence is extremely rare.

Comment: sex differences in age of onset depend on the type of crime
When self-reported delinquency was disaggregated into violence (figure 7.5), theft (figure 7.6), and substance-related offences (figure 7.7), different patterns emerged for different types of crime. Both males and females showed steadily increasing incidence of onset of all three types of offence with age. Cumulatively, by age 21 about 60 per cent of the sample had committed theft, 75 per cent had committed violence, and almost 90 per cent had committed a substance-related offence. At every age, more males than females had begun their involvement in theft and violence, but there were no sex differences in the onset of drug- and alcohol-related offences. Figure 7.7 shows that the sexes were virtually matched in age of onset of substance offences, which consisted of using or selling marijuana, using or selling harder drugs, and being drunk in a public place. This is consistent with the findings reported earlier in chapter 3, where we examined mean-level sex differences on dimensional measures of antisocial behaviour, and found that the sexes were more similar in their substance-related offending than in other types of offending.

Comment: sex similarity in onset among those who do onset
What is not apparent from the various cumulative onset figures is the remarkably *similar* age of onset among the subset of boys and girls who had participated in antisocial behaviour by the end of the study period. Among those convicted by age 21, the 103 boys were first convicted at a mean age of 17.7 years and the 38 girls were first convicted at a mean age of 17.9 years. Among those arrested as juveniles before age 17, the 101 boys were first

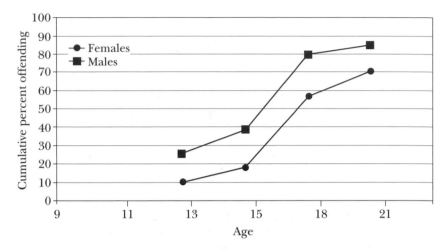

7.5 Age at first self-reported violent offences

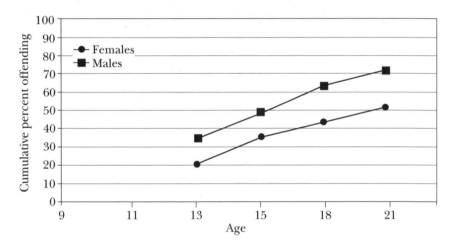

7.6 Age at first self-reported theft offences

arrested at a mean of 13.5 years and the 49 girls were first arrested at a mean of 13.7 years. Among those diagnosed with conduct disorder, the 148 boys were first diagnosed at a mean age of 14.7 years, and the 71 girls were first diagnosed at a mean age of 15.2 years. Among those self-reporting delinquent acts, the 512 boys first self-reported at a mean age of 13.3 years, and the 468 girls first self-reported at a mean age of 13.7 years. The overall pattern, regardless of measurement source, was for Dunedin Study males and females to onset antisocial behaviour within 2 to 6 months of each

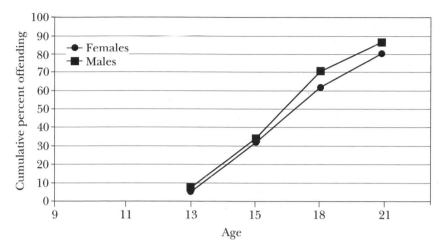

7.7 Age at first self-reported drug/alcohol offences

other. Because we found no other published studies, this pattern of sex similarity awaits replication checks.

Comment: caveats and conclusions

It is important to note that the mean onset ages in this chapter cannot be used as precise indicators because the Dunedin Study data do not cover the whole life course, and both 'left-hand' and 'right-hand' censoring will affect estimates of age of onset. As a contrast, consider that the mean age of onset of 'serious' self-reported delinquency in the Pittsburgh Youth Study (PYS) was 11.9 years for boys (OJJDP, 1998) compared to our estimate of 13.3 years. Because phase 13 was the first phase at which we administered a full self-report delinquency interview, the youngest age that could enter into our calculations of mean age of self-reported onset was 12 years, the age covered by the phase 13 reporting period. The PYS assessed self-report delinquency at age 7. As another contrast, the mean age of conviction onset in a Swedish cohort studied to age 29 was 21.3 years for women (Stattin, Magnusson, and Reichel, 1989), compared to our estimate of 17.9 years. Because our conviction data were last gathered at the end of phase 21 the oldest age that could enter into our calculations of mean age of conviction onset was 22. The Swedish study assessed convictions to age 29.

As these two comparisons with other studies show, the precise ages of onset may have been different if the Dunedin data were not age-censored. Thus, the mean ages of onset in this chapter should be considered in context and with appropriate caution. Nevertheless, our *self-report* data showed that virtually all of the Study members who will offend in the future had already onset by the end of the study period (figure 7.4). Thus, it is probably safe to assume that the trajectories represented in the figures in this chapter represent onset during the period when it happens for the majority of people who engage in antisocial behaviour at any time in the life course.

We began this chapter by making opposing predictions. On the one hand, if girls compared to boys have less of the antisocial trait, or less aetiological press toward antisocial behaviour, they might show onset at *older* ages. On the other hand, if the onset of antisocial behaviour is tied to pubertal timing, and because girls tend to complete puberty earlier than boys, they might show onset at *younger* ages. The data yielded decisive support for neither pattern. Although there are fewer females than males participating in antisocial behaviour at every age (except the year between age 14 and 15), those females who do participate appear to begin their antisocial activities at about the same age as the boys do. It is possible that both of the hypothesised influences on onset occur, but they cancel each other out so that neither effect is observable in our data. Restated, boys may have stronger causes for becoming antisocial before girls, but girls attain pubertal maturity before boys do, and the net result is that the sexes begin antisocial behaviour at about the same age.

Take-home messages

• Estimates of the age at which antisocial behaviour begins vary widely when different sources of data are consulted. For both males and females, onset measured via conviction data will lag three to five years behind onset measured via self-report interviews. Official data may be used to study individual differences in age of onset, but official data give an inaccurate picture of actual onset and they should not be used for this purpose.

• Self-report data reveal that adult onset of antisocial behaviour after adolescence is extremely rare among both men and women.

• At every age, more males than females are beginning theft and violence.

• At every age, males and females tend to begin in approximately the same numbers to engage in drug- and alcohol-related offences.

• Among young people who do begin antisocial behaviour before adulthood, age of onset is markedly similar between the sexes. Males and females onset within 6 months of each other.

Unanswered questions

- Why is adult onset of antisocial behaviour so rare, and what distinguishes such adult-onset offenders?
- Why are females so similar to males on substance-related offences?
- Why does the onset of antisocial behaviours peak during adolescence?

CHAPTER EIGHT

Sex effects in risk predictors for antisocial behaviour: are males more vulnerable than females to risk factors for antisocial behaviour?

In previous chapters we saw evidence that males are more antisocial than females. In the next three chapters we ask if the aetiology of antisocial behaviour differs for males and females. This chapter takes a first look at this question by testing the hypothesis that males are more vulnerable than females to individual, familial, and environmental risk factors for antisocial behaviour. The basic premise is that biological sex or psychological gender serve either to exacerbate the influence of the risk factor or conversely to protect the individual from its influence.

Three types of research designs have been used to try to address the question of whether certain risk factors have a greater influence on the development of antisocial behaviour in males versus females. One approach is to use behavioural genetic designs to examine whether there are any sex differences in the genetic and environmental aetiology of antisocial behaviour. The available evidence suggests that estimates are more similar than different among males and females for genetic and environmental liability for externalizing behaviour problems (Gjone, Stevenson, and Sundet, 1996; Gjone et al., 1996), conduct problems (Cadoret and Cain, 1980; Cadoret et al., 1995; Slutske et al., 1997), and crime (Baker et al., 1989; Gottesman, Goldsmith, and Carey, 1997). Two studies that have found sex differences in the magnitude of genetic and environmental influences on antisocial behaviour reached opposite conclusions (Eley et al., 1999; Silberg et al., 1994). In all, the general pattern appears to point to more similarities than differences between males and females, but occasional differences point to the need for continued research. However, whereas such behavioural genetic designs serve a useful function in alerting researchers to possible aetiological similarities (or differences) between the sexes, unless these studies incorporate specific measures of genes or the environment, they cannot identify where the similarities or differences lie.

A second approach to testing whether males are more vulnerable to some risk factors than females is to determine the extent to which antisocial behaviour in one family member is associated with similar behaviour in other family members of the same and opposite sex. Farrington *et al.* (1996) found substantial associations across the sexes. Twin studies can quantify this more satisfactorily by determining if the correlations for antisocial behaviour within opposite-sex pairs are the same as those within same-sex dizygotic pairs. Eaves *et al.* (2000) did this with oppositional-defiant and conduct disorder symptoms and found no evidence that the origins differed between boys and girls.

A third, and the most common, approach to testing if males are more vulnerable to some risk factors than females is to compare the risk predictors of antisocial behaviour across samples of males versus females. Such evidence as there is indicates that the factors associated with juvenile offending in girls are generally similar to those found in boys (Fergusson and Horwood, forthcoming; Rutter, Giller, and Hagell, 1998). But some studies also point to the greater vulnerability of one sex to some risk factors. For example, some studies report that coercive parenting may have a stronger effect on boys' externalizing behaviour problems (e.g. disobedience, lying, physical aggression, rule-breaking, and other delinquent acts) (McFadyen-Ketchum *et al.*, 1996), but others report the opposite pattern (Webster-Stratton, 1996). Some studies report that boys with externalizing behaviour problems perform worse on intelligence tests than girls (Fagot and Leve, 1998) but others report the opposite (Olson and Hoza, 1993). In a previously published investigation of the developmental antecedents of partner violence in the Dunedin Study, we found that male and female perpetrators had many shared vulnerabilities in their histories, but that female perpetrators had significantly worse histories of relationships in their family of origin than male perpetrators (Magdol *et al.*, 1998a). One extensive review of sex differences in behavioural, cognitive, biological, family, and environmental risk factors for conduct problems revealed conflicting research findings in each domain (Keenan, Loeber, and Green, 2000). On the whole, efforts to resolve the question of whether males are more vulnerable than females to some risk factors for antisocial behaviour are frustrated by the fact that sex differences in risk predictors are seldom tested formally, and more often than not conclusions are based on a comparison of p values associated with risk predictors within small groups of boys and girls.

In this chapter we test if the known predictors of antisocial behaviour confer significantly greater risk on the development of antisocial behaviour in males versus females. We focus on the most important risk factors for anti-social behaviour that have been enumerated in an authoritative review com-missioned by the US Office of Juvenile Justice and Delinquency Prevention (Hawkins *et al.*, 1998). The five most important domains of risk factors are: parental risk predictors (e.g., young mother, parental crime), family risk predictors (e.g., low socioeconomic status, harsh discipline), cognitive and neurological risk predictors (e.g., low intelligence), behavioural risk predic-tors (e.g., temperament, hyperactivity), and peer-relationships risk factors (e.g., peer rejection, peer delinquency). The Dunedin archive does not exhaust the universe of putative risk factors for antisocial behaviour, but it contains indicators from each of these important domains. In this chapter, we used the measured risk factors to predict within-sex individual differ-ences in antisocial behaviour and to test if these risk factors predicted more antisocial behaviour among males than females.

Method

The dependent variable: a composite measure of adolescent antisocial behaviour

The outcome variable in the analyses reported in this chapter (and subse-quent chapters) is a multi-source composite that combines seven different measures of the Dunedin Study members' antisocial behaviour: parent reports of antisocial behaviour at ages 13 and 15 (using the Revised Behaviour Problem Checklist at both age periods), teacher reports of anti-social behaviour at age 13 (using the Rutter Child Scale), self-reports of delinquent behaviour at ages 13, 15, and 18 (using the Self-Report Delinquency interview), and informant reports of antisocial behaviour at age 18. Details about each of these measures are provided in chapter 3. For the present study, all seven measures were standardized and combined into a single antisocial composite. This linear composite of these seven measures was reliable for both boys (0.86) and girls (0.77); for estimation of the reli-ability of a linear composite, see Nunnaly (1978, pp. 246–54).

The antisocial composite incorporated seven different measures to insure that multiple sources and ages were represented in the composite score. All seven measures were present for 877 Study members and six of the seven measures were present for 956 Study members (491 boys and 465 girls), 95 per cent of the birth cohort. We compared analyses based on these two dif-ferent subsamples, and the results did not differ in statistical significance or

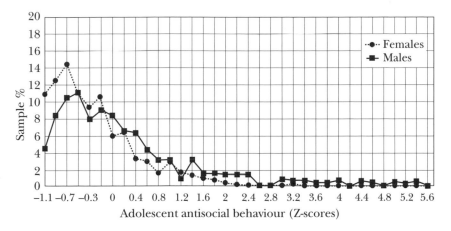

8.1 The cohort distribution of adolescent antisocial behaviour, by sex

in substantive terms. To maximize the number of cases, we thus base all further analyses on 956 cases.

Figure 8.1 shows the distribution of the composite measure of adolescent antisocial behaviour, which has been standardized to a mean of 0 and a standard deviation of 1. Boys had significantly higher scores on the composite measure of antisocial behaviour, t (954) = 7.96, $p<0.001$. Figure 8.1 shows that fewer girls were found at the extreme tail of the distribution. The magnitude of the sex difference in the antisocial behaviour scale, in standard deviation (SD) units, was 0.49, which can be regarded as a medium effect size (Cohen, 1992). It is important to compare this sex difference to those differences noted earlier in table 3.1. This comparison shows that sex differences for single-source, single-age measures of antisocial behaviour were about half the size (about 0.25 standard deviation) of the sex difference for our aggregated composite measure (0.49 SD). This comparison suggests two conclusions. First, it suggests that previous meta-analyses of sex differences in aggressive behaviour may have underestimated the magnitude of sex differences by using single-source measures taken at a single age. Second, it underscores the importance of the aggregation principle for developmental research (Rushton, Brainerd, and Pressley, 1983). Aggregation is not always appropriate, of course, but in the service of obtaining more reliable estimates of risk and protective factors in development investigators are better off creating aggregated scores by combining, within specified developmental periods, several measures of the same construct.

The risk predictors

On the basis of existing research and theory, we selected for study five domains of risk factors, where each domain includes multiple measures of risk factors. In this chapter, we describe each of the risk-predictor measures. An exhaustive review of each risk factor – how it is presumed to affect antisocial behaviour and how it has fared in past empirical evaluations – is beyond the scope of this book; here we very briefly note some routes by which each risk factor is thought to cause antisocial behaviour in children (for a recent review of these topics, see Loeber and Farrington, 1998; Rutter, Giller, and Hagell, 1998). Virtually all of the risk predictors have previously published evidence of their reliability and validity in the Dunedin Study, and appropriate papers are cited.

MATERNAL RISK PREDICTORS

There is evidence from a number of studies that maternal characteristics, identifiable during pregnancy or during the child's first few years of life, are relevant to the development of antisocial behaviour. Young motherhood may be linked to offspring antisocial behaviour through the poor quality of premature parenting, through economic stress, or because young mothers tend to be more antisocial (Maynard, 1997; Jaffee, forthcoming). Maternal low IQ as well as poor maternal reading skills may affect children's antisocial behaviour by compromising children's preparation to meet the demands of school (Mandel, 1997). Poor parental mental health may affect children's antisocial behaviour by compromising parental attention, affection, energy and judgement (Downey and Coyne, 1990; Rutter, 1990). Parental criminality may be linked to children's antisocial behaviour through genetic effects, socialization processes, or because this variable is a good proxy indicator for other unmeasured social and psychological disadvantages (Farrington, 1995). We assessed the risk conferred by these maternal characteristics via seven measures.

Mother's age at her first birth and *mother's age at the Study member's birth* were recorded at the birth of the Study member, in 1972–3. Details about these measures in the Dunedin Study are described by Jaffee *et al.* (2001).

Mother's IQ was assessed with the SRA verbal test (Thurstone and Thurstone, 1973) administered to the sample mothers when the children were 3 years old. Details about this measure in the Dunedin Study are described by Silva (1978).

Mother's reading skills were assessed using the Burt Word Reading Test (Scottish Council for Research in Education, 1976) when the children were three years old.

Mother's mental health problems were measured with the Malaise Inventory, a 24-item questionnaire that was completed by the Study members' mothers when the Study members were aged 7, 9, and 11. The questionnaire was developed by Rutter, Tizard, and Whitmore (1970; see also Rodgers *et al.*(1999)) to sample a variety of common symptoms of emotional disturbance, and is heavily weighted with items reflecting affective stress response (e.g., easily upset, miserable) and somatic symptoms (e.g., tiredness, headaches). Details about this scale in the Dunedin Study are described by McGee, Williams, and Silva (1985b).

Mother's neuroticism was assessed with the Eysenck Personality Inventory (Eysenck, 1964), administered to the sample mothers when the children were 3 years old. Details about this scale in the Dunedin Study are described by McKerracher, McGee, and Silva (1984).

Parental criminality was assessed via a questionnaire posted to parents when the Study members were young adults and the parents' ages ranged from 40 to 75. The parents were asked to report if they had ever been convicted of a crime; 12 per cent of the Study members' parents reported that they had.

FAMILY RISK PREDICTORS

There is evidence from a number of studies that harsh and erratic discipline practices, and more generally conflicted family environments, are linked to the development of antisocial behaviour (Dishion and Patterson, 1997; Dodge, Bates, and Pettit, 1990; Loeber and Stouthamer-Loeber, 1986; Patterson, DeBaryshe, and Ramsey, 1989; Straus, Sugarman, and Giles, 1997). Similarly, low socioeconomic status and unstable family circumstances may increase the risk of antisocial behaviour because they reduce parental resources for child-rearing, interfere with effective parenting, and upset parent–child attachment bonds (Brooks-Gunn and Duncan, 1997; Fergusson, Horwood, and Lynskey, 1992; McLanahan and Sandfeur, 1994). We assessed the risk conferred by these family characteristics via nine measures.

Deviant mother–child interaction was assessed at age 3. At this time, the mother was observed during a one-hour testing session and rated by an observer on eight categories. A point was assigned for each category on which the interaction appeared negative or inappropriate (e.g., if the mother's expression of affect was consistently negative, or if her evaluation of the child was constantly critical or derogatory, or if she was rough or inconsiderate in physically handling the child). Points across the eight categories were summed. Details for this scale in the Dunedin Study are described by Henry *et al.* (1996).

Harsh discipline was measured at ages 7 and 9 using a checklist of disciplinary behaviours. Parents were asked to indicate if they engaged in ten behaviours, such as 'smack [your child] or hit him/her with something', 'try to frighten [your child] with someone like his/her father or a policeman', and 'threaten to smack, or deprive [your child] of something'. Details for this scale in the Dunedin Study are described by Magdol *et al.* (1998b).

Inconsistent discipline was measured at ages 7 and 9 as part of an interview about how parents dealt with the Study child when he or she was naughty or misbehaved. Mothers evaluated their own discipline, as well as their husbands' discipline, on a 4-point scale (1 = always the same; 4 = very changeable).

Family conflict was measured at ages 7 and 9 with the Moos Family Relations Index (FRI; Moos and Moos, 1981), completed by the mothers of the Study members. The conflict subscale of the FRI contains items such as, 'In our family, we believe you don't ever get anywhere by raising your voice', and 'Family members sometimes hit each other'. Details for this scale in the Dunedin Study are described by Parnicky, Williams, and Silva (1985).

Number of caregiver changes experienced by the child was assessed through age 11. At each assessment year the parents were asked what changes in the family configuration had occurred since the last assessment. Responses included changes such as parent death or separation, father's girlfriend moving in, child sent to live with relatives, or foster care. These responses were summed to calculate the total number of caretaker changes by age 11.

Number of residence moves is the sum of residence changes experienced by the Study members by age 11 as reported by their primary caregivers (e.g., parents) at each interview from ages 5 through 11.

Years with a single parent indexes the number of years from birth to age 11 that the Study member lived with a single parent. Details about these last three measures are described by Henry *et al.* (1993).

Family socioeconomic status (SES) measured the average SES level of the Study members' families across the first fifteen years of the Dunedin Study. We used a six-point scale designed for New Zealand (Elley and Irving, 1976), where 1 = 'unskilled labourer' and 6 = 'professional'. Details about SES measurement in the Dunedin Study are described by Wright, Caspi, Moffitt, Miech, and Silva (1999).

Relationship with parents was assessed by a 12-item self-report measure taken from the Inventory of Parent Attachment (Armsden and Greenberg, 1987). The items measure whether or not adolescents feel they can trust their parents, communicate with their parents, and are not alienated from their parents. Each item is rated on a 4-point scale ranging from 1, 'almost never' to 4, 'almost always or always'. Details about this scale in the Dunedin Study are described by Nada-Raja, McGee, and Stanton (1992). The measure of relationship with parents was administered at ages 13 and 15. We combined the scores from both age periods.

CHILD NEURO-COGNITIVE RISK PREDICTORS

There is evidence from numerous studies that IQ, especially verbal skills, and individual differences in neuropsychological functions represent some of the most robust intrapersonal factors implicated in early disruptive behaviour (Hirschi and Hindelang, 1977; Moffitt, 1993b; Wilson and Herrnstein, 1985). The Dunedin findings (e.g., Moffitt, 1990a; White *et al.*, 1990), and other studies (e.g., Denno, 1990; Moffitt, Gabrielli, and Mednick, 1981) show that the relation between IQ and delinquency holds when IQ is measured well before the development of illegal behaviour. The relation between IQ and delinquency holds after controlling for socioeconomic status, race, academic attainment, and each child's motivation during the IQ test (e.g., Lynam, Moffitt, and Stouthamer-Loeber, 1993) and is not an artefact of slow-witted delinquents being more easily detected by police; undetected delinquents who are identified by interview have low IQ scores too (Moffitt and Silva, 1988b). We assessed the risk conferred by IQ via independent assessments of cognitive functions taken repeatedly from ages 3 to 13. In addition, we include measures of neurological abnormalities and heart rate in our list of risk factors because, as high-risk studies suggest, these factors which assess features of the central and autonomic nervous systems may be relevant to the development of disruptive and serious antisocial behaviour (Raine, 1994). In all, we assessed the risk conferred by neuro-cognitive characteristics via eight measures.

Neurological abnormalities were assessed at age 3. Each child was examined by a pediatric neurologist for neurological signs, including assessment of motility, passive movements, reflexes, facial musculature, strabismus, nystagmus, foot posture, and gait. This assessment was based on the procedures described by Touwen and Prechtl (1970); the results have been reported by McGee *et al.* (1982).

Intelligence was assessed at age 3 with the Peabody Picture Vocabulary Test (Dunn, 1965), at age 5 with the Stanford Binet Intelligence Scales (Terman and Merrill, 1960), and at ages 7, 9, and 11, with the Wechsler Intelligence Scale for Children – Revised (WISC – R; Wechsler, 1974). All tests were administered by trained psychometrists according to standard protocol.

Details about intelligence testing in the Dunedin Study are described by Moffitt *et al.*, 1993. We combined the WISC-R scores from the three age periods to form two overall scores: WISC-R IQ and Verbal IQ.

Neuropsychological memory scores at age 13 were constructed as a composite factor score from scores on the several trials of the Rey Auditory Verbal Learning Tests, measuring immediate and delayed recall of word lists. Details about this measure are provided by Frost, Moffitt, and McGee (1989).

Reading achievement was measured at ages 7, 9, and 11 by the Burt Word Reading Test (Scottish Council for Research in Education, 1976), a word-recognition reading test having normative standards for New Zealand children, which resembles the American Wide-Range Achievement Test of reading. Details about this measure in the Dunedin Study are described by Fergusson *et al.* (1996). We combined the (age-standardized) reading scores from the three age periods to form an overall score.

Heart rate was measured by nurse examiners at ages 7, 9, and 11. At each age, an average heart rate measure was derived from measures of resting heart rate taken by a nurse on three occasions during the course of a physical examination. We combined the (age-standardized) measures of resting heart rate from the three age periods to form an overall score.

CHILD BEHAVIOURAL RISK PREDICTORS

Already during toddlerhood and middle childhood, individual differences in 'difficult temperament' and hyperactivity play a major role in the development of antisocial behaviour. These temperamental qualities and associated hyperactive behaviours set in motion person-environment transactions – with parents, teachers, and peers, at home and at school – that help to sustain early emerging individual differences and elaborate them into antisocial outcomes (Caspi and Moffitt, 1995). Some researchers have also linked early internalizing problems to later antisocial behaviour (Moskowitz and Schwartzman, 1989; Kellam, Brown and Ensminger, 1983), although the mechanisms by which this may come about are less clear-cut (Kerr, Tremblay, Pagani and Vitaro, 1997). In all, we assessed the risk conferred by early emerging behavioural and emotional differences via six measures, gathered repeatedly during the first decade of life.

Difficult temperament was assessed in two ways, by parental reports and by observations made by psychological examiners. At age 3 mothers were asked whether the Study child was easy or difficult to manage. Response options were coded as 'easy all the time', 'easy most of the time', or 'very difficult'. At ages 3 and 5 children participated in a testing session that lasted approximately 90 minutes and involved cognitive and motor tasks. At each age, each child was tested by a different examiner who had no knowledge of the child's prior behavioural history. Following the testing session, the examiner rated the child's behaviour on a range of behavioural characteristics (e.g., fleeting attention, emotional lability). Based on factor analyses of the examiners' behavioural ratings, Caspi *et al.* (1995) identified a developmentally robust dimension that reflected individual differences in reactions to stress and challenge, in impulse control, and in the ability to persist in problem-solving. Children who scored high on this factor were emotionally labile, irritable, negativistic, rough, inattentive, and had difficulty concentrating.

Hyperactivity was measured with the Rutter Child Scales (Rutter, Tizard, and Whitmore, 1970; see chapter 3 for details), supplemented with items concerning inattention, impulsivity, and hyperactivity (see McGee, Williams, and Silva, 1985a for details). These additional items were derived from the Diagnostic and Statistical Manual of Mental Disorders (DSM-III) diagnostic criteria for Attention Deficit Disorder (American Psychiatric Association). The Rutter Child Scales were completed by parents and teachers at ages 5, 7, 9, and 11. The hyperactivity items were summed across the four age periods to derive, separately for parents and teachers, a measure indexing the Study children's levels of hyperactivity in different settings.

Internalizing problems were also measured with the Rutter Child Scales, using items that enquired about the major areas of a child's emotional functioning during the past year. Items include worries about many things, often appears miserable, unhappy, tearful, and rather solitary. These were completed by parents and teachers at ages 5, 7, 9, and 11. The relevant items were summed across the four age periods to derive, separately for parents and teachers, a measure indexing the study children's internalizing problems in different settings.

PEER-RELATIONSHIPS RISK PREDICTORS
Evidence from numerous studies points to the role of peer experiences and schools as relevant to the development of delinquency (Cairns and Cairns, 1994; Coie, Dodge and Kupersmidt, 1990; Parker and Asher, 1987; Tremblay *et al.*, 1995; Warr, 1993). We assessed the risk conferred by these factors via five measures.

Peer rejection measures the extent to which the child was disliked by other children. At ages 5, 7, 9, and 11 parents and teachers independently evaluated whether the child was 'not much liked by other children' using a 3-point scale. We created a scale by summing these ratings across the four age periods to derive, separately for parents and teachers, a measure indexing the Study children's level of peer rejection during the primary school years, as viewed by two different reporting sources.

Peer attachment measures the attachment of Study members to their peers, as assessed by a measure from the Inventory of Parent and Peer Attachment (Armsden and Greenberg, 1987) that parallels the parent relationship measure described earlier.

Peer delinquency, assessed at age 13, is the sum of fifty-eight items on the Early Delinquency scale (twenty-nine norm violations and twenty-nine illegal offences) on which the Study members had reported the behaviour of 'my friends and other people my age who I know'. The measure and its psychometric properties have been described by Caspi *et al.* (1993), who presented analyses showing that this measure of peer delinquency is not merely a proxy for one's own delinquency.

School involvement measures involvement in school activities at age 15 with a visual analogue scale. Study members were shown a card with five concentric circles. They were asked to suppose that 'the circle represents the activities that go on at your school' and queried: 'How far from the centre of things are you?' A value of 1 indicates little involvement in school activities and a value of 5 indicates 'the centre of things.'

Data analysis approach

Table 8.1 presents the correlations, separately for males and females, between the omnibus measure of adolescent antisocial behaviour and each of the risk predictors. Effect sizes for correlations can be interpreted as $r = 0.1$ is a small effect, $r = 0.3$ is a medium effect, and $r = 0.5$ is a large effect (Cohen, 1992). The age at which each of the risk predictors was measured is shown in the first column of table 8.1; recall that the composite measure of adolescent antisocial behaviour spans ages 13 to 18. As such, with the exception of five measures taken at age 13 or 15 (relationship with parents, attachment to peers, peer delinquency, involvement in school, and scores on the neuropsychological memory test battery), the risk predictors are prospective to the measure of antisocial outcome, covering *non-overlapping* assessment ages.

We tested the vulnerability hypothesis using moderated multiple regression analyses,

$$\text{ASB} = a + b_1 \text{Sex} + b_2 \text{RISK} + b_3 (\text{Sex} \times \text{RISK}) + e,$$

where ASB represents the Study members' scores on the omnibus measure of adolescent antisocial behaviour, b_1 and b_2 represent the main effects of the Study members' sex and their scores on the risk predictor, and b_3

indexes whether the effect of the risk predictor on adolescent antisocial behaviour varies as a function of the Study member's sex. The results of these sex-interaction tests are presented in the final column of table 8.1. Evidence for the differential vulnerability hypothesis would yield a significant interaction effect, in which the effect of the risk factor would be significantly greater on males' antisocial behaviour than on females' behaviour. We used ordinary least squares multiple regression to examine these sex differences.

Results

Maternal risk predictors
Among the seven maternal risk predictors tested, all were significantly correlated with males' antisocial behaviour and six were significantly correlated with females'. The results showed that boys and girls who were born to young mothers, to mothers with low IQ scores or poor reading skills, whose mothers had mental health problems, and whose parents had a history of criminality were at increased risk of developing antisocial behaviour. None of the sex-interaction terms in the multiple regression analyses were significant at $p < 0.05$, indicating that these maternal risk factors are most parsimoniously viewed as similar for males and females.

Family risk predictors
Among the nine family risk predictors tested, all were significantly correlated with males' antisocial behaviour and eight were significantly correlated with females'. The results showed that boys and girls whose mothers were negative and critical, who faced harsh discipline, inconsistent discipline, and family conflict, whose families moved frequently, who experienced multiple different caregivers and spent longer periods of time with a single parent, and who grew up in socioeconomically disadvantaged families were at increased risk of developing antisocial behaviour. In addition, a poor relationship with parents in adolescence was associated with greater antisocial behaviour among both boys and girls. These risk correlations were obtained using different measures of family risk, relying on different data sources, across the age period from 3 to 15. Although each of these family risk factors was a significant predictor of antisocial behaviour among both boys and girls, the multiple regression analyses indicated that most of the family risk predictors had a stronger effect on boys' than on girls' antisocial behaviour. Boys who experienced inconsistent discipline, who grew up in conflicted homes, who endured multiple caregiver changes, whose

Table 8.1. *Correlations showing how well thirty-five risk factors predict boys' and girl's antisocial outcome during adolescence*[a]

Childhood risk predictor	N males/females	Assessment age(s)	Boys' correlation	Girls' correlation	Sex interaction $p < 0.05$
Maternal risk predictors					
Mother's age at her first birth	483/457	birth	−0.23*	−0.23*	no
Mother's age at Study member's birth	490/462	birth	−0.14*	−0.19*	no
Mother's IQ	477/459	3	−0.13*	−0.07	no
Mother's reading level	481/455	3	−0.12*	−0.13*	no
Mother's Eysenck Neuroticism	489/464	3	0.18*	0.13*	no
Mother's psychiatric malaise	491/465	7, 9, 11	0.23*	0.24*	no
Parental criminality	449/434	lifetime	0.17*	0.13*	no
Family risk predictors					
Deviant mother–child interaction, observer-rated	491/465	3	0.13*	0.16*	no
Harsh discipline	478/452	7, 9	0.19*	0.27*	no
Inconsistent discipline	478/452	7, 9	0.23*	0.20*	yes (p=0.03)
Moos Family Conflict scale	491/465	7, 9	0.21*	0.16*	yes (p=0.02)
Caretaker changes	401/361	birth–11	0.33*	0.21*	yes (p<0.01)
Residence moves	450/424	birth–11	0.15*	0.09	yes (p=0.04)
Years with single parent	488/455	birth–11	0.24*	0.18*	yes (p=0.01)
Family socioeconomic status	491/464	birth–15	−0.22*	−0.18*	yes (p=0.01)
Relationship with parents	491/465	13, 15	−0.44*	−0.47*	no
Child cognitive and neurological risk predictors					
Neurological abnormalities	455/447	birth–3	0.09	0.08	no
Peabody Picture IQ	491/465	3	−0.11*	−0.11*	no
Stanford Binet IQ	474/449	5	−0.21*	−0.11*	yes (p=0.01)

WISC-R IQ	491/465	7, 9, 11	−0.21*	−0.12*	yes (p=0.01)
WISC-R VIQ	491/465	7, 9, 11	−0.19*	−0.11*	yes (p=0.02)
Neuropsych. memory score	378/349	13	−0.20*	−0.07	yes (p=0.01)
Burt reading test	491/465	7, 9, 11	−0.11*	−0.12*	no
Heart rate	431/401	7, 9, 11	−0.12*	−0.10	no
Child behavioural risk predictors					
Difficult baby, parent report	490/464	3	0.15*	0.16*	no
Undercontrolled temperament, observer-rated	491/465	3, 5	0.19*	0.13*	yes (p=0.02)
Hyperactivity, parent report	491/465	5, 7, 9, 11	0.28*	0.28*	no
Hyperactivity, teacher report	491/465	5, 7, 9, 11	0.35*	0.27*	yes (p=0.04)
Internalizing, parent report	491/465	5, 7, 9, 11	0.09	0.11*	no
Internalizing, teacher report	491/465	5, 7, 9, 11	0.10	0.06	no
Peer-relations risk factors					
Peer rejection, parent report	490/465	5, 7, 9, 11	0.25*	0.25*	no
Peer rejection, teacher report	482/454	5, 7, 9, 11	0.35*	0.19*	yes (p<0.01)
Peer attachment, self-report	491/465	13, 15	−0.13*	−0.11*	no
Peers' delinquency, self-report	379/348	13	0.39*	0.40*	no
School involvement, self-report	485/459	15	−0.25*	−0.12*	yes (p=0.01)
Cumulative for all risk predictors[b]					
Multiple correlation	491/465	birth–15	0.72*	0.69*	no

Notes:

[a] The outcome measure of antisocial behaviour is shown in figure 8.1

[b] To retain as many cases as possible for the analysis missing-data dummy indicators were included. See chapter 9, footnote 1, for details.

* The starred correlations were significant at p<0.01.

families moved a lot, who spent longer periods of time with a single parent, and who grew up in socioeconomically disadvantaged homes were are greater risk of developing antisocial behaviour than girls' who experienced these same family risks.

This suggestive pattern of findings fits with evidence from other research about sex differences in reactivity to environmental stress. For example, some evidence suggests that males may be somewhat more sensitive to stressors such as in-home crowding, divorce, and parental loss (Wachs, 1992). What is not clear from the evidence at hand, either in the Dunedin Study or in previous studies, is whether the apparent greater vulnerability of males represents a sex difference in reactivity to similar familial conditions or whether males are simply treated differently from females especially during times of familial stress (Rothbaum and Weisz, 1994).

Neuro-cognitive risk predictors
Among the eight neuro-cognitive risk predictors tested, seven were significantly correlated with males' antisocial behaviour and five were significantly correlated with females'. The results showed that boys and girls with compromised intelligence were at greater risk of antisocial behaviour. These risk correlations obtained using different measures of intelligence across a wide age period, from the Peabody test at age 3 to a neuropsychological memory test battery at age 13. These findings are in keeping with a critical mass of research showing that the correlation between scores on intelligence and related neuropsychological tests and antisocial behaviour is small but very robust (Moffitt, 1993b). Most of these previous studies and reports focused on males. The present findings add to this body of research by documenting that compromised intelligence is also a risk factor for females' antisocial behaviour.

Most of the eight neuro-cognitive risk factors were significant predictors of antisocial behaviour in both sexes, but the multiple regression analyses indicated that the measures of intelligence had a stronger effect on males' than on females' antisocial behaviour. We do not know whether these differential risk effects will withstand the rigours of replication in other studies, but the internal replication of these interaction effects across different measures of intelligence at different ages in the Dunedin Study suggests that these differential risk effects merit scrutiny.

In addition, the third panel of table 8.1 shows that neurological abnormalities and low resting heart rates were very modestly correlated with adolescent antisocial behaviour. Although only the correlation between heart rate and antisocial behaviour among boys was significant at $p < 0.01$, the remaining three correlations in table 8.1 were all marginally significant at p<0.10. The direction of these effects is in keeping with high-risk studies and experimental studies that point to the possible role of these neurological and physiological risk factors in the development of antisocial behaviour (Raine, 1994). The Dunedin results suggest that although the contribution of these factors may be small, they are equally relevant to understanding antisocial behaviour in both males and females.

Behavioural risk predictors

Among the six behavioural risk predictors tested, four were significantly correlated with males' and five with females' antisocial behaviour. The results showed that boys and girls with difficult temperament and with hyperactive behaviours were at greater risk of antisocial behaviour. These risk correlations obtained using different measures of behavioural risk, relying on different data sources, across the age period from 3 to 11. Parent and teacher reports of children's internalizing problems were only weakly and, on the whole, not significantly related to males' and females' antisocial behaviour in adolescence.

Although the patterns of findings were generally the same for males and females, the multiple regression analyses indicated that observer-rated difficult temperament and, to a greater extent, teacher reports of hyperactivity were more predictive of subsequent antisocial behaviour among males than among females. However, this pattern of findings was not replicated using parent reports. Reporters other than parents are better able to evaluate problem behaviours in relation to the population of boys and girls, and it may be that the sex-interaction effects detected in observers' and teachers' ratings should be given more weight.

Peer-relationships risk factors

The results show that boys and girls who were rejected by other children during the primary school years, who reported affiliating with delinquent peers, and who felt marginalised from school and conventional peers were significantly more likely to be involved in antisocial behaviour. Two of the sex-interaction terms in the multiple regression analyses were statistically significant, indicating that boys who were disliked by their peers in childhood (according to their teachers) were more likely to be involved in antisocial behaviour as adolescents, and that boys who were less involved in school were more likely to be involved in antisocial activities. As a caution, it should be noted that whereas in the other risk domains all of the risk factors were measured prospectively, three of the five peer-relations risk factors were measured at ages 13 and 15 and thus overlapped with the measurement of antisocial behaviour. As such, the final three rows of correlations in the peer-relations panel of table 8.1 may represent the effects of antisocial behaviour on peer relations as much as the effect of peer relations on antisocial behaviour.

Comment: are males more vulnerable than females to risk factors for antisocial behaviour?

Most of the risk factors for antisocial behaviour applied equally well to males and females in the Dunedin Study. Although our finding that males were more vulnerable to family adversity than females is in keeping with some previous research, it bears mention that these statistically significant interaction effects were quite small. For example, among the family risk predictors in table 8.1, the most robust interaction effect accounted for only 1 per cent of the variance in antisocial behaviour, and on average the sex-interaction terms explained less than 1 per cent of the variance in antisocial behaviour. Likewise, the sex-interaction terms for the neuro-cognitive and behavioural risk predictors also accounted for only about 1 per cent of the variance in antisocial behaviour. It is intriguing that boys with compromised intelligence, undercontrolled temperament, and hyperactivity were at greater risk of antisocial behaviour than girls with these risks, but these were very small effects. In fact, in chapter 12 we will investigate these same sex differences using the diagnosis of conduct disorder as the outcome variable, and we will see that only a few of the significant interaction effects reported here in chapter 8 will be replicated. Evaluated as a whole, then, the evidence suggests that sex differences in association between risk factors and antisocial behaviour are small and not very robust across different measurement strategies and statistical procedures.

Comment: how much variation in adolescent antisocial behaviour is explained by cumulative childhood risk?

The final panel of table 8.1 shows the multiple correlation between all the risk predictors and the omnibus measure of adolescent antisocial behaviour. The multiple correlations are the same for boys (R = 0.72) and girls (R = 0.69). They approach in magnitude the reliability of the measure of antisocial behaviour in adolescence (alpha = 0.86 and 0.77, respectively). This suggests that the risk factors reported in table 8.1 account for nearly all of the reliable variation in adolescent antisocial behaviour, within each sex.

It should be noted that we have not included several important childhood risk factors. We deliberately did not include a measure of childhood aggression as a risk predictor variable in this chapter because we view childhood aggression as an early manifestation of antisocial behaviour rather than a conceptually distinct risk factor. We have already shown in Chapter 6 that there is moderate continuity from measures of childhood antisocial behaviour to measures of adolescent antisocial behaviour. We note the omission of three other factors in particular. First, we did not assess child abuse (Smith and Thornberry, 1995; Widom, 1989b), although we did assess harsh discipline but did not find it to have a differential effect on males versus females. Moreover, other evidence shows that childhood maltreatment does not have differential effects on boys and girls, but instead leads to a broad range of adverse outcomes in both sexes (e.g., Malinosky-Rummell and Hansen, 1993). Second, we did not assess parental substance abuse (Farrington, 1995), although we did assess maternal mental health and parental criminality but did not find them to have differential effects on males versus females. We are unaware of any evidence to suggest that males are more vulnerable than females to parental substance abuse, but this possibility needs to be evaluated further. Finally, we focused mostly on mothers' characteristics because fathers were not interviewed routinely when the Dunedin Study members were growing up. Although fathers' behaviour was represented in the measures of family risk (i.e., parents' crime, discipline, family conflict, caretaker changes, socio-economic status, and relationship with parents), with the exception of conviction history we did not assess fathers' characteristics directly from the fathers. Research on assortative mating suggests that when a child's mother has poor mental health, criminal offending, and low IQ, his father is statistically likely to have these risk factors too (see chapter 14), suggesting that our maternal measures serve at least as a fair proxy for the characteristics of the Study members' fathers. Nonetheless, it is possible that there are sex-linked effects of risk factors on children and more attention needs to be devoted to the independent measurement of maternal and paternal risk predictors in future research. (We were able to examine separately the effect of maternal and paternal criminality on the Study members' antisocial behaviour, but did not find any sex-linked effects.)

Take-home messages

- The risk measures available in the Dunedin archive account for most of the reliable variation in the antisocial behaviour of both males and females.

- The same risk factors predict antisocial behaviour in both males and females; we did not detect any replicable sex-specific risk factors for antisocial behaviour.
- Family adversity, compromised intelligence, difficult temperament and hyperactivity have somewhat stronger effects on males' than on females' antisocial behaviour, but . . .
- These sex differences in association are relatively small and, at best, offer only weak support to the hypothesis that males are more vulnerable than females to risk factors for antisocial behaviour; in general, males and females are both vulnerable to the same individual, familial, and environmental risk factors for antisocial behaviour.

Unanswered question

- Why are male children somewhat more vulnerable than female children to certain risk factors for pathology?

CHAPTER NINE

Sex effects in risk predictors for antisocial behaviour: are males exposed to more risk factors for antisocial behaviour?

Chapter 8 showed that the risk factors for antisocial behaviour are more similar than different for the two sexes. Moreover, with a few exceptions – albeit consistent and theoretically interesting ones – males and females were equally vulnerable to the same risk factors. In this chapter we evaluate a different hypothesis: that males and females are *differentially exposed* to risk factors for antisocial behaviour and that these sex differences in exposure to risk account for sex differences in antisocial behaviour. According to this possibility, the risk factors for antisocial behaviour are the same in males and females, but males may be more antisocial than females because there is a sex difference in the level of the risk factors among males versus females.

To test this hypothesis we will first test if there are sex differences in the levels of each of the risk factors for antisocial behaviour and we will then evaluate if these sex differences in risk exposure can account for sex differences in antisocial behaviour. Our approach follows that devised by Rowe, Vazsonyi, and Flannery (1994, 1995). The basic idea is to determine whether differences in levels of risk factors for antisocial behaviour account for sex differences in antisocial behaviour. In a cross-sectional sample of 800 adolescents, Rowe and his colleagues found similar correlations in the two sexes between a host of risk factors and self-reported delinquency. Moreover, much of the difference between males and females in self-reported delinquency was explicable in terms of the higher level of the risk factors in males. For example, Rowe *et al.* (1995) reported that of the factors that showed a correlation with delinquency of 0.25 or greater, all but one (sexual experiences) were found among more males than females, and at higher levels among males. This applied to lack of maternal affection, low school achievement, impulsiveness, deceitfulness, and rebelliousness. However, inference from these findings was limited by a reliance on cross-sectional self-report data for all the variables, and by some lack of conceptual independence between the predictor and criterion variables. Moreover, because this was a highly select and homogeneous sample, much of the variation in delinquency may have been within the normal range, with very few individuals seriously delinquent. Nevertheless, the research strategy is an excellent one, and we adopt it here.

Method

Measures
The dependent variable was the composite measure of adolescent antisocial behaviour previously described in chapter 8. The thirty-five risk predictors were also described in chapter 8.

Data analysis procedure
Our analysis proceeded in two steps. In the first step, we tested if there were sex differences in the levels of risk factors for antisocial behaviour. To do this, we standardized all the risk factors on the whole sample to the same scale using the z-score transformation; each risk factor thus had a mean of 0 and a standard deviation of 1. We performed t-tests on each of the measures to test for mean-level differences between boys and girls (see table 9.1). Effect sizes of the sex differences in table 9.1 may be operationally defined as $SD = 0.2$ is a small effect size, $SD = 0.5$ is a medium effect size, and $SD = 0.8$ is a large effect size.

In the second step, we tested if the sex differences in the mean levels of the risk factors for antisocial behaviour accounted for the sex differences in antisocial behaviour. We did this by testing different multiple regression models in which we compared the sex differences in antisocial behaviour before and after controlling for sex differences in the risk factors for antisocial behaviour. Evidence for the differential exposure hypothesis would show that the sex differences in antisocial behaviour are considerably attenuated after controlling for differences between males and females in their levels of risk.

Results

Comparing boys and girls on the mean levels of risk factors
Table 9.1 shows the mean levels on risk factors for antisocial behaviour, for boys and girls separately. These are the same risk factors that chapter 8

(table 8.1) showed were significantly correlated with antisocial behaviour. The first two panels of table 9.1 show that boys and girls were equally exposed to the same maternal and family risk factors. Boys and girls were equally likely to be reared by young mothers and by mothers with low IQ and poor reading skills and they were equally exposed to parental psychopathology, criminality, family discord, family break-up, and economic hardship. At a family-wide level, there were no sex differences in boys' and girls' exposure to risk; indeed, one would not expect a child's sex to be related to indicators such as the poverty or residential stability of his or her family (especially since many members of the Dunedin birth cohort had siblings of the opposite sex at home!). Harsh discipline was the only family risk factor for which we found a mean-level sex difference; boys received harsher discipline than girls (d = 0.22). However, we cannot infer from this finding that harsher discipline caused the boys to become more antisocial than girls. Our earlier results showed that boys were more antisocial than girls at an early age (see table 3.1) and other research has shown that young children's antisocial behaviour evokes parents' efforts to control it (e.g., Lytton, 1990). Thus, it is possible that the Dunedin boys evoked at least some of this harsher behaviour from their mothers.

The third panel of table 9.1 shows that boys differed from girls on almost all the cognitive and neurological risk factors for antisocial behaviour. Boys suffered more neurological abnormalities (d = 0.19), they performed more poorly on the neuropsychological tests at age 13 (d = 0.33), and they were poorer readers than girls (d = 0.36). These findings are consistent with the hypothesis of greater neuro-developmental impairment in boys than girls (Eme, 1992). Because boys are known to lag behind girls in expressive language, boys should score more poorly than girls on the two tests that included expressive language, the Stanford Binet and the WISC-R. Boys did perform slightly worse than girls on the Stanford-Binet test at age 5 (d = 0.15) but there were no sex differences on the WISC-R, partly for the historical reason that items that differentiate boys and girls were systematically discarded from the Wechsler tests during test construction (Matarazzo, 1972), and partly because any mean-level sex difference in overall intelligence (g) is negligible (Jensen, 1998). Consistent with this, boys and girls did not differ on the Peabody (an intelligence test that involves no expressive language). In addition, the results in table 9.1 show that boys had significantly slower heart rates than girls (d = 0.34).

The fourth panel of table 9.1 shows that boys differed from girls on behavioural risk factors that are correlated with antisocial behaviour. There were small differences between boys and girls on observer-rated measures

Table 9.1. *Boys' and girls' mean levels on risk factors for adolescent antisocial behaviour*

Childhood risk factors[a]	N males/females	Assessment age(s)	Males' mean z-score	Females' mean z-score	Sex difference p<0.05
Maternal risk factors					
Mother's age at her first birth	530/497	birth	0.04	−0.04	no
Mother's age at Study member's birth	534/499	birth	0.05	−0.06	no
Mother's IQ	518/493	3	−0.04	0.04	no
Mother's reading level	522/491	3	−0.03	0.03	no
Mother's Eysenck neuroticism	533/499	3	−0.03	0.03	no
Mother's psychiatric malaise	520/492	7, 9, 11	0.01	−0.01	no
Parental criminality	467/458	lifetime	12%	12%	no
Family risk factors					
Deviant mother–child interaction, observer's ratings	535/502	3	0.03	−0.03	no
Inconsistent discipline	506/475	7, 9, 11	−0.01	0.01	no
Harsh discipline	506/475	7, 9	0.11	−0.11	yes
Moos Family Conflict scale	493/469	7, 9	0.02	−0.02	no
Caretaker changes	415/371	birth–11	−0.01	0.01	no
Residence moves	466/438	birth–11	0	0	no
Years with single parent	531/492	birth–11	−0.02	0.03	no
Family socioeconomic status	532/499	birth–15	0	0	no
Relationship with parents	501/469	13, 15	−0.03	0.04	no

Child cognitive and neurological risk factors

Neurological abnormalities	498/479	birth–3	0.09	−0.10	yes
Peabody Picture IQ	491/465	3	−0.01	0.01	no
Stanford Binet IQ	509/477	5	−0.07	0.08	yes
WISC-R IQ	511/480	7, 9, 11	0.04	−0.04	no
WISC-R VIQ	511/480	7, 9, 11	0.04	−0.04	no
Neuropsych. memory score	380/354	13	−0.16	0.17	yes
Burt word reading test	510/479	7, 9, 11	−0.18	0.18	yes
Heart rate	453/419	7, 9, 11	−0.16	0.18	yes

Child behavioural risk factors

Difficult baby, parent report	490/464	3	0.03	−0.03	no
Undercontrolled temperament, observer-rated	528/495	3, 5	0.07	−0.07	yes
Hyperactivity, parent report	521/492	5, 7, 9, 11	0.12	−0.13	yes
Hyperactivity, teacher report	524/492	5, 7, 9, 11	0.26	−0.28	yes
Internalizing, parent report	521/492	5, 7, 9, 11	−0.06	0.07	yes
Internalizing, teacher report	524/492	5, 7, 9, 11	0.01	−0.01	no

Peer relations risk factors

Peer rejection, parent report	534/502	5, 7, 9, 11	0	0	no
Peer rejection, teacher report	512/479	5, 7, 9, 11	0.02	−0.02	no
Peer attachment, self-report	501/471	13, 15	−0.38	0.40	yes
Peers' delinquency, self-report	381/352	13	0.18	−0.19	yes
School involvement, self-report	495/466	15	−0.07	0.07	yes

Note:

[a] The risk predictors were standardized for the whole sample as z-scores.

Table 9.2. *Explaining the sex difference in adolescent antisocial behaviour using the measures that showed significant sex differences from table 9.1*

Risk factors	Adolescent antisocial behaviour scale			Lifetime diagnosis of CD		
	Sex difference before risk variables entered	Sex difference after risk variables entered	Percentage of the sex difference explained	M:F OR before risk variables entered	M:F OR after risk variables entered	Percentage of the sex difference explained
Family risk[a]	0.49 SD	0.45 SD	9%	2.4	2.3	6%
Neuro-cognitive risk[b]	0.49 SD	0.40 SD	19%	2.4	2	18%
Hyperactivity risk[c]	0.49 SD	0.32 SD	35%	2.4	1.7	38%
Neuro-cognitive, hyperactivity, and family risk combined	0.49 SD	0.26 SD	47%	2.4	1.5	53%
Peer-relations risk[d]	0.49 SD	0.37 SD	25%	2.4	2	21%
All 4 risk types combined	0.49 SD	0.22 SD	56%	2.4	1.3	65%

Notes: N for the multivariate analysis with all risk factors combined was 491 boys and 465 girls. M:F OR = male to female odds ratio.

[a] Variable entered was: (1) harsh discipline.

[b] Variables entered were: (1) neurological abnormalities, (2) Stanford-Binet IQ (3) neuropsych memory, (4) Burt word reading, (5) heart rate.

[c] Variables entered were: (1) under-controlled temperament, (2) parent-rated hyperactivity, (3) teacher-rated hyperactivity.

[d] Variables entered were: (1) attachment to peers, (2) peers' delinquency, (3) involvement at school.

of difficult temperament during the preschool years (d = 0.14), larger differences between the sexes on parent reports of hyperactivity (d = 0.25), and still larger differences on teacher reports of hyperactivity (d = 0.54).

The final panel of table 9.1 shows that boys had significantly weaker attachments than girls, both to peers (d = 0.78) and to school (d = 0.14), and boys also had significantly more delinquent peers than girls (d = 0.37).

Do sex differences in risk levels account for the sex difference in antisocial outcome?

Next we tested if the mean-level sex differences in risk factors could explain mean-level sex differences in antisocial behaviour. These tests are shown in table 9.2. The rows of table 9.2 show different groupings of risk factors (e.g., family risk factors, neuro-cognitive risk factors). The columns of table 9.2 show whether these risk factors can account for the sex difference in antisocial behaviour. Thus, the first column of table 9.2 shows the magnitude of the sex difference in the omnibus measure of adolescent antisocial behaviour, expressed in standard deviation units (SD). The second column shows the magnitude of the sex difference in the omnibus measure of adolescent antisocial behaviour, also expressed in d units, *after* the risk variables have been entered into a multiple regression equation (Ordinary Least Squares). The third column shows the percentage of the sex difference in antisocial behaviour that was accounted for by sex differences in the risk factors for antisocial behaviour.[1]

---

[1] We entered into this regression analysis all the risk factors that showed a significant mean-level difference in the final column of table 9.1. As this table shows, many of the predictor variables had some missing data; the number of missing cases per variable ranged from 0 to 24 per cent (neuropsychological test battery at age 13). These data were missing for equal numbers of males and females. The predictor variables represent data gathered from multiple sources at multiple ages, and the same cases were not missing the same data. This pattern of missing data made list-wise deletion undesirable for our analyses that used all of the predictors at once. Instead, for the multivariate regression analyses we utilized missing-data indicators (Little and Rubin, 1987). For each variable that was missing some data, we created a corresponding dummy variable that indicated which cases were missing (1 = missing; 0 = observed). We then recoded respondents who were missing the original variable to the variable mean so that they would not be ejected from analysis, and both variables (recoded substantive variable and missing-data indicator) were included in the multivariate equations. In these multivariate equations, each substantive variable applies only to its observed cases. Each missing-data variable, when statistically significant, indicates that respondents missing data on this measure have different levels of antisocial behaviour than those not missing data. In each regression equation, the substantive variables and the missing-data indicators were entered simultaneously. Only one missing-data indicator was statistically significant ($r > 0.10$): Study members with missing data on the measure of parental criminality were more antisocial, suggesting that analyses of this particular variable may underestimate true effect sizes. For sensitivity analysis we further re-estimated our models (a) using only mean substitution and (b) using list-wise deletion (which excludes cases missing data for any variable in the analysis), but these re-estimations did not change the substantive results.

If risk factors might account for the sex difference in antisocial behaviour measured along a dimension, it is also important to test whether or not risk factors can account for sex differences in the prevalence of diagnosed conduct disorder. Considering both dimensional and diagnosis outcome measures provides a useful demonstration of the robustness of risk factors' effects on sex differences. Therefore, whereas columns 1–3 detail these steps using the adolescent antisocial behaviour scale as the outcome measure, columns 4–6 detail these steps using the lifetime diagnosis of conduct disorder as the outcome. Whereas columns 1–2 present the results in d units, columns 4–5 present the unadjusted and adjusted odds ratios taken from logistic regression equations.

The first column of table 9.1 shows that the magnitude of the sex difference in the antisocial behaviour scale, in standard deviation units, was 0.49. Likewise, the fourth column of table 9.2 shows that (as seen previously in table 4.2) males were more likely than females to meet the criteria for a conduct disorder by an odds ratio of 2.4.

The first four rows of table 9.2 test whether childhood risk factors could account for sex differences in antisocial behaviour measured in adolescence. Temporally, all of these risk factors were measured prior to the two measures of antisocial outcome. The family risk factor (shown in the first row of table 9.2) did not account for these sex differences in antisocial behaviour; in fact, family risk accounted for only 9 per cent of the sex difference in the antisocial behaviour scale and 6 per cent of the sex difference in the risk for conduct disorder. Neurocognitive risk factors (shown in the second row of table 9.2) accounted for 18 per cent to 19 per cent of the sex difference in antisocial behaviour. Hyperactivity risk factors, including undercontrolled temperament (shown in the third row of table 9.2), accounted for 35 per cent and 38 per cent of the sex difference in antisocial behaviour. The fourth row of table 9.2 shows that when the family, neuro-cognitive, and hyperactivity risk factors, which were all measured in the first eleven years of life, were entered into one regression model, they accounted for 47 per cent to 53 per cent of the sex difference in adolescent antisocial behaviour.

We next considered the risk factors associated with peer relations. (These were measured concurrently with antisocial outcome.) Peer-relationships risk factors (shown in the fourth row of table 9.2) accounted for 25 per cent and 21 per cent percent of the sex difference in adolescent antisocial behaviour. When all of the childhood and adolescent risk factors were combined into one regression model, they accounted for 56 per cent and 65 per cent of the sex difference in antisocial behaviour. Table 9.2 shows that these results were robust to measurement considerations, as the same results were obtained when using a continuously distributed composite measure of anti-social behaviour as when using categorical diagnoses.

Comment: why do risk measures explain only half of the sex difference in antisocial outcome?

It is reasonable to ask why we can explain only 56–65 per cent of the association between sex and adolescent antisocial behaviour. There are three reasons for this. First, there are limits on the analysis arising from imperfect measurement in both the dependent and independent variables. Second, there may be interaction effects among the various risk factors, and such interaction effects might explain part of the sex difference in outcome. Our effort to account for the association between sex and antisocial behaviour has been limited to studying the additive (combined) contributions of main effects. A much larger sample size than the Dunedin cohort would be required to assess the potential contribution of interaction effects among all possible pairs of the multiple risk factors we have studied here. Third, and most important, our analysis has left out several important explanatory variables. Indeed, we do not have measures of two factors thought to explain the sex difference in physical aggression: physical strength and testosterone. Despite these limitations, the results in table 9.2 show that mean-level differences between males and females in the most oft-cited risk factors for anti-social behaviour account for one-half to two-thirds of the propensity of males to behave in more antisocial ways than females.

Comment: the importance of hyperactivity and peers for the sex difference in antisocial behaviour

The most important contributing factor to sex differences in adolescent antisocial behaviour was the sex difference in childhood hyperactivity (including undercontrolled temperament). In chapter 8 we saw that hyperactivity was the most potent predictor of antisocial behaviour *within* both males and females. In this chapter we have seen that sex differences in hyperactivity and temperament also account for the most variation *between* males and females. Of course, this simply pushes the question back one step further: why is hyperactivity so much more common and severe in males? The answer to this critical question is unknown. Progress is being made in the description of sex differences in the genetic and environmental architecture of attention-deficit hyperactivity symptoms (Eaves, *et al.*, 2000; Faraone *et al.*, 1999; Rhee *et al.*, 1999; Swanson *et al.*, 2000). Genetic factors appear particularly important here, perhaps more so than with antisocial behaviour generally. Although the original suggestion that an extra Y chromosome led to violent crime was shown by epidemiological research to be mistaken (Witkin *et al.*, 1970), evidence is still emerging that the extra Y chromosome is associated with an increase in hyperactivity that predisposes to antisocial behaviour, albeit not usually of a violent type (Rutter, Giller and Hagell, 1998). It may be that gender differences in antisocial behaviour are linked to such genetic factors. It is also possible that temperamental and personality characteristics related to hyperactivity, such as novelty-seeking and impulsiveness, account for gender differences in antisocial behaviour, and we shall test this possibility in greater detail in chapter 10.

The second most important contributing factor to sex differences in antisocial behaviour was the sex difference in peer relations. Maccoby (1998) has drawn attention to evidence from a range of different sources that boys' social groups tend to be different from girls' in several important respects. Six key contrasts may be highlighted. First, boys' interchanges with same-sex peers are more domineering and bragging. Second, boys are more likely to engage in risk-taking and limit-testing activities. Third, boys' groups are more orientated to appearing unambiguously male. Fourth, boys' groups tend to be larger and more orientated around activities. Fifth, boys' groups tend to be more separate from the world of adults and its social controls. Sixth, within boys' groups, dominance and status are more important than in girls' groups. It would be misleading to overemphasize these differences, for there is considerable heterogeneity within boys' and girls' groups. Moreover, our analysis of the coincidence of girls' conduct problems with their puberty in chapter 4 suggested that, after puberty, opposite-sex intimate peer relationships may assume as much or more influence over problem behaviours as the same-sex peer groups which were influential before puberty. (We return to the question of intimate partners in chapter 14.) Nevertheless, the prevailing social cultures of all-male and all-female peer groups tend to be different, and the present findings, along with other studies of peer-group effects (Caspi *et al.*, 1993; Giordano, Cernkovich, and Pugh, 1986; Mears, Ploeger, and Warr, 1998), suggest that differential exposure to the influences of delinquent peers may account, in part, for sex differences in antisocial behaviour.

Comment: family adversity risk factors do not account for sex differences in antisocial behaviour

In chapter 8 we saw that family risk factors were predictive of antisocial behaviour *within* both males and females. In this chapter, however, we have seen that these factors account for very little of the variation *between* males and females. We considered the possibility that although family adversity does not contribute directly to the development of sex differences in antisocial behaviour, family adversity may account for sex differences in antisocial behaviour by buffering or exacerbating individual-level vulnerabilities in one sex more than in the other sex. For example, childhood hyperactivity may render boys at risk for antisocial behaviour regardless of their family background, but hyperactivity may affect girls' risk of antisocial behaviour only if girls are reared in an adverse environment, thereby widening the observed sex difference in antisocial behaviour.

To test this possibility, we examined the effect of hyperactivity on adolescent antisocial behaviour when family problems were present against when family problems were absent, and we repeated this analysis separately for boys and girls. (We focused on hyperactivity because it emerged as the most potent risk factor; see chapter 8.) Tables 8.1 and 9.1 list the various family risk factors considered in this book. We first derived a composite index of family adversity by counting how many of the family variables were suffered by each Dunedin Study member (e.g., being born to a teen mother, parental criminality, growing up in a low-SES family). We then examined whether childhood hyperactivity predicted later antisocial behaviour more strongly in the context of multiple adversities. The results from multiple regression analyses showed that hyperactivity (beta=0.40, $p<0.01$) and the family adversity index (beta=0.26, $p<0.01$) predicted adolescent antisocial behaviour. The interaction term between hyperactivity and family adversity was also statistically significant ($t=2.34$, $p<0.05$), although this interaction effect contributed less than 1 per cent of the variance in antisocial outcome. Thus, although hyperactivity predicted antisocial behaviour across the full range of family adversity, hyperactive children were somewhat more likely to become antisocial if they were reared in adverse conditions ($r=0.40$) than if reared in non-adverse conditions ($r=0.30$). The finding that hyperactive children who grow up in adverse conditions have slightly more antisocial outcomes has been reported previously for Dunedin males (Moffitt, 1990). Of particular interest for this chapter, however, is that the potentiation effect did not vary across boys and girls ($t=1.55$, $p=0.12$). Adverse family circumstances contribute to individual differences in antisocial behaviour, but not to sex differences in antisocial behaviour. A positive family does not protect girls more than boys, it protects both.

It is possible, of course, that we have underestimated the contribution of the family to the development of sex differences in antisocial behaviour because the Dunedin archive does not contain measures of some important parenting practices which parents may apply with differing vigour to sons versus daughters (Keenan and Shaw, 1997), particularly parental monitoring and supervision (Agnew, 1985; Dishion and McMahon, 1998; Thornberry, 1987). If parents worry that the consequences of delinquent peer affiliations are more harmful for girls than for boys (e.g., pregnancy, date-rape, kidnapping), they may discipline the transgressions by a daughter that would be considered beneath their notice for a son. Research suggests that parental supervision, which is negatively associated with delinquency in boys and in girls, may affect the sex–delinquency relationship, although this effect may be limited to the earliest stage of adolescence (e.g., Jang and Krohn, 1995; Simons, Miller, and Aigner, 1980). Sex differences in parental monitoring are also thought to be conditional on social class; working-class parents supervise daughters closely, whereas middle-class parents treat sons and daughters more alike (Hagan, Simpson, and Gillis, 1987; Hill and Atkinson, 1988).

However, before we attribute to parental monitoring the power to explain the sex difference in antisocial behaviour, it is important to recognize that parents' supervision and monitoring can be a *consequence* of an adolescent's behaviour, as opposed to the *cause* of it (Bell and Chapman, 1986; Lytton and Romney, 1992). For example, some research suggests that pubertal hormones activate both problem behaviour and parent–child conflict (Buchanan, Becker, and Eccles, 1992). Other research shows that the association between low parental monitoring and high adolescent delinquency falls to insignificance when the adolescent's prior history of conduct problems is controlled, suggesting that parents become lax and apathetic about monitoring as a consequence of youngsters' persistent transgressions (Dishion *et al.*, 1991). The notion that parental monitoring explains the behavioural difference between the sexes is based on the assumption that parents' active tracking and surveillance of daughters prevents the latter from becoming involved in antisocial behaviour. However, Kerr and Stattin (2000) challenged this assumption in a study of 1,186 14-year-olds. They found that parents' tracking, surveillance, and efforts to solicit information were not very effective in reducing adolescents' antisocial behaviour, and these strategies could even backfire if the adolescents felt controlled. Parents of non-delinquents were indeed more likely to be aware of their adolescents' daily activities compared with parents of delinquents, but this came about because the least delinquent adolescents were the most likely to *tell* their parents about their activities. In other words, adolescents actively control how well their parents monitor them. This finding suggests that because girls are less antisocial than boys and have less to hide, girls make it easy for their parents to monitor their behaviour. Thus, even though parents may know more about their teenaged daughters' lives than their sons', there is good reason to question the seemingly straightforward assumption that adolescent girls are less antisocial because they are more closely supervised by their parents.

This is an area in need of more research, and longitudinal studies of sons and daughters who are siblings would be an informative design. The Dunedin Study, with its focus on a single target child, did not allow us to compare parents' treatment of sons and daughters within the same household. Nevertheless, our conclusion that family adversity during childhood does not contribute to the development of sex differences in antisocial behaviour is probably correct. Family risk factors predict antisocial behaviour for both sexes, and both sexes are equally exposed to most family risks, therefore family factors cannot account for features that distinguish the antisocial behaviour of males: (1) the greater prevalence of males who exhibit antisocial behaviour, (2) the higher frequency and broader variety of criminal offending among males who do participate, and (3) the greater seriousness and violence of antisocial behaviours committed by males. Moreover, the data show that females' lesser antisocial involvement is not the product of a protective effect of family factors on girls. Instead, our findings suggest that girls are exposed to just as much family risk as boys are, but they are less antisocial because they are less likely to suffer from neuro-cognitive deficits, undercontrolled temperament, and hyperactivity, and because as teenagers they generally develop a better quality of relationship with peers who are less antisocial.

Take-home messages

- Boys have higher rates than girls of the most important risk factors for antisocial behaviours, including more compromised neuro-cognitive status, more hyperactivity, and more peer problems.
- Sex differences in the level of various risk factors account for one-half to two-thirds of the sex differences in antisocial behaviour.
- Sex differences in early-emerging undercontrolled temperament and hyperactivity problems account for more than one-third of the sex difference in antisocial behaviour.
- Sex differences in peer relationships account for one-quarter of the sex difference in antisocial behaviour.
- Family adversity contributes to individual differences in antisocial behaviour, but not to the sex difference in antisocial behaviour.

- The findings support the hypothesis that males are more likely to be anti social than females because they are exposed to greater levels of individual and interpersonal risk for antisocial behaviour.

Unanswered questions

- Why do more boys than girls suffer from hyperactivity; do genetic factors of some kind play a role?
- Why are boys' and girls' peer cultures so different?
- Studies of peer delinquency in adolescence should measure aspects of peers such as age, sex, and the nature and quality of relationships to discover how the strong statistical correlation between peer delinquency and self-delinquency comes about.
- Studies of male/female sibling pairs would inform the question of whether parents rear sons and daughters differently and thereby cause sex differences in adolescent delinquency. Such studies should be longitudinal to find out whether parenting styles influence youngsters' antisocial behaviour as against youngsters' behaviour influencing parenting styles.
- Variables studied here explained between one-half and two-thirds of the sex difference in antisocial behaviour. What explains the rest? Do pubertal hormones, physical size, or parental monitoring play a role?

CHAPTER TEN

Can sex differences in personality traits help to explain sex differences in antisocial behaviour?

In the previous two chapters we examined sex differences in the early risk predictors for antisocial behaviour. We continue this theme in this chapter by turning our attention to sex differences in the relation between personality and antisocial behaviour. A personality analysis of sex differences in antisocial behaviour may improve our understanding of the diathesis underlying antisocial disorders. Personality research has already described the nature of the propensity toward antisocial behaviour by organizing information about the individual differences in cognitions, motivations, emotions, and distinct styles of approach and response to the world that robustly predict criminal offending (Moffitt *et al.*, 1995). Just as males and females differ on their antisocial involvement on average (chapters 3 and 4), males and females are also known to differ on their personalities on average (Feingold, 1994). If population sex differences in personality traits could account for the sex difference in antisocial behaviour this conjunction would suggest that measured quantitative personality traits may be a window on to core diatheses underlying antisocial disorders. Such a window could deepen our understanding of antisocial propensity because findings about the origins of personality traits are rapidly emerging from several quarters in the behavioural sciences. Longitudinal studies attest to developmental links from early childhood temperament to later adult personality (Caspi, 2000; Caspi *et al.*, forthcoming). Biological correlates of personality traits are being uncovered by quantitative genetic research (Plomin and Caspi, 1999), molecular genetic research (Benjamin, Ebstein, and Belmaker, forthcoming), neurotransmitter research (Berman, Kavoussi, and Coccaro, 1997; Cloninger, Svrakic and Przybeck, 1993; Cloninger,

1998), and neuro-imaging studies of the brain (Davidson and Irwin, 1999; Raine *et al.*, 2000).

One personality profile has proved to play a particularly useful role in understanding antisocial behaviour: it features two primary personality factors called Constraint and Negative Emotionality. Our work, and the work of others, shows that this profile has replicated robustly across males and females, whites and African-Americans, adults and young adolescents, and samples from different nations, using either official or self-report measures of crime, and using several different instruments for assessing personality (Caspi *et al.*, 1994; Elkins *et al.*, 1997; Krueger *et al.*, 1994). The personality profile has been found to relate to a developmental trajectory of life-course persistent antisocial behaviour (Moffitt *et al.*, 1996). It prospectively predicts physical abuse of a partner (Moffitt *et al.*, 2000) as well as conviction for violent crime (Caspi *et al.*, 1997). Personality is most often assessed via self-reports to reveal how an individual perceives and describes him- or herself, but we have shown that when an informant who knows the subject well provides the personality data, the same criminal personality profile is obtained (Moffitt *et al.*, 1995).

To measure personality characteristics relevant to the crime-prone profile in the Dunedin Study we used the Multidimensional Personality Questionnaire (MPQ; Tellegen, 1982), one of the best-known contemporary structural models of personality traits (Church and Burke, 1994; Watson, Clark, and Harkness, 1994). The MPQ assessment is a systematic method of gathering psychological clues as to why behaviours occur by considering the attitudes, values, and beliefs that perpetrators have about themselves and others, the emotions perpetrators tend to experience readily, and the kind of activities and settings that perpetrators prefer.

As anticipated by many criminologists, antisocial behaviour is predicted by a lack of constraint. This personality characteristic is sometimes called 'low self-control', and it plays the starring role in one of the most important contemporary theories of crime (Gottfredson and Hirshi, 1990). In the MPQ system this personality factor is labelled 'Constraint' and operationalized when research participants describe themselves as reflective, cautious, careful, rational, and planful; when they say they endorse high moral standards and feel most comfortable in a conservative social environment; and when they say they avoid excitement and danger, preferring safe activities even if they are tedious.

A finding that was less anticipated by criminology theory was that self-control is not the lone star that predicts crime. A characteristic labelled

'Negative Emotionality' is just as essential. Although less well-known to crime theorists, Negative Emotionality has a rich empirical and theoretical nomological net in other behavioural sciences (Watson and Clark, 1984; Watson, Clark, and Harkness, 1994). In the MPQ it is operationalized when research participants describe themselves as nervous, vulnerable, prone to worry and unable to cope with stress; when they say they feel tense, fearful, and angry; when they feel suspicious, expect mistreatment, and see the world as being peopled with potential enemies; and when they say they seek revenge for slights, take advantage of other people, and find it fun to frighten others.

The goal of this chapter is to (a) test for sex differences in the way MPQ personality traits relate to antisocial behaviour, (b) test for sex differences in MPQ personality traits, and finally (c) test whether or not differences between the personalities of males and females can account for observed sex differences in antisocial behaviour. Although we follow the same analytic logic in this study of personality traits that we earlier used to study risk factors in chapters 8 and 9, we wish to note a distinction. In chapters 8 and 9 we looked at personal characteristics (e.g., hyperactivity, heart rate, IQ) that are thought to be expressed fully in childhood, and thus those characteristics were properly measured prospectively to our adolescent measure of antisocial behaviour. In contrast, in this chapter we look at personality traits, which are thought to have roots in childhood temperament but which continue to be shaped by subsequent experience in an ongoing process of construction. These traits are thought to become fully formed and stable sometime in late adolescence, and thus they are properly measured thereafter. As such, we measured personality traits at age 18.

Method

Measures of personality

As part of the phase-18 assessment, Study members completed a modified version of the Multidimensional Personality Questionnaire (MPQ; Tellegen, 1982). In all, MPQ data were gathered for 938 Study members; 862 Study members completed the MPQ at the research unit during the age-18 assessment, and 76 additional Study members returned a mailed version of the MPQ subsequent to the assessment.

The MPQ is a self-report personality instrument designed to assess a broad range of individual differences in affective and behavioural style. We chose to administer the MPQ because (1) it was developed and standardized with non-clinical populations; (2) it yields a comprehensive profile of human psychological differences along multiple personality dimensions; (3) its reliability and validity are well established, and (4) previous developmental and behavioural-genetic studies with the MPQ have established that the personality traits measured by this psychological test are heritable and stable (McGue, Bacon, and Lykken, 1993; Tellegen *et al.*, 1988). Thus, the traits assessed by the MPQ appear to reflect consistent and enduring patterns of behaviour in the general population.

MPQ scale names and descriptions of high scorers for each scale are presented in table 10.1. The scales' internal consistency alphas ranged from 0.63 to 0.80, and had an average value of 0.73. The scale intercorrelations for male Study members ranged from −0.30 to 0.50 with a mean absolute value of 0.16. The scale intercorrelations for female Study members ranged from −0.38 to 0.41 with a mean absolute value of 0.17. The low magnitudes of these inter-correlations are similar to those obtained with the original instrument and illustrate the relative independence of the ten MPQ scales (cf. Tellegen *et al.*, 1988). The ten scales constituting the MPQ can be viewed at the higher-order level as defining three distinct superfactors (Tellegen, 1985; Tellegen and Waller, forthcoming).[1] As shown in the last rows of table 10.1, *Constraint* is a combination of the Self-control, Harm avoidance, and Traditionalism scales. Individuals high on this dimension tend to endorse conventional social norms, avoid thrills, and act in a cautious and restrained manner. *Negative Emotionality* is a combination of the Aggression, Alienation, and Stress Reaction scales. Individuals high on this dimension have a low general threshold for the experience of negative emotions such as anxiety and anger, and tend to break down under stress. *Positive Emotionality* is a combination of the Social Closeness, Well Being, Achievement, and Social Potency scales. Individuals high on this dimension have a lower threshold for the experience of positive emotions and for positive engagement with their social and work environments, and tend to view life as being essentially a pleasurable experience.

Measures of antisocial behaviour

We examined two measures of antisocial behaviour: the first is the composite measure of adolescent antisocial behaviour described in chapter 8 and the second is the DSM-IV diagnosis of lifetime conduct disorder described in chapter 4.

---

[1] Tellegen's Absorption scale was not included in the MPQ version administered in the Dunedin Study.

A. ARE THE CORRELATIONS BETWEEN PERSONALITY AND ANTISOCIAL BEHAVIOUR THE SAME FOR MALES AND FEMALES?

Data analysis approach

To assess the relation between personality characteristics and antisocial behaviour, we calculated correlations between the composite measure of adolescent antisocial behaviour and the ten MPQ scales (and their three superfactors). We examined whether the personality correlates of antisocial behaviour differed between males and females by evaluating the statistical significance of sex-interaction terms in a multiple regression framework, as described earlier, in chapter 8.

Results

Table 10.1 shows that, among both males and females, antisocial behaviour was positively associated with the MPQ scales Aggression, Alienation, and Stress Reaction, suggesting that young men and women who were involved in a wide variety of antisocial behaviour were likely to take advantage of others, to mistrust others and to feel betrayed and used by their friends, and to become easily upset and irritable. Antisocial behaviour was negatively associated with the MPQ scales Self-control, Traditionalism, and Social Closeness, suggesting that young men and women who were involved in a wide variety of antisocial behaviour behaved impulsively rather than cautiously, preferred rebelliousness over conventionality, and had little need or capacity for warmth and close relationships. The overall multiple correlation between personality and antisocial behaviour was similar for males (R=0.57) and females (R=0.58). At the superfactor level, Constraint and Negative Emotionality emerged as robust correlates of antisocial behaviour among males and females.

Table 10.1 shows that there were a few gender differences in the personality correlates of antisocial behaviour. We examined whether the personality correlates of antisocial behaviour differed between males and females by evaluating the statistical significance of sex-interaction terms in a multiple regression framework. The results of these analyses are shown in the fifth column of table 10.1. Of the 13 sex-interaction terms tested, we found three sex differences at $p < 0.05$. The MPQ scales Harm Avoidance and Traditionalism (and to a lesser extent Self-control, $p = 0.07$), and their superfactor Constraint were more strongly related to antisocial behaviour among males than females. In sum, although convergence across the sexes

Table 10.1. *Age-18 Multidimensional Personality Questionnaire correlates of males' and females' antisocial behaviour during adolescence, and mean-level sex differences for the MPQ scales*

Personality scale	A high scorer is . . .	Males' correlation	Females' correlation	Sex interaction p<0.05	Which sex has higher levels of the trait, p<0.05
Self-control	reflective, cautious, careful, planful, rational	−0.29*	−0.28*	no	girls 0.34 SD
Harm avoidance	avoids excitement and danger, prefers safety even if tedious	−0.17*	−0.08	yes	girls 0.72 SD
Traditionalism	needs predictable environment, has high moral standards, conservative	−0.34*	−0.29*	yes	girls 0.21 SD
Aggression	willing to take advantage of others and cause them discomfort	0.47*	0.50*	no	boys 0.87 SD
Alienation	suspicious, feels mistreated, persecuted, threatened	0.35*	0.34*	no	boys 0.32 SD
Stress reaction	nervous, vulnerable, sensitive, prone to over-react, worries	0.22*	0.26*	no	girls 0.41 SD
Social closeness	sociable, needs and likes people, turns to them for comfort	−0.22*	−0.17*	no	girls 0.43 SD
Well-being	happy, cheerful, feels good about oneself and the future	−0.01	−0.11*	no	no sex diff.
Achievement	works hard, enjoys demanding projects, persists for long hours	0.01	−0.10	no	boys 0.22 SD

Social potency	forceful, decisive, influences others, enjoys leadership roles	0.10	0.09	no	boys 0.19 SD
Cumulative for all personality scales					
Multiple correlation		0.57*	0.58*	no	
MPQ Factor Scores					
Constraint	Control + Harm avoidance + Traditionalism	−0.36*	−0.30*	yes	girls 0.59 SD
Negative emotionality	Aggression + Alienation + Stress reaction	0.45*	0.46*	no	boys 0.28 SD
Positive emotionality	Social closeness + Well-being + Achievement + Social potency	−0.03	−0.10	no	no sex diff.

Notes: N for the correlations between personality and antisocial behaviour was 461 males and 440 females. For the comparison of boys' and girls' mean personality scores N was 478 males and 460 females.

* Significant at p<0.01.

was the most usual finding, the results also suggested that weak Constraint is more likely to be expressed in antisocial behaviour by males than by females.

B. HOW ARE THE PERSONALITIES OF MALES AND FEMALES DIFFERENT?

Data analysis approach

To compare the sexes' personality profiles, we first standardized all the personality variables to the same scale for the whole sample using the z-score transformation. Thus, each personality variable had a mean of 0 and a standard deviation of 1. Personality comparisons between males and females were performed using t-tests. The final column of table 10.1 reports sex differences in personality. Where the differences between males and females were significant at $p < 0.05$, the column shows the effect size d representing the standard deviation unit difference between the sexes.

Results

The Dunedin men and women differed in their personalities in ways suggested by previous research (Feingold, 1994). Of particular interest is the fact that sex differences in personality were most notable on Negative Emotionality and Constraint, the two superfactors most robustly related to antisocial behaviour. As table 10.1 shows, males were characterized by significantly higher levels of Negative Emotionality – a propensity to experience aversive affective states – and significantly lower levels of Constraint – difficulty inhibiting the expression of emotions and impulses.

C. DO SEX DIFFERENCES IN PERSONALITY ACCOUNT FOR SEX DIFFERENCES IN ANTISOCIAL BEHAVIOUR?

Data analysis approach

Following the statistical procedures suggested by Rowe *et al.* (1994; 1995) and outlined in chapter 9, we used regression analyses to examine whether mean-level differences between the sexes in the risk predictors (in this case, personality traits) could account for mean level differences between the sexes in their antisocial behaviour. We performed two sets of multiple regression tests. In the first (OLS) regression, we compared the effect of sex on antisocial behaviour before and after entering the MPQ personality traits into the model. In the second (logistic) regression, we compared the effect of sex on the risk of a lifetime diagnosis of conduct disorder before and after entering the personality traits into the model.

Results

The results are shown in table 10.2. Personality differences between males and females in Negative Emotionality and Constraint explained 96 per cent of the effect of sex on adolescent antisocial behaviour and 78 per cent of the effect of sex on the likelihood of developing conduct disorder.

Comment: implications of sex differences in personality for the study of antisocial behaviour

Our results suggest that, among both males and females, antisocial behaviour becomes increasingly likely among those persons high in negative emotionality *and* low in constraint. Negative emotionality is a tendency to experience aversive affective states such as anger, anxiety, and irritability (Watson and Clark, 1984). It is likely that individuals with chronically high levels of negative affect perceive interpersonal events differently than others do. They may be predisposed to process information in a biased way, perceiving threat in the acts of others and in the vicissitudes of everyday life. This situation may be worsened when negative emotionality is accompanied by an inability to modulate impulsive expression, a lack of constraint.

Unlike the developmental-antecedents analysis reported in chapters 8 and 9, the age-18 personality data reported in this chapter were not prospective. At best, our analysis of the link between personality traits and antisocial behaviour is concurrent, and to some extent participation in delinquency may have influenced the Study members' personality reports. However, elsewhere we have shown that a variety of temperament and personality measures are able prospectively to predict a variety of antisocial outcomes, in different longitudinally studied cohorts, across time-lags ranging from three to eighteen years (Caspi *et al.*, 1996; Caspi *et al.* 1997; Lynam *et al.*, 2000; Moffitt *et al.*, 2000).

Although the finding that sex differences in personality account for virtually all of the effect of sex on antisocial behaviour is statistically impressive, it only shifts the analysis to a different set of questions: what are the origins of sex differences in personality traits? In one sense, this analysis supplants one question with another question. In another sense, however, these results do represent a considerable advance, for a fair amount is becoming

Table 10.2. *Explaining the sex difference in adolescent antisocial behaviour using personality data from the Multidimensional Personality Questionnaire*

Family of risk factors	Sex difference in adolescent antisocial behaviour			Sex difference in the life-time diagnosis of conduct disorder		
	Before risk variables entered	After risk variables entered	Percentage of the sex difference explained	Before risk variables entered	After risk variables entered	Percentage of the sex difference explained
Personality[a]	0.46 SD*	0.02 SD	96%	OR = 2.4*	OR = 1.2	78%

Notes: N for the personality analyses was 461 boys and 440 girls. SD = standard deviation units, OR = odds ratio.

[a] Variables entered were the nine personality scales from table 10.1 that showed a sex difference: self-control, harm avoidance, traditionalism, aggression, alienation, stress reaction, social closeness, achievement, and social potency.

* Significant at p < 0.01.

known about the origins of personality traits (Caspi, 1998). Our findings imply that research on the origins of personality traits can be harnessed to understand antisocial behaviour.

At least three psychological theories of antisocial behaviour lead to the expectation that sex-specific personality profiles may help to account for sex differences in antisocial behaviour. First, according to the reformulated frustration–aggression hypothesis, aggression is a result of negative affect elicited by aversive events (Berkowitz, 1989). A dispositional extension of this hypothesis is that chronic levels of negative affect should have the direct result of increasing aggression. Thus, to the extent that males are significantly more prone than females to experience chronic levels of negative affect, they may also be more prone to aggress. This perspective is supported by our finding that sex differences in levels of Negative Emotionality account, in part, for sex differences in antisocial behaviour. Second, according to a cognitive-behavioural account, individual differences in the appraisal and interpretation of situations play a critical role in inhibiting or promoting aggression (Crick and Dodge, 1994; Link, Andrews, and Cullen, 1992). Thus, to the extent that males more than females perceive provocation in the action of others and are vigilant towards real or imagined threats, they may also be more prone to act aggressively. In fact, Bettencourt and Miller (1996) suggest that men may be more likely to interpret ambiguous or neutral situations as provoking, and may thus react aggressively even in the absence of a direct provocation. This perspective is supported by our finding that sex differences in levels of MPQ Alienation and Aggression account, in part, for sex differences in antisocial behaviour. Finally, according to self-control theory, the gender gap in crime may be accounted for by the fact that males have lower self-control than females (Burton *et al.*, 1998; LaGrange and Silverman, 1999). This perspective is supported by our finding that sex differences in levels of Constraint account, in part, for sex differences in antisocial behaviour.

Trait explanations are not an end; rather, they are 'place-holders' in an evolving search for fuller explanations of motivated behaviour (Fletcher, 1993; Wakefield, 1989; Zuroff, 1986). In this sense, developmental researchers can embed personality measures in process theories that lead to new and testable hypotheses about social, psychological, and biological phenomena. The importance of attempting to understand antisocial behaviour in terms of personality may become more apparent when considering the 'nomological net' surrounding personality and its development. In particular, data suggest that the personality traits that predict antisocial behaviour possess three important developmental features. First, behavioural-genetic studies have shown that the MPQ variables are partially heritable; more than 50 per cent of the variation in Negative Emotionality and Constraint can be attributed to genetic factors (Bouchard, 1994). Second, developmental studies have shown that the MPQ variables are predictable from temperament in early childhood; specifically, undercontrolled Dunedin 3-year-olds score significantly higher on adult measures of Negative Emotionality and significantly lower on adult measures of Constraint (Caspi and Silva, 1995). Finally, longitudinal studies have shown that individual differences in the MPQ traits are stable from adolescence through the adult years. Across an 8-year period, Negative Emotionality and Constraint yielded cross-age correlations of 0.60 and 0.67 among the Dunedin men and women (Roberts, Caspi, and Moffitt, forthcoming). Across a ten-year period in another study, Negative Emotionality and Constraint yielded cross-age correlations of 0.58 and 0.60 (McGue, Bacon, and Lykken, 1993), suggesting that these traits stay longitudinally consistent across adulthood. In all, the present findings, together with other studies of personality development, provide useful information about the psychological foundations of antisocial behaviour in adolescence, suggesting that (a) the same constellation of personality qualities characterizes antisocial males and females, (b) the origins of this personality constellation may be found early in life, (c) this constellation stabilizes during adolescence, and (d) sex differences in mean-levels of this constellation account for much of the sex difference in antisocial behaviour.

Take-home messages

- The personality trait correlates of antisocial behaviour are the same for males and females.
- There are substantial sex differences on those very personality traits that are associated with antisocial behaviour, with males having more Negative Emotionality and less Constraint than females.
- Sex differences in personality traits account for almost all of the sex differences observed in antisocial behaviour.

Unanswered questions

- More work is needed to apply newly emerging evidence about the origins and development of personality traits to the perennial problem of sex differences in antisocial behaviour.

CHAPTER ELEVEN

Sex and comorbidity: are there sex differences in the co-occurrence of conduct disorder and other disorders?

In this chapter, we compare the sexes on disorders and psychiatric conditions that co-occur with antisocial disorders during the developmental period from ages 11 to 21. We examine mental retardation, reading retardation, attention deficit-hyperactivity disorder (ADHD), anxiety disorders, depression and dysthymia, mania, eating disorders, alcohol and marijuana dependence, and schizophreniform symptoms. The chapter addresses three issues. How common is comorbidity among young people who have conduct disorder? What is the pattern of cumulative co-occurrence of conduct disorder with other disorders across the period of the life span we study, and does this pattern differ for males and females? Are there changing patterns of comorbidity with conduct problems across the repeated assessments of the study, and do those patterns differ for males and females?

In recent years awareness has increased about the phenomenon of comorbidity, the concurrent diagnosis of two or more mental disorders within the same individual. Epidemiological studies show that approximately half of all persons with a mental disorder have more than one diagnosable disorder (Clark, Watson, and Reynolds, 1995). The ubiquity of comorbidity has implications for research methodology, clinical practice, and diagnostic nosologies (Caron and Rutter, 1991; Angold, Costello and Erkanli, 1999). With respect to research methodology, it has been shown that comorbidity can confound developmental studies of the onset and course of a disorder (Sher and Trull, 1996). With respect to clinical practice, comorbid disorders compared to pure disorders have earlier onset, more chronic course, more complicating factors that impede compliance with treatment, poorer response to treatment, and poorer prognosis (Brown and Barlow, 1992; Clarkin and Kendall, 1992; Shea, Widiger, and

Klein, 1992; Verhulst and van der Ende, 1993). With respect to nosology, comorbidity raises questions about the validity of classification systems and the appropriateness of categorical approaches to the assessment of psycho-pathology (Krueger *et al.*, 1998; Wittchen, 1996). Indeed, the term comor-bidity refers to patients who have two separate diseases, but rates of overlap between some disorders are so high as to suggest that they may be different presentations of the same pathology process (Rutter, 1997). These many implications become even more critical when we appreciate that the term 'comorbidity' oversimplifies the situation. For example, at age 21, 47 per cent of diagnosed cases in the Dunedin cohort had comorbid disorders, but 56 per cent of those 'comorbid' cases had 3 or more disorders, while 53 per cent of those 'trimorbid' cases had 4 or more disorders, and 53 per cent of those 'quatromorbid' cases had 5 or more disorders. Unsurprisingly, more disorders went hand in hand with more severe life impairment (Newman *et al.*, 1998).

The study of sex differences in comorbidity is especially relevant to the developmental epidemiology of conduct disorder (Hinshaw, Lahey, and Hart, 1993). The presence of sex differences in co-occurring psychiatric fea-tures and conditions associated with conduct disorder would raise the pos-sibility that conduct disorder in males versus females represents a different syndrome with a possibly different course. Specifically, male conduct disor-der could be more severe and persistent because it is complicated by more comorbid conditions. Sex differences in co-occurring disorders and condi-tions among youth with conduct disorder would also suggest that there may be sex differences in the treatment responses of males versus females and that sex-specific regimens may need to be considered in treating conduct disorder.

Studies of comorbidity with conduct disorder have tended to focus on one disorder at a time, most often attention-deficit-hyperactivity (Lynam, 1996). However, although childhood-onset conduct disorder cases consti-tute most of the comorbid cases in the ADHD population, concurrent ADHD does not constitute a large share of comorbid cases in the conduct-disorder population. This is because the prevalence of ADHD is generally only half the prevalence of conduct disorder, and the increase in the inci-dence of conduct disorder during early adolescence coincides with a decline in the prevalence of ADHD. Because of the very low prevalence of ADHD among girls, comorbidity has usually been studied in all-male samples. One review has attended to sex differences in the relation between conduct disorder and ADHD, but it concluded that findings have been inconsistent (Loeber and Keenan, 1994).

Another shortcoming of studies of comorbidity with conduct disorder is that they have tended to focus on one cross-sectional diagnostic assessment at a time. A cross-sectional snapshot provides a potentially misleading picture, because arbitrary reporting windows exclude from the comorbid count emerging or recovering disorders that fall just below the threshold for diagnosis at the time of assessment, as well as episodes of disorder that fall outside the window by only weeks or months. Cumulative lifetime comorbidity across meaningful developmental periods would be more informative about conduct disorder, because a typical case of conduct disorder tends to outlast the one-year reporting period of most childhood epidemiological studies.

Moreover, as we have seen in chapter 4 of this book, both the incidence and prevalence of conduct problems wax and wane across the developmental period in which diagnoses of conduct disorder are usually made (ages 10–18). This pattern of fluctuation differs for males and females. Other disorders, too, show changing prevalence across childhood and adolescence, and thus what appears comorbid (or not) at one snapshot of a developing age group may differ quite a bit at another snapshot taken when the group is a couple of years younger or older. What is needed is an analysis of comorbidity with conduct problems that takes this developmental fluctuation into account by comparing repeated snapshots (Caron and Rutter, 1991).

With specific reference to sex differences, even less systematic information is available because studies of comorbidity with conduct disorder usually focus on one sex or pool the sexes. Our review of the literature revealed one widely held belief about a sex-specific comorbid relation: that antisocial behaviour is linked with depression among females. It has been suggested that although girls' underlying psychopathology may sometimes be expressed as antisocial behaviour in a limited way, or for a limited time, psychopathology among females is primarily channelled into internalizing problems such as depression (Zahn-Waxler, 1993), whether by gender-role socialization or as a natural consequence of sex differences in cognitive and emotional development (Keenan and Shaw, 1997). Reviews of studies point to some evidence for a sequence in which girls who have early conduct problems develop adult depression (Loeber and Keenan, 1994; Zoccolillo, 1992). As one example, retrospective diagnoses of conduct disorder among respondents in the Epidemiological Catchment Area Study predicted complementary patterns of adult diagnoses for the sexes; conduct disorder was followed by externalizing disorders for 73 per cent of men and 39 per cent of women, whereas conduct disorder was followed by internalizing disorders for 26 per cent of men and 73 per cent of women

(Robins, 1986). This hypothesis, then, calls for a look at how relations between conduct disorder and other disorders might change from adolescence to young adulthood. We do this in the present chapter with a special focus on depression.

The Dunedin Study's repeated-measures design lends itself to analysis of the cumulative lifetime co-occurrence of different disorders across the peak period of risk for conduct disorder. In addition, the design supports an analysis of how patterns of comorbidity might change during the period of risk, by comparing successive snapshot assessments. In this chapter we present findings from both of these types of analyses, maintaining our emphasis on testing for sex differences.

A. THE LIFETIME COMORBIDITY OF CONDUCT DISORDER: ANALYZING DIAGNOSTIC CATEGORIES

Measures

LIFETIME DIAGNOSES OF CONDUCT DISORDER

Cumulative lifetime diagnoses of DSM-IV conduct disorder at ages 11, 13, 15, and 18 were made for 154 boys and 72 girls, as described in chapter 4. The remaining 370 boys and 422 girls were the comparison group.

COGNITIVE MENTAL DISORDERS

A presumptive diagnosis of mental retardation was made using the accepted standard definition; if the averaged IQ score from three testings with the WISC-R (Wechsler, 1974) fell more than two standard deviations below the New Zealand mean IQ. A presumptive diagnosis of reading retardation was made using the lowest 10 per cent of the sample (Fergusson *et al.*, 1996) on the averaged age-standardized reading score from three testings with the Burt Word Reading Test (Scottish Council for Research in Education, 1976).

BEHAVIOURAL AND EMOTIONAL DISORDERS

Mental health was assessed in private standardized interviews, using the Diagnostic Interview Schedule for Children-Child version (DISC-C, Costello *et al.*, 1982) at the younger ages and the Diagnostic Interview Schedule (Robins *et al.*, 1981) at older ages, with a reporting period of 12 months at each age. Both instruments were adapted for the Dunedin Study. Modifications, procedures, reliability, validity, prevalence, and correlates have been described in detail for each age in a series of publications listed in the next paragraph. Diagnoses were made via computer algorithms following the then-current version of the Diagnostic and Statistical Manual of Mental Disorders (American Psychiatric Association, 1980;1987). Table 11.1 shows the ages at which each disorder was diagnosed; disorders were not assessed that were expected to yield fewer than 10 cases in our sample of 1,000 (e.g., ADHD was not assessed after age 15, psychotic disorders were not assessed before 21). The prevalence rates of mental disorders in the Dunedin sample closely match rates reported for people of similar age in other surveys (Costello, 1989; Kessler *et al.*, 1994).

At age 11, 792 Study members (77 per cent of the sample) were interviewed using the DISC-C and diagnosed using DSM-III; 18 per cent received a diagnosis (see Anderson *et al.*, 1987 for details). At age 13, 734 Study members (71 per cent) were interviewed using the DISC-C and diagnosed using DSM-III; 16 per cent received a diagnosis (see Frost, Moffitt, and McGee, 1989). At age 15, 943 Study members (92 per cent) were interviewed using the DISC-C and diagnosed using DSM-III; 22 per cent received a diagnosis (see McGee *et al.*, 1990). At age 18, 930 Study members (91 per cent) were interviewed using the Diagnostic Interview Schedule (DIS) and diagnosed using DSM-III-R; 41 per cent of the sample received a diagnosis (see Feehan *et al.*, 1994). At age 21, 961 Study members (94 per cent) were interviewed using the DIS and diagnosed using DSM-IIIR; 40 per cent of the sample received a diagnosis (see Newman *et al.*, 1996). Elsewhere, we have shown that the effects of missing cases on cumulative lifetime diagnoses are non-significant (e.g., Hankin *et al.*, 1998).

For this book the behavioural and emotional disorders diagnosed were grouped along the chapter groupings found in the *DSM*. These included: Attention Deficit Hyperactivity Disorder, Anxiety Disorders (Separation Anxiety, Generalized Anxiety Disorder, Obsessive-Compulsive Disorder, Panic Disorder, Agoraphobia, Social Phobia, and Simple Phobia); Depressive Disorders (Major Depressive Episode and Dysthymia); Manic Episode, Eating Disorders (Anorexia Nervosa and Bulimia Nervosa); Substance Disorders of Alcohol Dependence and Marijuana Dependence; and Schizophreniform Disorder, which consisted of the positive symptoms of Schizophrenia. Cases entered the diagnostic group if they had ever been given the diagnosis at any assessment phase of the study.

Data analysis approach

We calculated the overlap between lifetime diagnoses of conduct disorder and the other disorders using cross-tabulations within sex, which yield cell percentages and odds ratios. Odds ratios were used to test if the

Table 11.1. *Lifetime comorbidity among males and females who were ever diagnosed with DSM-IV conduct disorder during the longitudinal Study*

Comorbid Disorder	Age	Males			Females			Sex interaction $p < 0.05$
		No CD	CD	OR	No CD	CD	OR	
Mental retardation	7, 9, 11	0.3%	3%	12.0*	1%	3%	1.9	no
Reading retardation	7, 9, 11	10%	23%	2.6*	5%	10%	2.1	no
Attention-deficit hyperactivity disorder	11, 13, 15	3%	23%	8.6*	2%	9%	5.3*	no
Anxiety disorders	11, 13, 15, 18, 21	26%	45%	2.3*	47%	72%	2.8*	no
Depression/dysthymia	11, 13, 15, 18, 21	16%	35%	2.8*	36%	72%	4.5*	no
Mania	21	2%	4%	2.5	2%	5%	3.1	no
Eating disorders	18, 21	0%	1%	—	1%	9%	7.7*	—
Alcohol dependence	18, 21	19%	43%	3.2*	11%	31%	3.5*	no
Marijuana dependence	18, 21	8%	38%	6.5*	4%	27%	9.0*	no
Schizophreniform	21	2%	13%	9.9*	3%	9%	4.0*	no

Notes: N = 154 boys and 72 girls with conduct disorder vs. 370 boys and 422 girls not so diagnosed. OR = odds ratio.

* Significant at $p < 0.05$.

co-occurrence between disorders exceeded chance expectations, in view of the prevalence rate of each disorder. Odds ratios were considered significant at $p < 0.05$, as indicated on table 11.1, if their 95 per cent confidence intervals did not include 1. The statistical test for a sex difference in the pattern of comorbidity was conducted as a logistic regression model on the whole sample; if the model fit to the cross-tabled data improved significantly after we added a 'sex by conduct disorder' interaction term to the model, then there were significant sex differences.

Results

Conduct disorder in the Dunedin sample was characterized by substantial and significant comorbidity with all of the disorders we studied. Of the 226 Study members who had lifetime diagnoses of conduct disorder, 201 had at least one other diagnosable disorder between ages 11 and 21, yielding 90 per cent with comorbid disorders and only 10 per cent who appeared to have 'pure' conduct disorder. Among conduct-disordered Study members, 88 per cent of boys and 93 per cent of girls had comorbid disorders. Note that this is likely to be an underestimate, because not every mental disorder was assessed, and because episodic disorders may have occurred in the years between our assessment windows. In any case, our 90 per cent rate of comorbidity among conduct-disordered young people matches the 90 per cent rate of comorbidity among antisocial-personality-disordered adults in the American Epidemiological Catchment Area Study (Robins and Regier, 1991).

Table 11.1 shows the percentages of Study members with and without conduct disorder who had met the diagnostic criteria for other disorders. Considerable percentages of both males and females with conduct disorder suffered from anxiety, depression, and substance dependence during the age period studied. In addition, reading retardation and ADHD were especially common among boys with conduct disorder. Logistic regression analyses revealed no statistically significant sex differences in rates of lifetime comorbidity for any of the disorders. This finding is in agreement with other, larger, epidemiological studies, such as Hodgins *et al.* (1996), who found similar patterns for the sexes of overlap between lifetime conviction histories and psychiatric hospital diagnoses in 324,000 members of a Scandinavian cohort. The American Epidemiological Catchment Area survey found that overlap between adult diagnosis of antisocial personality disorder (ASPD) and other disorders was similar for men and women, although more women with ASPD had comorbid mania, schizophrenia and substance abuse disorders (Robins and Regier, 1991). McCord and Ensminger (1997) also report comorbidity in a large sample of male and female African-Americans.

Elsewhere, we have reported the co-occurrence of mental disorders in the Dunedin cohort with two other measures of antisocial behaviour: partner abuse (Danielson *et al.*, 1998) and violent crime (Arseneault *et al.*, 2000). In both reports the tendency for violence and mental disorder to co-occur was marked. At age 21, half of Dunedin Study members involved in partner violence had a psychiatric diagnosis, and one-third of those with a psychiatric diagnosis were involved in partner violence (Danielson *et al.*, 1998). Arseneault *et al.* (2000) reported that Study members with schizophreniform disorder or substance dependence disorders were 18 per cent of the Dunedin cohort at age 21, but that year they accounted for 55 per cent of the cohort's total violent offenders, 58 per cent of the cohort's 107 violent court convictions, and 54 per cent of the cohort's 2,403 self-reported violent offences. In both of these reports, as in this chapter, comorbidity patterns did not differ by sex.

Not shown in table 11.1 is the percentage of each disorder family with comorbid conduct disorder. These rates were: 50 per cent of mental retardation cases, 42 per cent of reading retardation cases, 29 per cent of anxiety cases, 33 per cent of depression cases, 42 per cent of mania cases, 53 per cent of eating disorder cases, and 43 per cent of alcohol-dependent cases also had conduct disorder. Three of the disorders appeared to be especially heavily concentrated in the portion of the sample who had conduct disorder: 68 per cent of ADHD cases, 62 per cent of marijuana-dependent cases, and 61 per cent of schizophreniform cases also had conduct disorder at some time in their lives.

Because the strong comorbidity between conduct disorder and schizophreniform disorder may seem surprising, readers may wish to know more about the content of this diagnostic group (for more about this group see Poulton *et al.*, 2000). The schizophreniform group constituted 4 per cent of the sample at age 21 (N = 39). Study members in this category responded 'yes, definitely' to interview questions about the positive symptoms of schizophrenia, endorsing at least two, and generally several more than two, bizarre beliefs such as 'someone was plotting against them or spying against them' and 'they were sent special messages through television or radio' and sensory experiences such as 'hearing voices that other people could not hear' and 'unusual feelings moving inside or on their body'. The interview ruled out plausible explanations, experiences resulting from alcohol or drugs, and experiences occurring during an episode of major depression. Structured psychiatric interviews for schizophrenia are known to identify a substantial number of cases who endorse psychotic-type beliefs and experiences, some of whom will become clinically schizophrenic and many of whom will not (Kendler *et al.*, 1996). After years of Study participation with proven confidentiality, Dunedin Study members may be unusually willing to reveal bizarre experiences and beliefs to our interviewers. Although we do not expect all members of the schizophreniform group to emerge with schizophrenia, Study data provide clear evidence that group members were far from being in good mental health at age 21; 87 per cent had suffered from mental disorder diagnosed at previous phases of the study, 77 per cent said symptoms interfered with their lives, 54 per cent had corroboration from a peer informant, 39 per cent had contact with mental health treatment services in the past year, and 10 per cent took prescribed psychotropic medication (Newman *et al.*, 1996). Although fewer than 4 per cent of the cohort, this schizophreniform group accounted for 10 per cent of the cohort's violent crime at age 21 (Arseneault *et al.*, 2000).

B. CROSS-AGE COMPARISONS OF COMORBIDITY WITH CONDUCT DISORDER: ANALYSING CONTINUOUS SYMPTOM SCALES

In the previous analysis of diagnostic data, we were obliged to use lifetime cumulative diagnoses because within any single assessment phase of the Dunedin Study statistical power was compromised by small cell sizes in three-way cross-classification tables (i.e., conduct disorder group by sex by comorbid disorder group). This shortage of power prevented us from examining developmental changes in patterns of comorbidity. To overcome this limitation, in analyses presented in this section we used continuously distributed symptom scales to measure each disorder. This allowed us to examine comorbid relations between disorders within each age 'snapshot' with adequate power. Moreover, as we saw earlier in chapter 4, the diagnostic cut-off points for conduct disorder appear to be arbitrary, with individuals above and below the cut-off having milder or more severe versions of the disorder along a continuum. This may apply to other disorders as well. We can take a more sensitive look at the disorder continuum by analysing symptom scales, as we do here.

Measures

ADOLESCENT ANTISOCIAL BEHAVIOUR

As described in chapter 8, this was a composite of z-standardized parent reports at 13 and 15, teacher reports at 13, informant reports at 18, and self-reports at ages 13, 15, and 18, with reliability (alpha) of 0.86 for boys (n = 491) and 0.77 for girls (n = 465).

SYMPTOM SCALES FOR DIFFERENT 'DISORDER FAMILIES'

Table 11.2 shows the disorders that were measured at two or more assessment phases between age 11 and age 21 in the Dunedin study: ADHD, anxiety, depression, and substance dependence (alcohol and marijuana). Although not every disorder was measured repeatedly in the Dunedin Study, these were the four disorders that accounted for the highest rates of comorbidity with conduct disorder in the sample, according to table 11.1. Symptom scales were created at each age by summing the scores (coded 0 = no, 1 = sometimes, 2 = definitely) from interview items assessing symptoms of each disorder. Both internal consistency and two-month test–retest reliabilities exceed 0.70 for all scales.

Data analysis approach

We calculated the relation between adolescent antisocial behaviour and the other symptom scales using Pearson correlations within sex. Effect sizes may be assessed as r = 0.1 is a small effect, r = 0.3 is a medium effect, and r = 0.5 is a large effect. The statistical test for a sex difference in the pattern of comorbidity was conducted as a multiple regression model on the whole sample, as described in chapter 8. If the squared multiple correlation increased significantly after we added a 'sex by conduct disorder' interaction term to the main effects model, then there were significant sex differences.

Results

Overall, table 11.2 appears consistent with table 11.1, suggesting that there were no major sex differences in the associations between antisocial behaviour and other disorders, whether categorical or dimensional measurement approaches were used. However, contrary to table 11.1, the age-specific analyses in table 11.2 revealed one sex difference that was not only statistically significant, but robust across three phases of the longitudinal study, and thus warranted interpretation. As shown in the third part of

Table 11.2. *Comorbidity among males and females: correlations between continuously distributed scales of diagnostic symptoms and the composite measure of adolescent antisocial behaviour*

Comorbid Symptom Scale	Age	Males' correlation	Females' correlation	Sex interaction $p<0.05$
ADHD	11	0.37*	0.25*	no
	13	0.46*	0.35*	no
	15	0.43*	0.40*	yes
Anxiety	11	0.30*	0.12*	no
	13	0.22*	0.12	no
	15	0.11*	0.14*	no
	18	0.19*	0.24*	yes
	21	0.12*	0.13*	no
Depression	11	0.34*	0.22*	no
	13	0.17*	0.19*	no
	15	0.21*	0.35*	yes
	18	0.20*	0.23*	yes
	21	0.15*	0.19*	yes
Substance dependence	18	0.53*	0.43*	no
	21	0.16*	0.34*	no

Notes: This table reports continuous symptom scales for disorders assessed at two or more ages in the study. The continuous measures of mental retardation (IQ) and of reading retardation (the Burt Reading test) are shown on table 8.1 as significant childhood predictors of antisocial behaviour. The continuous measures of manic and schizophreniform symptoms are shown on table 13.1 as significant age-21 outcomes of adolescent antisocial behaviour.
* Significant at $p<0.01$.

table 11.2, for girls a relation between antisocial behaviour and depression emerged at age 15 and continued thereafter. On the one hand, this pattern may have been obscured in table 11.1 by our use of lifetime diagnoses which lumped diagnoses of depression at ages 11 and 13 with depression at later ages (15, 18, and 21). On the other hand, it is possible that girls' antisocial behaviour is initially associated with sub-diagnostic levels of depression symptoms that only gradually reach diagnostic threshold as girls age into young adulthood. That possibility is examined next.

C. DOES A SPECIAL RELATION BETWEEN ANTISOCIAL BEHAVIOUR AND DEPRESSION EMERGE WITH AGE AMONG FEMALES?

The belief is widespread that girls' antisocial behaviour is transformed into depression as girls grow into women. However, the epidemiological evidence for this is not as solid as it could be. Evidence for this claim comes (a) from studies in which depressed adult women have retrospectively recalled past conduct symptoms (e.g., Robins, 1986; Robins and Price, 1991), (b) from a comparison across two samples assessed in different developmental periods, but that unfortunately also varied in other ways including nationality (Zoccolillo, 1992), and (c) from one observation of an untested trend in symptoms from childhood to adolescence (Offord, Alder and Boyle, 1986). Although none of the three pieces of evidence is conclusive because each method is problematic, taken together they are suggestive. The Dunedin Study provided the opportunity to add to this literature a formal test of sex differences in changing levels of depression across repeated assessments from childhood to adulthood within the same individuals who had conduct disorder.

Measures
We used the lifetime conduct disorder diagnosis and the depression diagnoses and symptom scales (standardized within age to a common metric; z-scores) from each Study phase. These measures were described earlier in this chapter.

Data analysis approach
We tested the significance of the sex difference in the age-related rate of increase of depression symptoms in two ways. First, we compared the rate of diagnosed depression as it changed across age 11, 13, 15, 18 and 21 for four groups, males and females, with and without conduct disorder. This analysis is shown in figure 11.1. Second, we examined the relative severity of depression symptoms by conducting a repeated-measures Analysis of Variance with lifetime conduct disorder (yes, no), sex (male, female) and age (11, 13, 15, 18, 21) as factors and the continuous depression symptom scale as the dependent variable. A significant three-way interaction term would reveal whether conduct disorder is increasingly associated with more severe depression for girls as they grow into adult women. This analysis is shown in figure 11.2.

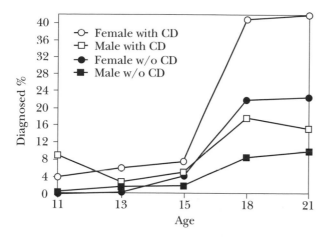

11.1 Changing prevalence of depression by sex and history of conduct disorder (CD)

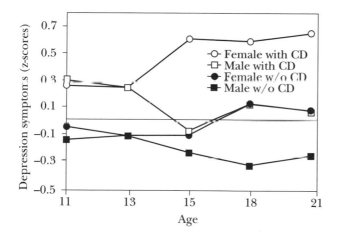

11.2 Changing depression symptoms by sex and history of conduct disorder (CD)

Results

Figure 11.1 shows that the prevalence of diagnosed depression increased between adolescence and young adulthood. The increase affected both males and females, and Study members with conduct disorder and those without. However, the highest rate of adult depression, at age 21, was attained by females with a history of conduct disorder. Moreover, conduct

disorder males showed an initial elevated rate of depression at age 11 relative to the other groups, which is consistent with Zoccolillo's (1992) observation that sex similarity in the lifetime overlap of conduct disorder and
depression conceals a pattern in which conduct-disorder boys are depressed
before puberty whereas conduct-disorder girls are depressed after puberty.

Figure 11.2, in which the symptom scales were standardized to z-scores
within each assessment age, removes from view the sample-wide rise in
depression with increasing age. This figure reveals that the *relative* severity
of depression worsened more for girls with conduct disorder than for any
other group, including boys with conduct disorder and girls without
conduct disorder. The figure also shows that, although all girls experienced
an increase in depressive symptoms as they grew older, girls without conduct
disorder began this increase after age 15, whereas girls with conduct disorder began it earlier, between ages 13 and 15. The test of the three-way
repeated-measures ANOVA interaction term showed that this sex difference
was significant, $F (4,2472) = 2.3, p = 0.05$.

Comment: whither the depression of women with a history of conduct problems?

Dunedin women with a history of conduct disorder suffered inordinately
from depression; 72 per cent of them had a depressive illness at some time
in the transition from adolescence to adulthood (versus 35 per cent of
males; table 11.1), and 42 per cent of them suffered a major depressive
episode in the year prior to their twenty-first birthday (versus 15 per cent of
males; figure 11.1). Which comes first, depression or conduct disorder?
Recall that data presented in chapter 8 showed that parents' and teachers'
reports of internalizing behaviour problems (depression and anxiety)
between ages 5 and 11 did not predict adolescent conduct problems for boys
or girls. However, in this chapter, adolescent conduct problems did predict
adult depression, and did so more strongly for women than for men. We
conclude that the emergence of depression among conduct-disordered
females represents a temporal ordering. Depression does not precede
conduct problems; rather, depression emerges and worsens subsequent to
conduct problems. This relation was quite powerful; one in every four
Dunedin women who were diagnosed with depression at age 21 was formerly diagnosed as a conduct-disordered girl, and their depression symptoms were 0.58 SD worse than those of women who had not had conduct
disorder. Our findings suggest that the experience of conduct problems
may be one heretofore unrecognized source of the rising incidence of

major depressive episodes known to plague women making the transition to adulthood (Hankin *et al.*, 1998).

The reason for this growth in depression for girls with an antisocial history is unknown. Do girls, more so than boys, reflect on their own past antisocial victimization of others with guilt and self-loathing? Theories of gender-specific moral development suggest this process (Eisenberg and Lennon, 1983; Zahn-Waxler, Cole, and Barrett, 1991). Do girls who venture into antisocial behaviours receive more criticism and rejection from family, friends, and other socializing agents for the same behaviours that a boy might perform with relative impunity? Theories of gender-specific socialization suggest this process (Block, 1983). Do the drugs and alcohol used during peri-pubertal episodes of conduct problems interact with females' neuro-hormonal systems, triggering the imbalances implicated in bio-genic depression (Buchanan, Becker, and Eccles, 1992; Tieger, 1980)? Is adolescent antisocial behaviour merely a prodromal phase of emerging depression for girls, and thus a part of the female internalizing syndrome (O'Connor *et al.*, 1998), bearing only a temporary resemblance to the male externalizing syndrome, a resemblance that is more apparent than real? Does the link between conduct disorder and depression arise, in part, from post-partum depression or the lifestyle constraints inherent in responsibility for small babies? As we shall see in chapter 13, early responsibility for child-rearing is disproportionately shouldered by young women with an antisocial history. These questions are an important focus for future developmental research on girls' conduct disorder.

Take-home messages

- Comorbid disorders commonly appear alongside conduct disorder, for both males and females; only 10 per cent of lifetime conduct disorder cases are 'pure'.
- The disorders most often found co-occurring with conduct disorder are anxiety, depression, substance dependence, ADHD, and reading retardation.
- Two-thirds of young people who develop ADHD, marijuana dependence, and schizophreniform symptoms also experience conduct disorder, making these four disorders virtually part and parcel of an antisocial syndrome in adolescence/young adulthood.
- In addition to high rates of comorbidity for young people with conduct disorder, research also shows high rates of comorbidity for other forms

of antisocial behaviour: criminal violence, partner abuse, and antisocial personality disorder.
- The sexes are more similar than different in their comorbidity patterns across disorders and ages.
- The only sex-specific pattern is that for females depression appears to follow conduct problems. The depression of antisocial females grows more severe as they enter adulthood.

Unanswered questions

- Why do antisocial disorders evidence more comorbidity (approximately 90 per cent of conduct disorder and antisocial personality disorder cases) than other mental disorders? What is the significance of this ubiquitous comorbidity for theory, research methods, and clinical practice?
- Is there an adolescent syndrome comprised of conduct disorder, ADHD, substance dependence, and schizophreniform symptoms?
- Further explanation is needed, of the link between antisocial behaviour and the bizarre beliefs and sensory experiences associated with schizophrenia.
- What process accounts for the developmental progression from conduct problems to major depression in young women?

CHAPTER TWELVE

Do girls who develop antisocial behaviour surmount a higher threshold of risk than their male counterparts?

For a long time, many researchers have been attracted to the hypothesis that females who develop antisocial behaviour surmount a higher threshold of risk than males and are therefore more severely afflicted. This hypothesis goes by many names, including group resistence, the threshold effect, and the gender paradox. Because the hypothesis holds such wide appeal, it is worth revisiting the logic behind it. The hypothesis is built on the factual observation that fewer females than males act antisocially. Because this is true, then the deduction is made that some factor has raised the threshold that females must pass before they convert antisocial attitudes, feelings, or motives into actual antisocial actions. A higher threshold implies that the few females who have indeed passed their high threshold were pushed over it by stronger causes than were the males who passed their low threshold. Generally the female threshold is presumed to be raised by gender-role socialization of females against aggression, at the level of the culture. The push over the threshold is presumed to come from psycho-biological or developmental factors, at the level of the individual. The hypothesis is typically addressed empirically by comparing the strength of aetiological variables across groups of antisocial females and males, looking for evidence of more severe aetiology among females. If more severe aetiology is found for girls, then the inference is made that a higher threshold for girls exists.

The criminologist Thorsten Sellin (1938) referred to this line of reasoning as the 'group resistence' hypothesis. He argued that criminals who belong to groups whose members normally have strong social resistence to crime (e.g., females) most embody the causes of crime which originate from individual psychopathology. Sellin noted that criminal members of groups with weak group resistence to crime (e.g., males) are likely to be acting in concert with the socialization received by the whole group. Males are socialized towards aggression, females are socialized away from it, and therefore an aggressive female is deviant, whereas an aggressive male is conforming. Christiansen (1977) applied Sellin's idea to compare twin concordance rates for crime across strong and weak resistence groups, observing in a national sample of twins that there was apparently a somewhat greater genetic press for those who passed their group's crime threshold among individuals from rural, high-social-class, and female groups (groups with high resistance to crime), as compared to urban, low-social-class, and male groups (groups with low resistance to crime). This hypothesis that female offenders must suffer greater genetic liability to push them over their sex's higher threshold for crime was later systematically tested in an adoption design (Baker *et al.*, 1989). Model-fitting revealed that the genetic effect on criminal conviction works at the same strength for men and women (i.e., similar correlations). However, the biological mothers who were convicted, relative to the fathers, were slightly more likely to have an adopted-away child who became criminal, which is consistent with a modestly higher mean-level risk among the few females who were convicted.

Eme (1992) systematically reviewed the evidence for what he termed the 'gender paradox' hypothesis. This version of the hypothesis states that the sex less frequently afflicted with a childhood disorder may have a more defective genetic and/or environmental background and a more deviant manifestation of illness, presumably because members of this sex surpassed a higher threshold to obtain their diagnosis. With respect to conduct disorder, Eme's comprehensive review uncovered no adequately designed research to offer empirical support for the so-called paradox. This absence of research on the paradox in antisocial disorders was presented in the context of a review of other disorders for which males also outnumber females: autism, mental retardation, reading disability and ADHD. Although more research was available for these disorders, findings as often went against the paradox hypothesis as for it.

Silverthorne and Frick (1999) applied the gender paradox idea to support their assertion that all girls who engage in diagnosable antisocial conduct have experienced severe aetiological histories. They suggested that although antisocial girls are generally adolescent-onset, they have aetiological backgrounds that are virtually identical to the backgrounds of the subtype of childhood-onset males. As we shall see in chapter 16, several studies have documented the fact that childhood-onset males suffer worse aetiological histories than adolescent-onset males. Thus, Silverthorne and Frick (1999) argued that diagnosed females are a homogeneous group who have much worse aetiology than those of diagnosed antisocial males in general. Silverthorne and Frick (1999) implicated family risk factors, neuro-cognitive problems, hyperactivity, and callous, unemotional personality styles as especially severe for delinquent girls. Other researchers support this view, extending it to the particular prediction that females with conduct disorder will be more likely than males with conduct disorder to experience comorbid conditions of hyperactivity, anxiety, and substance abuse (Loeber and Keenan, 1994).

As we have seen in chapter 11, Dunedin Study females with conduct disorder did not experience significantly more comorbid ADHD, anxiety, or substance abuse disorders than their male counterparts, or more of any other disorders for that matter. However, it remains possible that the other environmental and individual aetiological factors implicated by Eme (1992) and Silverthorne and Frick (1999) would show a paradoxical effect arising from a higher threshold for female conduct disorder. In this section, we test the gender paradox hypothesis by examining a variety of risk factors.

Method

Measures

Conduct disorder was defined for this analysis as lifetime DSM-IV diagnosis from ages 11 to 18, according to the presence of five or more symptom criteria, as described earlier in chapter 4 (n = 154 males and 72 females). The comparison group was Study members who were clearly free of conduct disorder from age 11 to 18, according to meeting fewer than three diagnostic criteria at every assessment age (n = 194 males and 266 females). Subclinical cases (i.e., Study members who had never reached diagnostic threshold for a conduct disorder diagnosis, but who had also not been free from subclinical symptoms either, having three or four symptoms at one or more phases) were excluded from analysis in this chapter (n = 176 males and 156 females). By excluding subclinical cases, we ensured that the healthy comparison groups of males and females were well matched to each other, and provided a clear contrast against the diagnosed groups.

Childhood risk predictors were the same maternal, family, neuro-cognitive, behavioural, and peer variables described earlier in chapter 8.

Personality scales were the same scales from the Multidimensional Personality Questionnaire described earlier in chapter 10.

Data analysis approach

The threshold/paradox hypothesis is addressed by comparing the difference between groups of Study members with and without conduct disorder on risk variables, while testing for evidence of a more extreme group difference within females than males. We conducted for each risk variable a two by two ANOVA, with sex (male, female) and diagnosis (yes, no) as group factors. We tested the statistical significance of a 'sex by diagnosis' interaction term using an alpha cut-off of $p < 0.05$, which at this sample size could detect a small effect size. We standardized to z-scores each of the risk predictors and personality scales, so that mean difference scores may be compared across males and females using a common metric across all the variables.

Results

Table 12.1 presents the results. For forty-three of the forty-five variables tested, there was no evidence of a significantly stronger effect of conduct disorder diagnosis for girls, and thus no evidence for the threshold/paradox hypothesis. Apparently, Dunedin sample girls who met diagnostic criteria for conduct disorder had not experienced a uniquely strong aetiological push to pass the threshold for the diagnosis.

Two of the forty-five variables did show a stronger relation to conduct disorder for females than males: self-reported relationship with parents at age 15 and the MPQ Achievement scale at age 18. This number of significant interactions could have emerged by chance. Nonetheless, in the event that these turn out to be replicable findings, it is useful to note that they may be interpreted from perspectives other than the gender threshold/paradox. For example, it is possible that conduct-disordered behaviour, which violates female gender-stereotypes and also signals that a daughter may be at risk for pregnancy, disrupts smooth parent–child relations more for 15-year-old daughters than for sons.

Four of the forty-five variables showed a significantly stronger relation to conduct disorder for males than for females: family conflict at ages 7–9, IQ at age 5, teachers' reports of hyperactivity at ages 5–11, and teachers' reports of peer rejection at ages 5–11. Thus, for the three domains of family conflict, neuro-cognitive deficits, and hyperactivity, which have been specified in prior accounts of the threshold/paradox hypothesis, there is modest evidence that males may actually have surmounted a higher threshold than females to earn a diagnosis of conduct disorder.

Table 12.1. *Mean difference on risk factors between Study members who attain a lifetime DSM-IV diagnosis of conduct disorder (5+ symptoms) and Study members with no diagnosis (fewer than 3 symptoms). The threshold hypothesis states that females must experience worse levels of risk factors than males to get the same diagnosis*

Childhood risk predictor[a]	Boys 154 with CD vs 194 with no CD (SD difference)	Girls 72 with CD vs 266 with no CD (SD difference)	Do CD girls have higher risk levels p<0.05
Maternal risk predictors			
Mother's age at Study member's birth	0.39 SD*	0.51 SD*	no
Mother's age at her first birth	0.54 SD*	0.59 SD*	no
Mother's IQ	0.39 SD*	0.33 SD*	no
Mother's reading level	0.28 SD*	0.40 SD*	no
Mother's Eysenck neuroticism	0.30 SD*	0.20 SD	no
Mother's psychiatric malaise	0.36 SD*	0.44 SD*	no
Parental criminal conviction	15% vs. 10%	19% vs 10%	no
Family risk predictors			
Deviant mother–child interaction, observer rating	0.31 SD*	0.34 SD*	no
Harsh discipline	0.38 SD*	0.48 SD*	no
Inconsistent discipline	0.40 SD*	0.43 SD*	no
Moos Family Conflict Scale	0.66 SD*	0.28 SD*	no, boys do
Caretaker changes	0.57 SD*	0.64 SD*	no
Residence moves	0.20 SD*	0.10 SD	no
Years with single parent	0.31 SD*	0.50 SD*	no
Family socioeconomic status	0.45 SD*	0.50 SD*	no
Relationship with parents	0.80 SD*	1.16 SD*	yes
Child cognitive and neurological risk predictors			
Neurological abnormalities	0.22 SD	0.16 SD	no
Peabody Picture IQ	0.41 SD*	0.26 SD*	no
Stanford Binet IQ	0.56 SD*	0.26 SD*	no, boys do
WISC-R IQ	0.57 SD*	0.32 SD*	no
WISC-R VIQ	0.54 SD*	0.30 SD*	no
Neuropsych. memory score	0.49 SD*	0.26 SD	no
Burt Word Reading Test	0.44 SD*	0.29 SD*	no
Heart rate	0.11 SD	0.26 SD	no

Table 12.1 (*cont.*)

Childhood risk predictor[a]	Boys 154 with CD vs 194 with no CD (SD difference)	Girls 72 with CD vs 266 with no CD (SD difference)	Do CD girls have higher risk levels p<0.05
Child behavioural risk predictors			
Difficult baby, parent report	0.31 SD*	0.49 SD*	no
Undercontrolled temperament, observer rated	0.41 SD*	0.15 SD	no
Hyperactivity, parent report	0.53 SD*	0.49 SD*	no
Hyperactivity, teacher report	0.98 SD*	0.52 SD*	no, boys do
Internalizing, parent report	0.03 SD	0.06 SD	no
Internalizing, teacher report	0.18 SD	0.09 SD	no
Peer relations risk factors			
Peer rejection, parent report	0.47 SD*	0.26 SD*	no
Peer rejection, teacher report	0.73 SD*	0.20 SD*	no, boys do
Peer attachment, self-report	0.34 SD*	0.28 SD*	no
Peers' delinquency, self-report	0.85 SD*	1.02 SD*	no
School involvement, self-report	0.35 SD*	0.29 SD*	no
Personality trait scales			
Self-control	0.64 SD*	0.61 SD*	no
Harm avoidance	0.35 SD*	0.13 SD	no
Traditionalism	0.67 SD*	0.50 SD*	no
Aggression	0.92 SD*	1.00 SD*	no
Alienation	0.95 SD*	0.82 SD*	no
Stress reactivity	0.59 SD*	0.63 SD*	no
Social closeness	0.48 SD*	0.26 SD*	no
Well-being	0.02 SD	0.20 SD	no
Achievement	0.03 SD	0.31 SD*	yes
Social potency	0.12 SD	0.20 SD	no

Notes: for the risk predictors, the ages of measurement and sample numbers are the same as reported in table 8.1. All personality scales were measured at age 18.
[a] The risk predictors were standardized for the whole sample as z-scores.
* Difference between CD group and non-disordered group within sex is significant at p<0.05.

Silverthorne and Frick (1999) suggested that girls with conduct disorder will have an especially unemotional, callous personality style. Within the domain of personality studied here, the widest sex discrepancies we observed were for the MPQ scales called Harm-avoidance (thrill-seeking vs. fearful) and Social closeness (callous vs. affection-seeking). On these measures, girls diagnosed with conduct disorder were more fearful and less callous than their diagnosed male counterparts, and indeed conduct disordered girls did not differ significantly from non-disordered girls on Harm-avoidance. Although this sex-linked pattern was not statistically significant, it is notable that it took the direction opposite to the threshold/paradox prediction.

As a final observation, it is important to note that the findings in our tests of the threshold/paradox hypothesis using categorical diagnosis as the measure of antisocial behaviour (table 12.1) are consistent with findings presented earlier in chapters 8 to 10 (see tables 8.1, 9.1 and 9.2, and 10.1), which used a continuous scale to measure antisocial behaviour. Taken together, these analyses suggest that although fewer females than males indeed become antisocial, antisocial females do not pass a higher threshold that requires a stronger aetiological press. Rather, the Dunedin data show that fewer females become antisocial, despite having the same threshold as males, because females experience lower levels of risk factors exerting the same or weaker aetiological press.

Comment: resolving our disconfirmation of the threshold hypothesis with the prior literature

The threshold/paradox hypothesis has been around for a long time and is inherently appealing, to us as well as to others. In the Dunedin Study we found no evidence for it, and some evidence against it. Being the apparent exception in the literature, we are obligated to provide an account here as to why previous proponents of the hypothesis may have been mistaken. The studies that have been consistently cited as evidence that antisocial females have worse family backgrounds than males had persuasive epidemiological or longitudinal designs (Baker *et al.*, 1989; Christiansen, 1977; Robins, 1966). However, all of them examined females who were *officially* designated by courts as antisocial during the first half of this century, when paternalistic judicial policies and practices did indeed enforce a higher threshold for females to be adjudicated or placed in formal treatment. Females, relative to males committing similar antisocial acts, were more likely at that time to be returned to their families for private control (Johnson and Scheuble, 1991; Nagel and Hagan, 1983). Thus, the females who appeared in the research data because they were adjudicated or treated prior to the 1970s probably did have a more severe and deviant level of disorder than the males, but we believe that this reflects an historical artefact of case definition rather than a law of nature.

More recent literature, based on more contemporary samples, has also been cited as evidence for the threshold/paradox hypothesis. For example, recent articles cite eighteen references attesting that delinquent females have worse family backgrounds, neuro-cognitive problems, or comorbid conditions than males (Loeber and Keenan, 1994; Silverthorne and Frick, 1999). A close look reveals that five of these are themselves non-empirical discussions of the threshold/paradox hypothesis that did not involve data. Of the remaining thirteen, girls alone were studied in nine, and from only four studies could the evidence for the threshold/paradox result from a comparison of the sexes. Virtually all of the comparisons between the sexes were conceptual; statistical significance testing of sex effects was generally not conducted. Moreover, because the female groups were invariably very small, findings for girls were probably extreme and unstable. In sum, it appears that Eme (1992) was accurate in concluding that there is no good empirical evidence for the threshold/paradox hypothesis of girls' conduct problems. The evidence may have been more apparent than real, comprised of artefacts of history, measurement, and method that have attracted notice because they happened to fit a notion that has held some inherent appeal.

Take-home messages

- The threshold/gender paradox hypothesis finds no support in this sample. Compared to males, females with conduct disorder do not have more comorbid disorders, worse family backgrounds, more severe neuro-cognitive problems, more extreme hyperactivity, or more antisocial, unemotional, or callous personalities.
- Although fewer females than males indeed become antisocial, females do not pass a higher threshold that requires a stronger aetiological press. Rather, fewer females become antisocial, despite having the same threshold as males, because they experience lower levels of risk factors exerting the same or weaker aetiological press.

CHAPTER THIRTEEN

Sex differences in the effects of antisocial behaviour on young adult outcomes

In chapters 8 and 9 we saw evidence that the aetiology of adolescent antisocial behaviour may be more similar than different for males and females. But aetiological similarity does not preclude males and females, once they are involved in antisocial behaviour, from developing different outcomes. As one example of this divergence, chapter 11 showed that once involved in antisocial behaviour, females but not males are at risk for adult depression. In this chapter, we examine whether antisocial problems in boys and girls predict the same or different outcomes in adulthood.

One possibility is that a history of antisocial behaviour has *fewer* negative consequences for females than for males. A reason for this expectation has to do with the pressure of social norms. Evidence for the influence of sex-role norms on outcomes emerged from the Fels Research Institute studies (Kagan and Moss, 1962). A number of continuities were found from childhood to adulthood, but they were related to the sex of the individual and the sex-appropriateness of the behaviours being assessed. For example, passivity and dependency showed continuity for female subjects but not for male subjects, whereas aggression showed continuity for male subjects but not for female subjects. These findings suggest that individuals who deviate from socially and culturally expected patterns of behaviour are often disliked and are thus likely to be coerced into more modal patterns – what Cattell (1973) has called 'coercion to the biosocial mean'. Passivity is acceptable for females but not for males; aggression is acceptable for males but not for females. As Kagan and Moss (1962, p. 269) note, 'the individual's desire to mold his overt behaviour in accordance with the culture's definition of sex-appropriate response is a major determinant of the patterns of continuity and discontinuity in his development'. As such, antisocial behaviour may have less long-lasting and damaging consequences for females than males because females, in whom such behaviour is less tolerated, may be more pressured to conform.

A second possibility is that a history of antisocial behaviour predicts *different* outcomes for females than males. Some evidence suggests that antisocial behaviour among girls may predict more 'feminine' outcomes, whereas for boys it may predict 'masculine' outcomes. In fact, Robins (1986) has speculated that previous studies purporting to show better outcomes for antisocial girls than boys may have done so because researchers chose to study male-specific outcomes, such as aggression. When the outcome domain is broadened to include other psychiatric features, such as depression and related somatic conditions, some studies suggest that antisocial girls are equally at risk of poor adult outcomes. Within psychiatric circles this has given rise to nosological and aetiological questions, such as whether internalizing and externalizing disorders share a common liability among women (Bohman *et al.*, 1984; Lilienfeld, 1992; Zoccolillo, 1992).

A third possibility, suggested by Magnusson, Stattin, and Allen (1985), is that antisocial behaviour has *similar* consequences for females and males, but these similar outcomes may have been obscured in previous studies by researchers who adopted a 'deviance model' rather than a 'social-role model' to study the outcomes of antisocial behaviour. In essence, previous studies may have reported sex differences in outcome because they have 'pathologized' antisocial behaviour and measured only mental illness and crime. It is possible that once the outcome domain is broadened to include measures of success or failure in the normative psychosocial tasks of the young adult age period, antisocial behaviour will be found to disrupt equally the development of females and males (Bardone *et al.*, 1996; 1998; Pajer, 1998; Serbin *et al.*, 1991).

To evaluate these three possibilities, we assessed the Dunedin Study members as they made their transition from adolescence to young adulthood. Here we examine various aspects of the developmental tasks during this transition: in domains of educational attainment, labour-force participation, residential patterns, and union- and family-formation, which are outcome measures from a social role model. We then shift our focus to examine mental health problems, physical health, and problems with substance abuse, outcome measures from a deviance model. We conclude by focusing on attitudes and experiences related directly to crime, outcome measures from a male-specific model.

Methods

Predictor variables

The *continuous measure of adolescent antisocial behaviour*, introduced in chapter 8, was used as one of the predictor variables in this analysis. Briefly, this measure was a composite of parent-report at ages 13 and 15, teacher-report at age 13, informant-report at age 18, and self-report at ages 13, 15, and 18. The measure's reliability was 0.86 for boys and 0.77 for girls. It had present data for 491 boys and 465 girls.

The *lifetime diagnosis of conduct disorder*, introduced in chapter 4, was also used as a predictor. Cumulative lifetime diagnoses of DSM-IV conduct disorder (five or more concurrent symptoms) at ages 11, 13, 15, and 18 were made for 154 boys and 72 girls.

Outcome measures

MEASURES OF EDUCATION BY AGE 21

We used two outcome variables to index educational attainment. The first measure of educational attainment was *age at leaving high school*. Members of this birth cohort (1972–3) could legally leave school as early as age 15. Approximately 12 per cent of the Dunedin Study members left school by age 16 and nearly 30 per cent left school by age 17, but the majority of the Study members remained in school through age 18. The measure of age of leaving school came from the Life History Calendar, which is also the source of several other variables in this chapter. The Life History Calendar is a large grid on which life pathways (e.g., education) are represented as rows, while the columns of the grid denote time units (months) during which events may have occurred (e.g., ending of high school education). The result is continuous, monthly information about life pathways and transition events occurring between each Study member's fifteenth birthday and the age-21 interview. Methodological studies have found that the retrospective reports gathered via the Life History Calendar are very reliable (Caspi *et al.*, 1996). The second measure of educational attainment indexes whether the Study members *enrolled in a tertiary education programme*. Compared to the US, which has historically had relatively open access to tertiary education, the rate of tertiary education enrolment in New Zealand is relatively low, although it has been rising rapidly throughout the 1990s among more recent birth cohorts; by the time of the age-21 interview, 19 per cent of the Study members had enrolled in a four-year college or university.

MEASURES OF WORK BY AGE 21

The first measure related to the work domain is a ten-item scale indexing *perceived opportunities for future success in life,* developed for the OJJDP three-site study in the United States (Huizinga, Loeber and Thornberry, 1993). It includes items such as 'The job market is usually good to people like me', and 'If a person like me works hard they can get ahead.' The scale was reliable (alpha = 0.60). The second measure of work is a twelve-item Index of Job Desirability developed on the basis of research findings about what workers value most in a job (Jencks, Perman, and Rainwater, 1988). For example, there are questions about whether the job allows the Study member to work overtime, whether it offers opportunities for advancement, and whether it offers paid holidays (Wright *et al.*, 1999). The third measure of work assesses the *duration of unemployment between ages 18 and 21.* Using the Life History Calendar, Study members were asked if there were any periods of a month or more when they were not employed but were seeking employment, thus excluding periods when they were full-time students or homemakers.

ESTABLISHING ONE'S OWN HOME BY AGE 21

To chart the transition of the Study members into independent living arrangements, we used five outcome variables. *Age at first leaving home* (for one month or more) came from the Life History Calendar. Most of the Study members (80 per cent) had left home by age 21. We assigned Study members who had not left home by age 21 the value of age 22. From the Life History Calendar we also obtained a measure of *number of residence moves* between ages 18 and 21 to index residential instability and a measure of *number of cohabitation partners* to index relationship instability. Study members were considered to have cohabited if they lived for a month or more with a partner in an intimate but unmarried relationship. *Welfare dependence* was measured with the Study members' reports, at age 21, of the types of governmental income they had received in the past year, including family support, accident compensation payments, domestic purposes benefit, unemployment benefit, and sickness or invalid's benefit. We summed the number of benefits received to form an index of sources of welfare support. Finally, we recorded whether or not the Study member *had a child* before their twenty-first birthday; 77 Study members had a total of 94 children.

MEASURES OF RELATIONSHIP WITH A PARTNER

Study members who reported involvement with a partner at the time of the age-21 assessment or within the past year were interviewed about qualities of that relationship. For the purposes of this study, an intimate relationship was defined as a relationship with a romantic partner during the past 12 months that had lasted for at least a month. Eighty-three per cent of the Study members reported that they were involved in such an intimate relationship during the past 12 months. Study members who had not been involved in an intimate relationship for at least a month were excluded from this part of the interview because they could not provide information about a specific partner. *Satisfaction with partner* was assessed using fourteen interview questions concerning the respondent's satisfaction with the different domains in the relationship (e.g., finances, sex, division of labour, future plans, shared time). Answers were coded 0 = not happy, 1 = somewhat happy, 2 = very happy, and summed. The scale was reliable (alpha = 0.80). *Relationship quality* was assessed using forty interview questions about shared activities and interests, the balance of power, respect and fairness, emotional intimacy and trust, and open communication. Answers were coded 0 = almost never, 1 = sometimes, and 2 = almost always, and summed. The scale was reliable (alpha = 0.90). *Conflicts with partner* was assessed by summing a list of eighteen topics of conflict in the relationship, such as that over in-laws, children, money, religion, or sex. The conflict scale was reliable (alpha = 0.84). Two measures of physical abuse were obtained from all Study members who either reported involvement with a partner or who reported dating in the past year. Only eighty Study members who had not dated in the past year were excluded from this part of the interview. As described in chapter 5, the set of questions about partner abuse was embedded in a 50-minute standardized interview about intimate relationships. The *physical abuse perpetration* measure was the sum of responses to thirteen items dealing with physical violence that the Study member reported committing against a partner. The *physical abuse victimization* scale contained the same items, but here the Study member was asked to report about victimization experiences at the hands of a partner. Responses to items on both scales were recorded 0 = no and 1 = yes. The scales had reliabilities (alpha) of 0.76 and 0.82, respectively (see Moffitt *et al.*, 1997).

MEASURES OF MENTAL HEALTH AT AGE 21

We used five outcome measures to assess the Study members' mental health at age 21. We used data from the Diagnostic Interview Schedule at age 21 (see chapter 11) to create four continuously distributed symptom scale scores: *anxiety symptoms, psychosis symptoms, mania symptoms,* and *depression symptoms.* Each of these scales was created by summing the Study member's scores on interview symptom items relevant to each domain; all scales had reliabilities (alphas) greater than 0.70. In addition, as part of the mental-health interview, Study members were asked about *suicide attempts* they had made during the past twelve months. Attempts were counted whether or not they had required medical attention.

MEASURES OF PHYSICAL HEALTH AT AGE 21

To assess *medical problems*, Study members completed a standard medical intake questionnaire in which they indicated which of the following thirteen medical problems they had experienced during the past year: anaemia, arthritis, cancer, hepatitis, diabetes, serious back trouble, heart trouble, kidney/bladder infections, epilepsy, acne, colitis, menstrual problems, and migraines. To get a *subjective health rating*, Study members rated their health on a scale from 1 (very good) to 5 (very poor). Using the 18 to 21 years of age reporting period on the Life History Calendar, Study members also reported *periods of disability*. We created a variable by summing the number of months during which the Study members reported being unable to carry out their normal activities as a result of an illness or an injury.

MEASURES OF SUBSTANCE ABUSE AND DEPENDENCE AT AGE 21

As part of the mental health assessment at age 21, the number of different types of drugs (excluding alcohol and nicotine) that the Study member used in the past year was recorded via a self-report checklist. The list of drugs included marijuana, opiates, stimulants, sedative-hypnotics, and psychedel-ics. In addition, we used data from the mental health assessment at age 21 (see chapter 11) to create two continuously distributed symptom scale scores, one each for *marijuana dependence* and *alcohol dependence*. Both scales had reliabilities (alphas) greater than 0.70.

MEASURES OF ATTITUDES ABOUT CRIME AND CRIMINAL BEHAVIOUR

The presence of *delinquent peers* was measured with a six-item scale used in the US National Youth Survey that asked the Study members how many of their friends (1 = none, 5 = all) were not good citizens, had personal prob-lems, broke the law, had problems with alcohol, had problems with drugs, and had problems with aggression (Elliott, Huizinga, and Menard, 1989). The reliability (alpha) of this scale was 0.79. *Self-concept as an offender* was measured by asking Study members to compare themselves to age peers on a visual ladder scale where 0 = I do many fewer illegal things than the average person my age, and 10 = I do many more illegal things than the average person my age. *Perceived risk of detection for crime* was measured by asking Study members to indicate how often they thought they would get caught for a specific crime committed on ten different days (e.g., 'If you shoplifted from a store on ten different days, how many times do you think you would probably get caught for shoplifting?'). The interview inquired about seven different crimes, including shoplifting, marijuana use, car theft, assault, burglary, drink-driving, and fraud. Respondents indicated their responses on 0 to 10 continuous scales, presented visually. The reliability (alpha) of this scale was 0.72. The importance of *informal sanctions* was measured with a twenty-eight-item scale based on self-ratings of whether the Study members believed their relationships with friends and family, their job prospects, and their ability to find an ideal mate would be affected if people knew that the Study members had shoplifted, used marijuana, stolen a car, hit someone in a fight, committed a burglary, driven while drunk, and used a stolen bank card. The response format was 0 = no, 1 = maybe, 2 = yes. The reliability (alpha) for this scale was 0.91. A measure of illegal behaviour was obtained using the standardized survey instrument of *self-report illegal behaviour* developed by Elliott and Huizinga (1989). This instrument, administered during private individual interviews, enquired about forty-eight different offences. The psychometric properties and descriptive epidemiology of this instrument in the Dunedin sample are described in detail by Moffitt, Silva, Lynam, and Henry (1994). The score recorded for each Study member represented the variety of different offences committed in the past year. *Self-reported violence* was a subscale made up of the seven items that measured simple assault and aggravated assault against intimates, simple assault and aggravated assault against others, robbery, gang-fighting, and forced sex. Using the Life History Calendar, Study members were asked to report whether they had been arrested and whether they had been incarcerated. We created two variables. The first summed, between ages 18 to 21, the *number of months with an arrest*, and the second summed the *number of months with an incarceration*. Using the same 18 to 21 years of age reporting period on the Life History Calendar, Study members also reported incidents of *crime victimization*. We created a variable by summing the number of months during which the Study members self-reported being victims of a property or personal crime.

Data analysis approach

Table 13.1 presents the correlations, separately for male and female Study members, between the continuous measure of adolescent antisocial behaviour and each of the adult outcomes measured during the age-21 interview. Effect sizes can be interpreted as r = 0.1 is a small effect, r = 0.3 is a medium effect, and r = 0.5 is a large effect.

Table 13.1. *Young adult outcomes of males' and females' antisocial behaviours during adolescence*

Young adult outcome	N males/females	Assessment age(s)	Males' correlation	Females' correlation	Sex interaction p<0.05
Schooling					
Age left high school	476/460	15–18	−0.42*	−0.38*	no
Enrolled in college/university	479/460	21	−0.21*	−0.16*	no
Work					
Perceived opportunities for future success in life	468/448	21	−0.32*	−0.20*	no
Index of job desirability	479/458	21	−0.17*	−0.01	no
Months of unemployment	475/459	18–21	0.40*	0.09	yes
Establishing one's own home					
Age left parents' home	476/460	15–21	−0.41*	−0.35*	no
Number of residence moves	467/447	18–21	0.30*	0.16*	no
Number of cohabitations	467/447	18–21	0.23*	0.23*	no
Parent of a child before age 21	467/447	15–21	0.42*	0.26*	no
Sources of welfare support	478/460	21	0.32*	0.29*	no
Relationship with partner					
Satisfaction with partner[a]	357/392	21	−0.24*	−0.26*	yes
Relationship quality scale[a]	357/391	21	−0.21*	−0.24*	no
Conflicts with partner[a]	362/393	21	0.27*	0.19*	no
Physical abuse perpetration	459/441	21	0.29*	0.38*	yes
Physical abuse victimization	460/440	21	0.30*	0.33*	yes
Mental health					
Anxiety symptoms	467/447	21	0.12*	0.13*	no
Psychosis symptoms	470/449	21	0.29*	0.19*	no

Mania symptoms	459/444	21	0.31*	0.26*	no
Depression symptoms	453/439	21	0.15*	0.19*	yes
Suicide attempter	465/445	21	0.13*	0.20*	yes
Physical health					
Medical problems	470/449	21	0.07	0.19*	yes
Subjective poor health	466/449	21	0.24*	0.25*	yes
Months disabled	460/449	18–21	0.17*	0.10	no
Substance abuse and dependence					
Variety of illicit drugs used	470/449	21	0.41*	0.35*	no
Marijuana dependence symptoms	461/444	21	0.47*	0.31*	yes
Alcohol dependence symptoms	458/438	21	0.37*	0.26*	no
Self-reported attitudes and experiences related to crime					
Peers' delinquency	466/448	21	0.38*	0.36*	yes
Self-concept as an offender	462/445	21	0.37*	0.26*	no
Perceived risk of detection for crime	463/445	21	−0.12*	−0.10	no
Perceived informal sanctions against crime	466/448	21	−0.36*	−0.33*	yes
Self-reported delinquency at 21	467/448	21	0.52*	0.52*	no
Self-reported violence at 21	467/448	21	0.45*	0.37*	no
Months with an arrest	460/444	18–21	0.41*	0.35*	yes
Months with incarceration	460/444	18–21	0.38*	0.20*	yes
Crime victimization	459/444	18–21	0.12*	0.11	no

Notes: The antisocial predictor measure covered the period up to the 18th birthday, whereas the age 18–21 outcome measures began the month following the 18th birthday; thus there is no temporal overlap between predictor and outcomes.

[a] These measures are available only for those Study members who were involved in a relationship during the past 12 months.

* Correlation was significant, $p < 0.01$.

We tested for sex differences in a multiple regression framework,

$$A = a + b_1 Sex + b_2 ASB + b_3 (Sex \times ASB) + e,$$

where A represents the Study members' adult outcomes, b_1 and b_2 represent the main effects of the Study members' sex and adolescent antisocial behaviour (ASB) on their adult outcomes, and b_3 indexes whether the effect of antisocial behaviour on adult outcomes varies as a function of the Study member's sex. The results of these gender-interaction tests are presented in the final column of table 13.1. We used ordinary least squares multiple regression to examine sex differences on continuously distributed outcome variables and logistic regression for dichotomous outcome variables.

Table 13.2 presents the adult outcomes of girls and boys who attained a diagnosis of conduct disorder, and therefore were closely matched on the severity of their antisocial symptom behaviours. The analysis for each outcome variable was a two (no diagnosis vs. diagnosis) by two (male vs. female) ANOVA, testing for main effects of diagnosis and also for interactions between diagnosis and sex. The first four columns of table 13.2 show group means for the four cells, and the fifth column shows whether nor not there was a significant difference between diagnosed and undiagnosed Study members' adult outcomes. Effect sizes for group differences can be interpreted as 0.2 SD is a small effect, 0.5 SD is a medium effect, and 0.8 SD is a large effect. The sixth column of table 13.2 shows whether or not there was a significant interaction between diagnosis and sex. The final column shows results of a planned contrast between conduct-disordered males and females.

Results

Overview
The findings depicted in tables 13.1 and 13.2 make three major points. First, the pervasiveness of the ill-effects of adolescent antisocial behaviour on adult outcomes across many domains is striking. All but one of the thirty-five outcome measures revealed a worse outcome for Study members with a history of antisocial behaviour (continuously measured) or with a past diagnosis of conduct disorder. Second, the similarity of the ill-effects of adolescent antisocial behaviour for both males and females is striking. There were few significant gender interactions, indicating that seldom did antisocial members of one sex have a worse outcome than antisocial members of the other sex. The continuous measure of antisocial behaviour generated ten interactions out of thirty-five possible, and the diagnosis of conduct disor-

der generated only five interactions out of thirty-five possible. Third, the outcomes that did differentiate conduct-disordered males and females appeared to be gender-stereotyped. Conduct-disordered males had significantly worse outcomes than conduct-disordered females in the domains of work and criminal justice, and also in the domain of substance abuse. In contrast, conduct-disordered females had much worse outcomes than conduct-disordered males in the domains of establishing a home and relationship with a partner, and in depression and physical health.

We comment on specific longitudinal follow-up results next, in sections corresponding to the measurement domains outlined in the *Outcome Measures* section.

Comment: educational attainment

Tables 13.1 and 13.2 show that adolescent antisocial behaviour was a robust predictor of truncated education. Antisocial adolescents left high school at an earlier age and were less likely to enrol in a college or university degree programme relative to other adolescents. To illustrate the correlational analysis shown in table 13.1, one SD unit increase on the standardized (z-score) composite measure of adolescent antisocial behaviour was associated with males leaving high school 4.6 months earlier and with females leaving high school 6.1 months earlier. Similarly, a unit change on the composite measure of antisocial behaviour reduced the likelihood that both males and females would enrol in university by an odds ratio of 2 in both cases. With respect to diagnosed conduct disorder, almost one-third of youths without conduct disorder attended university, whereas only about one-tenth of conduct-disordered youths attended.

In related research, we examined the educational attainment of Dunedin Study members in greater detail (Miech *et al.*, 1999). We took overall educational attainment by age 21 and broke it into its three separate transition points, because the factors influencing educational drop-out may differ at various points in the educational system. We first examined whether conduct disorder influenced Study members' performance on the New Zealand School Certificate Examinations, which are taken by age 16 and determine promotion in secondary school. Of our sample of Study members, 87 per cent earned a School Certificate; however, adolescents who met criteria for a diagnosis of conduct disorder by age 15 were less likely to earn a School Certificate by an odds ratio of 4.5. Among those who earned a School Certificate, 76 per cent also earned a Sixth Form Certificate, which is comparable to a high school degree in the United States; however, adolescents

Table 13.2. *Mean levels of standardized young-adult outcomes at age 21 for males and females who had attained a lifetime diagnosis of conduct disorder between ages 11 and 18*

Young adult outcome[a]	Female means		Male means		CD effect $p < 0.05$	Sex interaction $p < 0.05$	Do CD females and CD males differ? $p < 0.05$
	no CD n = 422	CD n = 72	no CD n = 370	CD n = 154			
Schooling							
Age left high school	0.12	−0.67	0.22	−0.56	yes	no	no
Enrolled in college/university	26%	13%	28%	11%	yes	no	no
Work							
Perceived opportunities for future success in life	0.03	−0.41	0.20	−0.35	yes	no	no
Index of job desirability	0.06	0.01	0.04	−0.26	yes	no	males worst
Months of unemployment	−0.08	0.08	−0.18	0.63	yes	yes	males worst
Establishing one's own home							
Age left parents' home	0.07	−0.54	0.24	−0.51	yes	no	no
Number of residence moves	−0.04	0.24	−0.18	0.41	yes	no	no
Number of cohabitations	0.05	0.55	−0.26	0.20	yes	no	females worst
Parent of a child before age 21	7%	29%	2%	17%	yes	no	females worst
Sources of welfare support	−0.11	0.57	−0.16	0.43	yes	no	no
Relationship with partner							
Satisfaction with partner	0.06	−0.51	0.13	−0.20	yes	no	females worst
Relationship quality scale	0.16	−0.37	0.02	−0.33	yes	no	no
Conflicts with partner	−0.04	0.35	−0.12	0.20	yes	no	no
Physical abuse perpetration	0	0.91	−0.24	0.14	yes	yes	females worst
Physical abuse victimization	−0.14	0.46	−0.08	0.36	yes	no	no

Mental health

Anxiety symptoms	0.07	0.28	−0.17	0.09	yes	no	no
Psychosis symptoms	−0.11	0.42	−0.16	0.48	yes	no	no
Mania symptoms	−0.19	0.54	−0.12	0.56	yes	no	no
Depression symptoms	0.07	0.64	−0.22	0.07	yes	no	females worst
Suicide attempter	1%	6%	1%	5%	yes	no	no
Physical health							
Medical problems	0.18	0.76	−0.31	−0.11	yes	yes	females worst
Subjective poor health	−0.03	0.74	−0.21	0.23	yes	yes	females worst
Months disabled	−0.04	0.14	−0.10	0.30	yes	no	no
Substance abuse and dependence							
Variety of drugs used	−0.23	0.33	−0.09	0.67	yes	no	males worst
Marijuana dependence symptoms	−0.27	0.32	−0.09	0.85	yes	yes	males worst
Alcohol dependence symptoms	−0.33	0.17	0.07	0.66	yes	no	males worst
Self-reported attitudes and experiences related to crime							
Peers' delinquency	−0.23	0.49	−0.08	0.62	yes	no	no
Self-concept as an offender	−0.34	0.24	0.04	0.74	yes	no	males worst
Perceived risk of detection for crime	0.37	0.21	−0.29	−0.46	yes	no	males worst
Perceived informal sanctions against crime	0.25	−0.4	0.03	−0.57	yes	no	no
Self-reported offending at 21	−0.44	0.29	0.02	1.02	yes	no	males worst
Self-reported violence at 21	−0.25	0.46	−0.12	0.76	yes	no	males worst
Months with an arrest	−0.17	−0.06	−0.05	0.63	yes	yes	males worst
Months with incarceration	−0.15	−0.11	−0.08	0.66	yes	yes	males worst
Crime victimization	−0.13	0.04	0.10	0.10	no	no	no

Notes: For the outcome variables, the measurement ages and the numbers of subjects are shown on table 13.1.

[a] The continuously distributed adult outcome measures were standardized for the whole sample as z-scores, so the group means shown are in SD units.

with a conduct disorder who had managed to earn a School Certificate were significantly less likely to earn a Sixth Form Certificate by an odds ratio of 2.5. Finally, among those who earned a Sixth Form Certificate, 37 per cent continued to a university education; however, adolescents with conduct disorder who overcame the odds against them and secured a Sixth Form Certificate were less likely to continue to a university education by an odds ratio of 2.3. These results held up even after controlling for socioeconomic background, individual differences in intelligence, and the presence of other comorbid mental disorders, such as depression, anxiety, and attention-deficit disorder. Moreover, there were no significant sex differences in these results. As such, the longitudinal findings from the Dunedin Study suggest that antisocial behaviour directly increases the risk that both males and females will fail at every educational transition and thereby seriously damage their own future life chances.

Comment: work patterns

Tables 13.1 and 13.2 show that adolescent antisocial behaviour was a significantly better predictor of work problems among males than females. Although both antisocial males and females perceived fewer opportunities for future occupational success in their lives, the work lives of antisocial males were significantly more chequered by age 21 than those of females. To illustrate, a unit change on the composite measure of adolescent antisocial behaviour shown on table 13.1. was associated with three months of unemployment among males in contrast to one month of unemployment among females. With respect to diagnosed disorder shown in the last column of table 13.2 ('work' panel), males experienced more unemployment than females in general, but conduct-disordered males suffered the most.

Part of the reason for the stronger effect of adolescent antisocial behaviour on males' labour-force activities is that many of the more antisocial females in the sample had already taken themselves out of the labour force before age 21. One important factor that takes young women out of the labour force for varying amounts of time is childbirth. Although, as we shall see in a later section, adolescent antisocial behaviour increased the risk of early parenthood among both males and females in the sample, overall more women (10 per cent) than men (6 per cent) had a child by age 21 (df $=954$, $p < 0.01$), and whereas women responded to the arrival of the child by withdrawing from the labour force, men did not. It is not appropriate to conclude that female adolescent antisocial behaviour is inconsequential for women's work lives; it is simply the case that antisocial behaviour among females reduces their risk of exposure to the workplace because they are more likely to have made an early transition into parenting. This finding underscores the life-course principle of interdependence: the effects of behaviour on transitions in one life domain cannot be understood apart from interdependent transitions in other life domains (Elder, 1998).

The mechanisms by which antisocial behaviour increases the risk of employment difficulties are not as obvious as would appear at first glance. Although earlier we saw that antisocial behaviour reduced the likelihood that adolescents will continue their formal education beyond the end of compulsory schooling, the employment difficulties of antisocial youth do not arise from lack of education alone. In related research with the Dunedin Study, we showed that adolescent antisocial behaviour continued to predict strongly the risk and duration of unemployment in young adulthood even after we adjusted for the fact that antisocial youth lost out in education (Caspi *et al.*, 1998). The direct influence of antisocial behaviour on unemployment may reflect at least three processes. First, youth who express nonconformity via antisocial behaviour may also reject conventional roles, including employment. Secondly, antisocial youth may selectively obtain the kinds of jobs that have high turnover. Thirdly, antisocial youth may get into trouble in the workplace because they have poor job performance and bring conflict to relationships with co-workers and supervisors. Understanding these mechanisms is important for designing effective programmes to smooth the transition from school to work for high-risk youth (Caspi *et al.*, 1998).

Comment: living arrangements and patterns of union formation

Tables 13.1 and 13.2 show hardly any sex differences in the effects of adolescent antisocial behaviour on living arrangements and patterns of union formation in young adulthood. Instead, the tables highlight the fact that both antisocial males and females were equally at risk for turbulent times (i.e., there were no significant interactions between sex and antisocial behaviours or sex and conduct disorder diagnosis). The last column of table 13.2 ('establishing one's own home' panel) reveals that conduct-disordered females cohabited with more partners and had more babies than conduct-disordered males, but this simply reflected the fact that all females were more likely than all males at this age to cohabit and have children.

Antisocial adolescents were significantly more likely to move out of their parents' house at an earlier age; an SD unit increase on the composite measure of adolescent antisocial behaviour was associated with males and females leaving home 9 and 8 months earlier, respectively, than their non-antisocial peers. Table 13.1 shows that partly as a result of leaving home at an earlier age, antisocial adolescents, both males and females, experienced vulnerable housing situations as measured by higher rates of residential turnover during the three-year period between their eighteenth and twenty-first birthdays. In related research with the Dunedin sample, we have shown that Study members with high levels of antisocial behaviour in adolescence had significantly higher rates of involuntary doubled-up housing during their transition into adulthood (Wright et al., 1998). Involuntary doubled-up housing occurs when persons who have no place to stay are taken in by other people, usually temporarily. The person being taken in typically has experienced financial or social difficulties and does not consider the doubled-up situation to be home; thus doubling-up has been shown to be a common precursor to homelessness. Even after controlling for social background characteristics (e.g., educational attainment, parental income) as well as numerous measures of social ties to their parents, we found that Dunedin Study members with high levels of antisocial behaviour in adolescence had rates of doubled-up housing around 140 per cent more than that of their non-antisocial peers, and those Study members who had, by age 15, been in trouble with the police had rates of doubled-up housing more than 200 per cent that of their peers. Regardless of other social or personal disadvantages, the process by which young adults establish initial independent housing as they move out of the parental home is compromised to a large and significant extent by their earlier history of antisocial behaviour, and this is equally true for males and females.

Antisocial adolescents were also more likely to become involved in cohabiting relationships. Between the ages of 18 and 21, antisocial males and females were 1.5 and 1.8 times more likely than their peers to cohabit. These were not necessarily stable and long-term arrangements, as we found that antisocial males and females were 2.0 and 2.6 times more likely to have cohabited with more than one partner during this time period. Whether or not antisocial youth were involved in cohabiting relationships, these adolescents were also at greater risk of becoming young parents. Antisocial males and females were 2.7 and 2.8 times more likely to become parents by age 21. Table 13.2 shows that almost one-third of conduct-disordered females had become young mothers.

Although antisocial youth appeared to be 'growing up faster' by forming their own households and by assuming adult roles at an earlier age, they were not necessarily becoming more independent. In fact, table 13.1 shows that adolescent antisocial behaviour predicted social welfare use by age 21:

a measure of dependence on and cost to society. For example, antisocial males and females were 1.8 and 2.4 times more likely to have received social welfare assistance from multiple government sources.

Adolescent antisocial behaviour was also associated with more conflicted relationships in young adulthood. By age 21, antisocial adolescents, male and female alike, were involved in less satisfying and more conflicted relationships. As table 13.1 shows, antisocial adolescents were also involved in mutually violent relationships; both males and females reported that they physically abused their partners and that they were abused by their partners. The significant sex interactions on both tables 13.1 and 13.2 reveal, moreover, that the Study members who were most deeply involved in unsatisfying relationships and in partner abuse were the females who had shown antisocial behaviour or attained a diagnosis of conduct disorder as adolescents.

The link between childhood and adolescent antisocial behaviour and adult partner violence has been all but unmentioned in the literature on family violence. However, to our knowledge there are now at least six independent replications of this predictive relation (Capaldi and Clark, 1998; Farrington, 1994; Giordano et al., 1999; Huesmann et al., 1984; Magdol et al., 1998b; Simons et al., 1998). In combination, these studies show that childhood conduct problems, even when measured in the first decade of life, foretell relationship violence equally well in the adult lives of both males and females. The finding that young people who have a history of antisocial conduct problems are likely to employ similar aggressive tactics later in their primary adult relationships suggests the hypothesis that the causes of conduct disorder are also the root causes of partner violence. As such, interventions conceptualized as treatments for conduct problems gain even more urgency if they are reconceptualized as primary prevention for future domestic violence.

Furthermore, conduct disorder predicts not only partner violence, but also a host of other undesirable outcomes including, as we have already seen, childbearing at a young age. This is illustrated by the Dunedin Study. Prior to the twenty-first birthday, 8 per cent of the Study members had one or more children, and 39 per cent of those young parents were involved in an abusive relationship, as compared to 15 per cent of the non-parents. It remains unclear whether parenthood coincides with partner violence because child-rearing stresses parents, because violence is provoked by conflict over the children (Jaffe, Wolfe, and Wilson, 1990), or merely because young people who are aggressive are selectively likely to leave home early, cohabit early, and bear children early (Bardone et al., 1996; Jaffee, forthcoming). Whatever the reason, these demographic statistics suggest that young children and partner violence are concentrated together in the same segment of the population, with the result that many children witness adults' partner violence (Fantuzzo *et al.*, 1997). Physical violence between partners, while harmful to its victims, places children of these households at risk for abuse and may set the stage for the inter-generational transmission of violence (Fergusson and Horwood, 1998; Moffitt and Caspi, 1998).

Comment: mental and physical health
The findings in this section echo and extend the earlier findings about comorbid disorders in chapter 11. Whereas the earlier analysis showed concurrent patterns of comorbidity between conduct disorder and other psychiatric conditions, tables 13.1 and 13.2 show the prospective prediction from adolescent antisocial behaviour to mental and physical health outcomes at age 21. Among both males and females, adolescent antisocial behaviour predicted elevated adult symptoms of anxiety, psychosis, and mania, as well as self-ratings of poorer health and self-reports of disability. The link between antisocial behaviour and physical health problems is attracting research attention (Bardone *et al.*, 1998; Farrington and Junger, 1995; Laub and Vaillant, 2000; Pine *et al.*, 1997), although the pathways that connect antisocial behaviour to poor physical health outcomes have not been thoroughly examined. Health psychologists may help to advance understanding of these linkages by focusing on specific health outcomes. For example, in the Dunedin Study, we found that a disproportionate burden of risky sexual intercourse and sexually transmitted diseases (STDs) among adolescents and young adults is borne by individuals with an antisocial history (Ramrakha *et al.*, 2000). Public-health officials and clinicians need more research-based evidence about how and why these phenomena co-occur in order to design compelling preventions and to deliver effective health services.

Sex differences emerged in relation to several adult outcomes. Table 13.2 shows that a diagnosis of conduct disorder predicted more depression symptoms, more medical problems, and a worse subjective rating of health for females. Table 13.1 shows that the continuous measure of adolescent antisocial behaviour predicted more depression symptoms, suicide attempts, medical problems and a worse subjective rating of health among females than males. To illustrate, a SD unit increase on the composite measure of adolescent antisocial behaviour predicted an increase of three depressive symptoms among females but only one such symptom among males. Likewise, adolescent antisocial behaviour was associated with 1.3 medical conditions among females but only 0.5 such conditions among males. Finally, antisocial females were 3.9 times more likely than peers to attempt suicide in contrast to antisocial males, who were 1.6 times more likely than peers to try to take their own lives. These findings confirm the hypothesis that antisocial behaviour is more closely related to the spectrum of somatization and depressive disorders among females than it is among males (Lilienfeld, 1992). The emergence of women's depression from their earlier conduct disorders was discussed in chapter 11.

Comment: substance abuse and dependence

Tables 13.1 and 13.2 show that adolescent antisocial behaviour was a robust predictor of drug use and substance dependence in young adulthood among both males and females. Both antisocial males and females were significantly more likely to use a wider variety of illicit drugs than were their peers. Likewise, both males and females were significantly more likely to report symptoms of dependence related to their use of marijuana and alcohol. These findings fit squarely with other longitudinal studies that document an association between early antisocial behaviour and substance use problems (e.g., Elliott, Huizinga, and Menard, 1989; Hawkins, Catalano, and Miller, 1992; Kandel, Simcha-Fagan, and Davies, 1986). One significant sex interaction was observed; both tables 13.1 and 13.2 show that males with a history of antisocial behaviour were the most likely of all Study members to be drug-dependent. The last column of table 13.2 reveals that conduct-disordered males used a wider variety of drugs and had more symptoms of alcohol dependence than conduct-disordered females, but this simply reflected the fact that all males were more likely than all females to abuse drugs and alcohol at age 21.

Comment: attitudes and experiences related to adult crime

The final panels of table 13.1 and table 13.2 show that males and females with a history of antisocial behaviour in adolescence were both likely to have delinquent peers in young adulthood, to develop self-concepts as offenders, to estimate the risk of crime as low, and to expect few sanctions against crime from their social networks. In short, antisocial adolescents, both males and females, grew up to be young adults who perceived few deterrents against engaging in antisocial behaviour, were surrounded by antisocial peers, and came to hold attitudes that favoured involvement in antisocial behaviour. Consistent with this social-psychological portrait, the tables show that antisocial behaviour in adolescence was a useful predictor of self-reported criminal offending among both males and females. Moreover, antisocial behaviour in adolescence was useful in predicting self-reported violent offending among both males and females.

However, two gender differences in the prediction of criminal outcomes from past behaviour were observed and replicated in both tables 13.1 and 13.2. Despite the attitudinal and behavioural similarities of males and females, in adulthood males with a history of adolescent antisocial behaviour had significantly different experiences with the criminal justice system: they were significantly more likely than females to be arrested and incarcerated during the 3-year period between ages 18 and 21. For example, an SD unit increase on the measure of adolescent antisocial behaviour was associated with an increase of 1.5 arrests among males but only 0.3 arrests among females.

In sum, in the area of crime itself, the young adult outcomes of antisocial behaviour did show some sex differentiation. Adolescent antisocial behaviour exerted a similarly strong effect on the subsequent attitudes and behaviour of both males and females, but males with a history of antisocial behaviour appeared to encounter more difficulties with legal sanctions. A small part of this may be due to sex differences in police and judicial sanctioning wherein police officers and judges are marginally more likely to imprison men than women (Steffensmeier, Kramer, and Streifel, 1993). However, it is more likely due to the fact that on average males are involved in more frequent, severe, violent antisocial behaviour than females (see chapter 5). This is illustrated in the final column of table 13.2, which shows that the mean level scores of males with conduct disorder were much worse than the scores of their female conduct-disordered counterparts on self-reported crime, violent offending, criminal self-concept, and the expectation that they will not be detected in criminal activities. Whatever the reason for this sex difference in the outcome of adolescent antisocial behaviour, it is probably the case that males with a history of adolescent antisocial behaviour are more likely to experience cumulative disadvantages, socially and psychologically, as a result of brushes with the law. A record of conviction or imprisonment may strain relationships, decrease social support, and raise barriers that block young men in their subsequent efforts to find jobs and housing (Nagin and Waldfogel, 1995).

Comment: interpreting gendered outcomes in a life-course perspective
Will the Dunedin males and females continue to diverge into sex-stereotyped worlds of work (for men) and family (for women) as they grow older? We suggest not. We have observed that, during the period of transition from adolescence to young adulthood, males lag developmentally a few

years behind females in entering the domain of family roles. However, we think that the Study men will catch up in a few years when they get around to taking up the developmental task of forming their own homes and families. Then, the formerly conduct-disordered men may show poor outcomes in these domains that troubled mostly women at age 21.

Our age-21 outcome measures give a snapshot of the young men while they were in this temporary period of developmental delay. At age 21, the Dunedin men's and women's experiences with partners and children set their lives apart both qualitatively and quantitatively. For example, among Dunedin 21-year-olds, women had been with a partner on average for 20.2 months, whereas men had been with a partner on average for only 12.8 months (df=869, p<0.01). Among those with a committed partner, the women's partners were two years older than they were on average, whereas the men's partners were a year younger than they were on average (df=562, p<0.01). With respect to moving in together, 34 per cent of women, but only 18 per cent of men, had cohabited with a partner (df=955, p<0.01). Thus, men at 21 were much less likely than women to have settled into a shared living arrangement with a mature partner. The women were more likely to be settled with children too. Among women 10 per cent had become mothers before 21, whereas among men 6 per cent had become fathers (df=954, p<0.01). More telling, the women who were mothers had lived with their children 96 per cent of the months in the child's life, whereas the men who were fathers had lived with their children on average only 55 per cent of the months of their child's life (df=75, p<0.01). Thus, among young men, biological fatherhood was not necessarily synonymous with taking on a settled and responsible parenting role (see also Jaffee *et al.*, forthcoming).

We expect the young men in the sample to catch up with the young women and enter the family domain later in their twenties. When the former conduct-disordered men catch up, it is reasonable to expect that, like the former conduct-disordered women at 21, they will show poor outcomes relative to the family domain with respect to partners (such as relationship conflict and dissolution) and children (such as poor parenting). The same logic may be applied also to the women in our analysis. Our age-21 outcome measures tapped the young women when they were already forming new families, especially if they had a history of antisocial behaviour, and were thus out of the workforce while caring for preschool children. It is possible that when these women join the workforce in a few years they will show poor outcomes relative to the work domain, much like the former conduct-disordered men at 21.

The idea of following up children who displayed antisocial behaviour to measure their adult outcomes has a long and rich legacy. A number of fine studies have pioneered findings, some following participants well into midlife, far beyond the young adult stage we have shown in this chapter (e.g., Farrington, 1994; Pulkkinen, 1996; Sampson and Laub, 1993; for a valuable anthology, see Robins and Rutter, 1990). This work continues today in several contemporary cohorts who have been followed through adolescence in the 1980s and 1990s and who are now reaching adulthood (see Farrington, 1998, appendix, for a summary of these ongoing studies). These and other similar longitudinal studies should be watched for fresh findings about the adult outcomes of antisocial youth.

Comment: foretelling the future

Scientists and laypersons alike are especially fascinated by two questions about crime: the first question concerns the onset of crime, or in everyday parlance, 'How early can we tell?' Efforts to answer this question are concerned with risk assessment and the identification of high-risk children who might be candidates for intervention. We tried to shed light on this issue in chapters 7–12, and will revisit it again later in the book. The second question concerns desistance from crime, or, in everyday parlance, 'When will they get better?' Efforts to answer this question are concerned with identifying key turning-points in life-course development. At this point in the longitudinal Dunedin Study we are unable to address this question because, at age 21, our Study members are still too young for us to study their desistance from crime. The reason for this can be best appreciated with reference to the relation between age and antisocial behaviour. When rates of crime are plotted against age, the rates for both prevalence and incidence of offending appear highest during late adolescence; they peak sharply at about age seventeen and begin to drop off only in their early twenties (Blumstein, Cohen, and Farrington, 1988). Not surprisingly, not enough Dunedin study members desisted from their antisocial behaviour between the ages of 20 and 21, the period covered by our Phase 21 assessment. The nature of desistance is also influenced by historical changes, and there is some suggestion that among more contemporary birth cohorts, desistance may be delayed even further, into the late twenties. The delay in desistance (or prolongation of involvement in antisocial behaviour) is attributable to the emergence, in the Western world and in recent years, of a new developmental stage in the life course (Arnett, 2000). This new developmental stage is called 'emerging adulthood' and it occurs between adolescence and young adulthood. It is characterized by role-less floundering, in which young adults neither perceive themselves to be adults (or adolescents) nor choose to occupy any of the adult roles historically favoured by their same-age peers in prior cohorts (e.g., marriage) and which are thought to be implicated in the process of desistance. 'Emerging adulthood' is characteristic of the Dunedin cohort, who are coming of age in a period when the turning-points that bring about desistance from crime are still far in their futures. For New Zealand males at the turn of the millennium the mean age of first marriage is 29, the mean age at first child is 31, jobs are remote because of the 18 per cent unemployment rate for those under age 24, and military service is distinctly uncommon.

Desistance is the least understood developmental process in life-course research on crime, and its study is rife with conceptual and methodological difficulties (Laub and Sampson, forthcoming). For example, does desistance mean slowing down one's frequency of offending or reducing the seriousness of one's offending? Is desistance simply the absence of recidivism or does it also involve a psychological change in attitudes and values? Related to these questions are numerous unresolved questions about how to measure and model desistance. Sampson and Laub (1993) have generated the most compelling theoretical perspective on desistance from criminal behaviour. According to their theory of age-graded informal social controls, desistance is not simply maturational reform in which youth 'age out of' crime; rather, desistance is due to the fact that at key points in the life course salient life events (e.g., a good marriage, a stable job, new opportunities offered by military service) engender social bonds that exert informal social controls on criminals and thus help them to reform their ways. This generative theory has garnered empirical support, and will be the focus of our longitudinal research as we continue to follow up members of the Dunedin Study. We have predicted that some offenders with the most serious antisocial histories, rather than turning over a new leaf when they encounter wives and jobs, may abuse their wives and steal from their employers. In contrast, offenders with less damaging pasts should have what it takes to embrace opportunities for desistance from crime (Moffitt, 1993a). Although, as already explained, we cannot yet study desistance in the Dunedin cohort, the results in tables 13.1 and 13.2 throw open a set of interesting questions about the process by which social bonds may help to deter individuals from crime.

First, the results show that good relationships and promising jobs are negatively correlated with antisocial behaviour; that is, at least in this period of emerging adulthood, few antisocial youths are on the road to experiencing those salient life events that can help them to turn their lives around. In related research in the Dunedin Study, we have shown that only about one-quarter of the Study members with a propensity to antisocial behaviour had scores above average for their cohort on the types of social ties that might deter crime, compared to about three-quarters of the other Study members (Wright *et al.*, forthcoming). This suggests that although the formation of certain social bonds *can* generate turning-points in the life course, it does not *do* so for the majority of antisocial persons because these persons are unlikely to encounter salubrious bonds in the first place. As suggested by previous research, new social bonds and their resulting social capital can be potentially effective agents of change, but – as suggested by the results in this chapter – their creation, whether through the individual's own initiative or by means of planned intervention programmes, will require very firm personal resolve as well as generous resources in order to battle against the forces of cumulative disadvantage.

Second, given the significant impact, yet the diminished frequency, of such social bonds among persons with a serious antisocial history, a critical issue for future research is to examine how some antisocial individuals form prosocial bonds. Do antisocial persons form prosocial bonds in a similar, or different, manner from prosocial individuals? Are there specific characteristics or circumstances that aid some antisocial persons in the formation of these bonds? Answers to these questions will help to shed light on one of the least understood and common features of adult development, leaving youthful crime behind (Laub and Sampson, forthcoming).

Take-home messages

- The data provide no support for the hypothesis that a history of antisocial behaviour has fewer consequences for females than for males. Antisocial behaviour has disruptive effects on both females and males as they make the transition from adolescence to adulthood.
- There is support for the hypothesis of sex-differentiated outcomes during the transition to young adulthood. In particular, antisocial behaviour among young men is significantly more likely to be associated with subsequent problems in work, substance abuse, and legal arenas, whereas antisocial behaviour among young women is significantly more likely to be associated with relationship problems, depression, tendency to suicide, and poor physical health.

Unanswered questions

- What processes explain the effects of adolescent antisocial behaviour on men's failure in the worlds of education and employment?
- What processes explain the link between adolescent antisocial behaviour and women's poor physical health?
- How do antisocial youths' difficulties in establishing their own homes and families mediate the transmission of social problems to the next generation?
- Does the experience of antisocial behaviour in the first two decades of life continue to bedevil psychosocial adjustment beyond young adulthood, perhaps well into midlife?
- What adult experiences promote change for antisocial youths who attain healthy outcomes?

CHAPTER FOURTEEN

Sex, antisocial behaviour, and mating: mate selection and early childbearing

Thus far we have reported evidence that as they enter adulthood females, relative to males, commit fewer crimes, are less likely to be involved in serious or violent crime, and their antisocial disorders are less likely to persist beyond adolescence into adulthood (see chapter 13). The exception to this pattern is that young women are as likely as young men to be involved in violence within their intimate relationships (see chapter 5). This suggests the need to examine in greater detail the types of men with whom antisocial females form intimate relationships. In addition, it has been remarked that although women who have conduct problems are seldom serious and violent offenders, they are the mothers who produce the next generation of serious and violent males (Henry *et al.*, 1993; Tremblay, 1991). An examination of assortative mating may help us to understand how this might occur.

By age 21, many of the Dunedin Study members were involved in committed intimate relationships with partners and, through *de facto* unions and marriages, some Study members already moved from their families of origin into new families of 'destination'. In this chapter, we examine who pairs off with whom and test whether antisocial females, as well as antisocial males, are likely to form unions with other antisocial persons. We also examine the consequences of assortative mating for the persistence of antisocial behaviour into adulthood, as well as the implications of this assortative mating for reproduction.

A great deal of developmental research on friendship formation in childhood and adolescence has explored who befriends whom. This research shows that antisocial girls and antisocial boys are both likely to form friendships with antisocial peers (e.g., Bjerregaard and Smith, 1993; Dishion, Andrews, and Crosby, 1995; Ennet and Bauman, 1994; Kandel, Davies, and

Baydar, 1990). Cairns and Cairns (1994) suggest that affiliation with antisocial peers consolidates deviant behaviour patterns and guides norm formation, and in this way such peer affiliations contribute to behavioural continuity over time. Union formation – or, who mates with whom – is equally important to study because it has both intra- and inter-generational implications. Assortative mating – the tendency for people to form unions with similar others – has *intra*-generational consequences because similarities between members of a couple create an environment that reinforces initial tendencies. Persons who marry a partner similar to themselves are less likely to change (Caspi and Herbener, 1990). Assortative mating has *inter*-generational consequences for both genetic and social reasons. Because people form unions with other people like themselves, the resulting couples differ more from each other on average than they would if people mated randomly. When assortatively mated couples reproduce, entire families increasingly differ from each other as a result of genetic and environmental modes of inter-generational transmission (Krueger *et al.*, 1998). As such, the study of assortative mating has developmental implications for understanding continuity across the life course and continuity between the lives of parents and their children. In this chapter, we examine the mating patterns of antisocial adolescents.

The Partners Study

Sample

In 1993, when the Dunedin Study members were 21 years old, we added a new component to the Dunedin research by assessing the union- and family-formation activities of the Study members. For this purpose, we expanded the sampling frame to include the partners of the Study members.[1] Prior to the age-21 interview, Study members were invited to bring their intimate partner (defined as someone they had been dating for at least six months, were living with, or had married) to the research unit. A total of 474 Study members indicated that they were involved with a partner who met the criteria, and 76 per cent (360) of the partners agreed to participate in the interviews. Of the couples who were interviewed, 52 per cent were in dating relationships, 41 per cent were in cohabiting relationships, and 7 per cent

---

[1] An additional inter-generational component of the Dunedin Study focuses on the children of the Study members as these children reach 3 years of age, the same age at which the Study members were themselves enrolled in the longitudinal study. Enrolment in this component of the Study is carried out on a rolling basis and data collection is ongoing; Jay Belsky is the Principal Investigator.

were married. The average relationship length was 26 months, with 73 per cent of the relationships having lasted for more than one year and 45 per cent having lasted for more than two years.

The 360 Study members with partners who participated were compared to the 114 Study members with partners who did not participate. The two groups did not differ significantly in mean educational attainment [$t(446) = 0.32$, $p = 0.75$] or in the average ages of their partners [$t(468) = 1.32$, $p = 0.19$]. In addition, the two groups did not differ significantly on the measures of personality, perceived consequences and attitudes, and antisocial behaviour examined in this book; the relevant t-values ranged from 0.18 to 1.56, all p values > 0.11. Study members with participating partners were in relationships of longer duration [$t(450) = 3.04$, $p = 0.001$] than were Study members whose partners did not participate. Female couple members were significantly younger (M $= 20.68$, SD $= 1.27$) than were male couple members (M $= 22.23$, SD $= 2.83$), [$t(359) = 9.91$, $p < 0.001$]. All original Study members were 21 years old, although the original men tended to have younger women as partners, whereas the original women tended to have older men as partners.[2]

Members of each couple were interviewed separately and privately, with confidentiality guaranteed, by different interviewers who were blind to the responses provided by the other member of the couple. Members of each couple did not know in advance the content of their partner's interview schedules. This eliminated the chance that couples would confer about their responses prior to the interview.

Measures

ADOLESCENT ANTISOCIAL BEHAVIOUR

As described in chapter 8, this was a composite of z-standardized parent reports at 13 and 15, teacher reports at 13, informant reports at 18, and self-reports at ages 13, 15, and 18, with reliability of 0.86 for boys (n $= 491$) and 0.77 for girls (n $= 465$). The time period covered by this measure was prospective to the Study members' relationships with their partners.

PARTNERS' SOCIAL CHARACTERISTICS

The partners' *reading achievement* was measured by the Burt Word Reading Test (Scottish Council for Research in Education, 1976) that was administered at earlier assessments to the Study members. *Educational attainment* was

---

[2] As expected from population prevalence rates of homosexuality reported from recent surveys of sexual behaviour (e.g., Laumann *et al.*, 1994), our sample of 360 couples included three same-sex couples, who were included in the analyses reported here.

measured on a 9-point scale, ranging from 1 (no high-school qualification) to 9 (university attendance). The partners' *fathers' socioeconomic
status* was measured using a 6-point scale designed for New Zealand occu-
pations (Elley and Irving, 1972), ranging from 1 (unskilled labour) to 6
(professional).

THE PARTNERS' ANTISOCIAL BEHAVIOURS AND ATTITUDES

The Self-Report Delinquency Interview described in chapter 3 was used
to assess participation in *illegal behaviour*. Here we focus on two measures.
The first is a measure of the variety of delinquent offending, which indicates how many of forty-eight different criminal behaviours the partner
committed at least once during the past twelve months. The second is a
measure of *violence*, which indicates how many of seven different violent
offences the partner committed at least once during the past twelve
months. In addition, we asked the partners to report the number of times,
since age 17, that they had been *convicted of criminal charges* in a court of
law. The partners were also interviewed about their *perpetration of physical
abuse* against the Study members. The physical abuse scale includes thirteen physical violence items, and was described earlier in chapter 5. The
partners' attitudes about crime were measured with the same protocol
that was used with the Study members themselves. This interview protocol yielded three measures, as described in chapter 13: *self-concept as an
offender, perceived risk of detection, and perceived informal social sanctions
against crime.*

PARTNERS' PERSONALITY

The partners completed the same modified form of the Multidimensional
Personality Questionnaire (MPQ) that was completed by original Study
members when they were 18 years old, as described in chapter 10. Here we
focus on the three higher-order MPQ superfactors: *Negative Emotionality,
Positive Emotionality*, and *Constraint* (see table 10.1 for further details).

Data analysis approach

Our analysis examines whether the Study members' antisocial behaviour
during adolescence predicted the characteristics of the partners with whom
they became involved in a serious relationship at age 21. Table 14.1 presents
the correlations, separately for male and female Study members, between
antisocial behaviour measured in adolescence and partners' characteristics
measured in adulthood. We tested for sex differences in a multiple regression framework,

Table 14.1. *Assortative mating: how well did the Study members' past antisocial behaviours during adolescence predict the characteristics of the partners with whom they were involved in a serious relationship at age 21?*

Characteristics of the partner the Study member brought to the Unit at age 21	Men's correlation n = 134	Women's correlation n = 213	Sex interaction p<0.05
Partner's social characteristics			
Educational attainment	−0.35*	−0.28*	no
Reading test score	−0.15*	−0.13*	no
Father's SES	−0.32*	−0.25*	no
Partner's antisocial behaviours			
Past-year self-reported delinquency	0.33*	0.33*	no
Past-year self-reported violence	0.27*	0.34*	no
Physical abuse perpetration against the Study member	0.32*	0.26*	no
Self-reported criminal charges at court	0.21*	0.38*	no
Self-concept as an offender	0.13	0.23*	no
Perceived risk of detection for crime	−0.01	−0.07	no
Perceived informal sanctions against crime	−0.39*	−0.33*	no
Partner's Personality			
Negative emotionality	0.29*	0.21*	no
Positive emotionality	−0.18*	−0.11	no
Constraint	−0.12	−0.08	no

Note:
* Correlation was significant, p<0.05.

$$P = a + b_1 Sex + b_2 ASB + b_3 (Sex \times ASB) + e,$$

where P represents the partners' characteristics, b_1 and b_2 represent the main effects of the Study members' sex and antisocial behaviour (ASB) on the partners' characteristics, and b_3 indexes whether the effect of antisocial behaviour on mate choice varies as a function of the Study member's sex. The results of these gender-interaction tests are presented in the final column of table 14.1.

Results

The results in table 14.1 show that an adolescent history of antisocial behaviour influenced the nature of the partner with whom Study members formed an intimate relationship as young adults. With regard to the social characteristics of their partners, both antisocial males and females were significantly more likely to later form unions with partners who were poorer readers, who had less formal education, and who came from more socioeconomically disadvantaged backgrounds. With regard to antisocial behaviour, both antisocial males and females formed unions with partners who were themselves involved in criminal behaviour. In addition, antisocial males and females were significantly more likely to become involved in an intimate relationship with partners who physically abused them. Table 14.1 also shows significant associations between the Study members' antisocial history and their partners' attitudes toward crime. The partners of antisocial Study members viewed themselves as significantly more antisocial and also perceived fewer social sanctions for engaging in crime. Finally, table 14.1 shows that both antisocial male and female adolescents were significantly more likely to form unions with partners who had elevated scores on Negative Emotionality; according to their personality profile, the partners of antisocial adolescents had a low general threshold for the experience of negative emotions such as anger, and tended to perceive the world around them as malevolent.

Comment: the intra-generational implications of assortative mating for antisocial behaviour

The results from analyses of mating patterns show that antisocial adolescents were significantly more likely later to pair off with partners who were disadvantaged and antisocial. There were no significant sex differences in these patterns of association; antisocial adolescent males and females were equally likely to pair off with antisocial partners in young adulthood. There are several ways in which this assortative pairing off can come about (Engfer, Walper, and Rutter, 1994). First, antisocial people may be more likely to meet each other simply because they come from a similar class background, but elsewhere we have controlled for social class origins and ruled out this possibility (Krueger *et al.*, 1998). Second, some antisocial people make an active choice of a similar partner who shares their values and therefore will not disapprove of their antisocial lifestyle. A third possibility is that conventional, prosocial individuals often avoid social contact with antisocial people and thus people with an antisocial history find that their field of potential partners is constrained to people like themselves.

Whatever the process, an important question for life-course research is what happens when two antisocial persons form a union. Specifically, what effect does pairing off with an antisocial mate have on the persistence of one's own antisocial behaviour? There are at least two possibilities. A 'social-influence' effect suggests that when an individual pairs off with an antisocial partner, the antisocial partner will contribute to and encourage that individual's own antisocial behaviour in adulthood. A 'social-amplification' effect suggests that the pairing of two antisocial persons will create a dangerous liaison, with the result that antisocial partners will promote the persistence and escalate the antisocial behaviour of those individuals who are already prone to antisocial behaviour.

We tested these two hypotheses in a multiple regression framework,

$$\text{ASB at age } 21 = a + b_1(\text{Adolescent's ASB}) + b_2(\text{Partner's ASB}) + b_3(\text{Adolescent's} \times \text{Partner's ASB}) + e,$$

where the outcome variable is the Study member's self-reported antisocial behaviour at age 21. The first coefficient, b_1, represents the effect of enduring criminal propensity, according to which the Study member's adolescent antisocial behaviour remains stable from youth to adulthood. The second coefficient, b_2, represents the social-influence effect of the partner, according to which the partner's antisocial behaviour contributes to the Study member's own adult antisocial behaviour above and beyond the Study member's criminal propensity. The third coefficient, b_3, is the effect of the product of the first two terms and represents a social-amplification effect, according to which pairing off with an antisocial partner promotes further antisocial behaviour among criminally-prone individuals. The results of this regression model are presented in table 14.2, separately for male Study members and their partners and for female Study members and their partners.

The results show three noteworthy findings. First, as we have already seen in chapter 13, there is a good deal of continuity in antisocial behaviour from adolescence to adulthood. The male and female Study members who were most antisocial in adolescence continued to be so in adulthood. Second, the results provide clear support for the social-influence hypothesis. When male and female Study members paired off with an antisocial partner, the result was that they themselves were more likely to engage in antisocial behaviour in adulthood. For both men and women, the regression results show that a

Table 14.2. *The effect of assortative mating on the continuity of antisocial behaviour: results of a hierarchical multiple regression analysis showing the effects of adolescent antisocial behaviour and partner's antisocial behaviour on self-reports of offending at age 21*

| | Predicting age-21 crime among: | | | | | |
| | Male Study members (N=134) | | | Female Study members (N=211) | | |
Independent variables	β	t-value	p	β	t-value	p
Study member's own antisocial behaviour in in adolescence	0.47	6.86	0.001	0.47	8.30	0.001
Partner's antisocial behaviour	0.33	4.87	0.001	0.30	5.29	0.001
Study member's antisocial behaviour in adolescence in interaction with partner's antisocial behaviour	0.14	1.10	0.27	0.18	2.25	0.02

longstanding criminal propensity and having an antisocial partner contributed *additively* to adult involvement in crime. Apparently, pairing off with an antisocial partner adds fuel to the fire. Third, the results provide qualified support for the social-amplification hypothesis. The absence of an interaction effect in the regression model estimated for male Study members and their partners suggests that antisocial men continue to behave antisocially regardless of whether their female partner was antisocial. In contrast, the presence of an interaction effect in the regression model estimated for female Study members and their partners pointed to a social-amplification effect for women.

Figure 14.1 plots the interaction between female Study members' adolescent antisocial behaviour and their partner's antisocial behaviour in predicting women's self-reported crimes at age 21. The x-axis measures adolescent antisocial behaviour in standard deviation units and the y-axis measures criminal behaviour at age 21 in terms of the number of self-reported types of crime. The slope of the top line represents the coefficient obtained by regressing self-reported crime at age 21 on adolescent antisocial behaviour

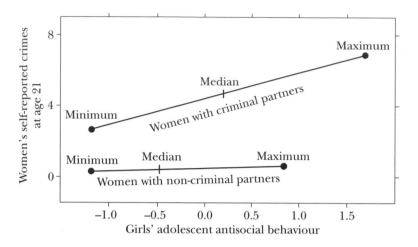

14.1 The continuity of antisocial behaviour among women, as a function of their male partner's criminal behaviour

for only those women with criminal partners. The slope of the bottom line represents the adolescent antisocial behaviour coefficient for women with non-criminal partners. Both lines slope upwards, but the line for women with a criminal partner slopes upwards more steeply, demonstrating a strong social-amplification effect. Apparently, only antisocial girls who pair off with antisocial men go on to become antisocial women. This pattern has also been reported in a study of English women; whether at-risk girls had good or poor adjustment as adult women depended on the qualities of their male partners (Quinton *et al.*, 1993).

Figure 14.1 can also be used to demonstrate the process of assortative mating by using the plotted regression lines as box-whisker plots. Each of the regression lines indicates the median, minimum, and maximum values of adolescent antisocial behaviour for the group of women who paired off with criminal partners and for those who paired off with non-criminal partners. (We used penultimate values for the minimums and maximums to avoid outliers.) As shown in figure 14.1, the median adolescent antisocial behaviour of women with criminal partners was much higher than that of the women with non-criminal partners. Similar differences occurred with the endpoints. This unequal distribution of adolescent antisocial behaviour in the two groups of women, combined with the social-amplification effect, demonstrates that antisocial girls are selectively more likely to become involved with antisocial men which, in turn, reinforces and amplifies their own antisocial behaviour into adulthood.

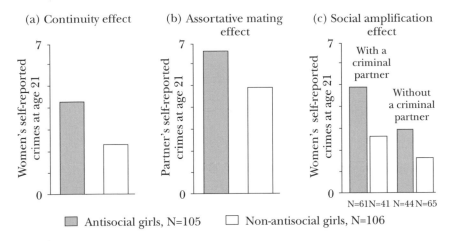

14.2 How assortative mating with antisocial men shapes women's lives

Figure 14.2 summarizes these various effects more plainly.[3] Panel (a) shows that antisocial girls commit more crimes in adulthood than their non-antisocial peers (continuity effect). Panel (b) shows that antisocial girls are more likely than non-antisocial girls to become involved with men who commit more crime in adulthood (assortative mating effect). Panel (c) shows that the partners' criminal behaviour moderates the persistence of girls' antisocial behaviour into adulthood (social amplification effect); it is the antisocial girls with criminal partners who remain persistent offenders. The persistence of antisocial behaviour among women thus depends on whether or not the woman pairs off with an antisocial man, but the important caveat (which is evident in the non-equal cell sizes in panel (c) of figure 14.2) is that, through the process of assortative mating, antisocial girls are more likely to encounter such men and are thus less likely to desist from antisocial behaviour. The results thus implicate antisocial men as the engines in women's transition from juvenile delinquency to adult crime.

Comment: the inter-generational implications of assortative mating for antisocial behaviour

Before turning to consider the intergenerational implications of assortative mating, it should be noted that we have focused in this chapter on

---

[3] For illustrative purposes only, we here divided girls into two groups on the basis of a median split on the measure of their adolescent antisocial beahviour. Likewise, we divided the partners into two groups on the basis of a median split on the measure of their own self-reports of crime at the phase-21 assessment.

assortative mating among young adults, when the original Study members were 21 years old. Chances are that many of these couples will not stay together and most of them may never have children together. Indeed, only seventy-seven Study members (8 per cent) from the original birth cohort had children by the time we interviewed them at age 21, and for assortative mating to have inter-generational consequences, reproduction must occur. Although this may seem to limit the generalizability of our findings, we have already shown (in chapter 13) that members of the cohort who had children by age 21 were significantly more antisocial than those who had not yet had children, and this was true for both males and females. Among the seventy-seven Study members who had children before age 21, 58 per cent had a prior diagnosis of conduct disorder. Conduct-disordered Study members were 22 per cent of the cohort, but they produced 60 per cent of the ninety-four offspring born before the cohort members turned 21. In contemporary cohorts, parenting before age 21 represents high risk for both parents and children (Maynard 1997).

Because adolescent antisocial behaviour is so strongly associated with early childbearing, studying assortative mating in young parents may help us to understand the origins and persistence of the most severe forms of antisocial behaviour. That is, the young participants in our research who have already reproduced appear to be creating children who are at unusually high risk for antisocial behaviour – by virtue of having been born to a parent who was more antisocial than his/her peers; by virtue of having been born to a parent whose *partner* was also antisocial; and by virtue of having been born to a parent who was young and inexperienced. We also know from chapter 13 that antisocial Study members as adults had other problems known to compromise parenting: for example, unstable housing, poor literacy, substance abuse, domestic violence, depression, and ill health. Moreover, a parent who has given life to a child need not remain *present* to contribute to the child's rearing experience; father *absence* is a good predictor of children's problems (Henry *et al.*, 1996). Chapter 13 noted that Dunedin men who had fathered a child had lived with them on average only 55 per cent of the months of the child's life. Elsewhere we have shown that the best predictor of father absence among these men was a developmental history of antisocial behaviour, and most absent young fathers are seriously antisocial men (Jaffee *et al.*, forthcoming).

The most intriguing implication from our findings about assortative mating for antisocial behaviour has to do with understanding how risk for antisocial behaviour is transmitted across generations. The reason is that positive assortative mating increases the ratio of between- to within-family variance in antisocial behaviour. Stated somewhat differently, positive assortment on a genetically influenced phenotype, such as antisocial behaviour (e.g., Rutter *et al.*, 1998), creates families whose members are similar with respect to that phenotype, but different from other families with respect to that phenotype. Thus, if successive generations mate assortatively, trait-relevant genes will become concentrated within families. Consider the hypothetical 'first generation', in which families are headed by parents who are correlated for the trait-relevant genes. These genes are passed on to their offspring, who receive a 'double dose' of the genes due to their correlated parents, and then go on to mate assortatively with persons with similar, trait-relevant genes, and so on, 'concentrating' the relevant genetic variance within families. Take height as an example. Whole families clearly differ from other families in terms of height, yet families are made up of persons who are similar in height. Part of the explanation for this phenomenon is likely to lie in the positive assortative mating that occurs for this trait. Now consider antisocial behaviour, where analyses reveal that families clearly vary in terms of their antisocial behaviour, yet are made up of persons who are very similar with regard to their antisocial behaviour (Farrington *et al.*, 1996; Rowe and Farrington, 1997).

The contribution of assortative mating to the creation of such 'crime-prone families' may be understood as the result of the joint effects of 'active' and 'passive' correlations between genotypes and environments (Plomin, DeFries, and Loehlin, 1977). An active genotype–environment correlation may be thought of as 'niche picking' (Scarr and McCartney, 1983) in which people choose social environments that are consonant with their endowments. Assortative mating is an active gene–environment correlation, in which people affiliate with mates who are similar to themselves. This active genotype–environment correlation in the parental generation is expressed as a passive genotype–environment correlation in the children's generation. Passive genotype–environment correlation occurs because parents' heritable characteristics influence both the genotypes they transmit to their child and the kinds of rearing they are able to provide. If parents are assortatively mated for antisocial behaviour, this produces a 'double whammy' effect (Scarr and McCartney, 1983); their children are transmitted heritable vulnerability factors and are also reared in a criminogenic home environment. Nature and nurture thus become a tightly tied bundle through the pairing of antisocial males with antisocial females. The evidence suggests that although women are seldom serious and violent offenders, *both* men and

women must be studied in an effort to understand the aetiology of antisocial behaviour.

Take-home messages

- Both males *and* females who have an antisocial history are more likely to
  form unions with members of the opposite sex who are involved in
  crime and who hold attitudes that encourage antisocial behaviour.
- Adolescent antisocial males *and* females also form intimate relationships
  with partners who have little education, are poor readers, and who
  abuse them physically. Such cross-trait assortative mating promotes
  socioeconomic problems for young families and endangers the physical health of the women and their children.
- Forming an intimate relationship with an antisocial partner during the
  transition to adulthood increases the likelihood that both members of
  the couple will be involved in illegal behaviour in adulthood.
- The persistence of antisocial behaviour among women depends on
  whether or not the woman pairs off with an antisocial man. Antisocial
  girls who form unions with antisocial men are at risk for making the
  transition from juvenile delinquency to adult crime. In contrast, antisocial girls who avoid criminal men are less likely to persist in their antisocial lifestyle, but they are also a minority of such girls because the
  process of assortative mating conspires to unite antisocial girls with antisocial men.
- Antisocial males and females selectively reproduce at a young age, with an
  antisocial mate. Conduct-disordered Study members were one-fifth of
  the cohort, but they produced nearly two-thirds of the offspring born
  to the Dunedin cohort members as teenage parents.
- The twin roles of assortative mating and selective reproduction must be
  taken into account when investigating the persistence of antisocial
  behaviour across the life course and across generations. Females
  should be included in studies to build knowledge about the aetiology
  of antisocial behaviour.

Unanswered questions

- If antisocial young adults are moderately likely to seek out antisocial partners, how can this be reconciled with the theory that bonding with a
  prosocial partner accounts for desistence from crime during young
  adulthood?

• Research into the consequences of teenage parenthood should begin to address the implications of the strong link between antisocial behaviour and teenage parenthood. Most of the infants born to teenage parents have at least one antisocial parent, and many are born to two antisocial parents.

CHAPTER FIFTEEN

Evaluating the recommendation to relax the criteria for diagnosing conduct disorder in girls

In this chapter we address a debate in the field about the best way to diagnose conduct disorder among females. Should the sexes be diagnosed using the same criteria, as is now done? Or should the diagnostic criteria for females be relaxed to a milder standard than the criteria for males?

Leading one side of this debate, Zoccolillo (1993) has argued for gender-specific criteria, recommending that fewer symptoms should be required for diagnosing girls than boys. This argument is based on the clinical observation that girls with levels of symptoms that would be considered mild for a boy (and below DSM's diagnostic threshold) nevertheless often experience clinically significant problems in their health and social functioning. In one study that evaluated the recommendation to relax the diagnostic criterion, doing so predictably raised the prevalence rate of conduct disorder for a sample of 10-year-old girls, but also netted more of the sample's girls who had a history of early-onset pervasive behaviour problems in kindergarten (Zoccolillo, Tremblay, and Vitaro, 1996). This result suggested that relaxing the diagnostic criteria for girls may augment sensitivity of the conduct-disorder diagnosis to consequential female cases. However, no boys were studied, so we do not know whether relaxed criteria might have benefited measurement validity for both sexes at age 10.

On the other side of this debate, Zahn-Waxler (1993) has argued that we should reject the recommendation for relaxing conduct-disorder diagnostic criteria for girls. She pointed out that a similar logic might well be applied to male depression. Should males, because they seldom meet full criteria for depression, in future be allowed to attain a diagnosis of depression with fewer symptoms than required for females? Zahn-Waxler suggests that efforts to diagnose more females with conduct disorder are misguided, and divert scientific attention away from the more important goal of uncovering why genuinely fewer females than males manifest antisocial behaviour.

To resolve the debate over whether gender-specific versus gender-neutral criteria should be used for diagnosis, what is needed is a systematic comparison of the relative predictive validity of diagnoses made using conventional versus relaxed diagnostic criteria, for both sexes (Gaub and Carlson, 1997; see also Hartung and Widiger, 1998). Zoccolillo recommended that 'Using same-sex comparisons and assigning the same proportion of males and females to the deviant category can be a powerful test of whether or not there should be prevalence differences in CD' (1993, p. 75). He also suggested using adult outcome as the benchmark for validating the diagnosis of girls using fewer symptoms than required for boys, noting that relaxed diagnostic criteria for girls would be justified 'if the same proportion of deviant boys and girls selected by this method go on to continued antisocial or deviant behaviour . . .' (1993, p. 75). The analyses in this chapter examine whether girls whose conduct-disorder symptoms are at a subclinical level will later exhibit adult outcomes that are just as maladaptive as the outcomes of diagnosed boys.

Both Zoccolillo (1993) and Zahn-Waxler (1993) suggested that it is wise to broaden our focus to outcomes beyond the antisocial domain (antisocial personality and crime), and we agree. In chapter 13, we tested for sex differences in a variety of domains of young adult outcomes following adolescent antisocial behaviour. The pattern of findings in chapter 13 suggested that some outcomes might be sex-stereotyped. An antisocial history among males predicted subsequent problems in domains of work, substance abuse, and the justice system. An antisocial history among females predicted subsequent problems in domains of forming one's own home, partner relationships, depression, suicide, and physical health. Therefore, while we tested Zoccolillo's hypothesis that females with subclinical conduct problems would have outcomes as poor as conventionally diagnosed males, we allowed for the possibility that the females' poor outcomes might be in different domains from the males' outcomes.

Zoccolillo's (1993) writings would suggest that poor outcomes of girls with subclinical conduct problems may best be observed in feminine domains. However, here we extended our analysis further to ask whether, conversely, males with subclinical conduct problems might also have outcomes as poor as conventionally diagnosed females, if we allow for the possibility that males' poor outcomes are in masculine sex-typed domains. It is critical to show that subclinical levels of conduct problems predict poor outcomes only for females. If not, the recommendation that the diagnostic criteria need to be relaxed solely for girls would be misleading clinically and unhelpful scientifically.

Method

Measures

CONDUCT DISORDER

Cumulative lifetime diagnoses of DSM-IV conduct disorder were made for 154 males and 72 females, according to the presence of five or more symptoms of conduct disorder at one or more of the phases of the Study (11, 13, 15, and 18), as described in chapter 4 of this book. For comparison, the subclinical cases were defined as the 176 males and 156 females who had a lifetime 'sub-clinical diagnosis'; they had never met criteria for a diagnosis but they had shown 3 or 4 symptoms of conduct disorder at one or more phases of the study. By defining males and females as subclinical or diagnosed cases using the same numbers of symptoms, we could disentangle the effects of symptom severity from the effects of sex differences.

YOUNG ADULT OUTCOMES

Measures were described earlier in chapter 13 for the domains of schooling, work, establishing one's own home, relationship with a partner, mental health, substance abuse, physical health, and experiences and attitudes related to crime. All young adult outcome measures were standardized to a common z-metric based on the whole sample. Thus, tables 15.1 and 15.2 allow visual comparisons between the groups on the extremity of their mean young adult outcomes.

Data analysis approach

The analysis for each outcome variable was a one-way ANOVA with planned comparisons between pairs of groups: subclinical females versus diagnosed males, and subclinical males versus diagnosed females.

Results

Testing Zoccolillo's hypothesis

We followed the analytic strategy suggested by Zoccolillo's hypothesis which predicts that subclinical girls are the functional equivalent of diagnosed boys. We compared the outcomes of females with subclinical conduct problems (3–4 symptoms) versus the outcomes of males with diagnosed conduct disorder (5 or more symptoms) to test whether their outcomes were similar.

These results are shown in table 15.1. For 23 of the 35 outcome measures related to conduct disorder, the diagnosed boys scored significantly worse than subclinical girls. This should come as no surprise, because the boys had worse conduct symptoms. However, as Zoccolillo predicted, the sub-clinical girls and the diagnosed boys did have similar levels of maladjustment on some measures. Subclinical girls scored poorly and similarly to diagnosed boys on twelve measures: university attendance, cohabitation, having a child, three measures of problems in their partner relationships, anxiety, suicide and depression, and two measures of health. Thus, when the outcome scores of subclinical girls were as poor as the outcome scores of diagnosed boys, this happened mainly for outcomes that were feminine sex-typed.

Reversing Zoccolillo's hypothesis

We reversed the analytic strategy suggested by Zoccolillo's hypothesis, to ask whether subclinical boys are ever the functional equivalent of diagnosed girls, according to their later outcomes. We compared the outcomes of males with subclinical conduct problems (3–4 symptoms) versus the outcomes of females with diagnosed conduct disorder (5 or more symptoms) to test whether their outcomes were also similar. These results are shown in table 15.2. For twenty-one of the thirty-five outcome measures related to conduct disorder, the diagnosed girls scored significantly worse than sub-clinical boys. This should come as no surprise because the girls had worse conduct symptoms. However, unexpectedly the subclinical boys and the diagnosed girls did have similar levels of maladjustment on fourteen measures. Subclinical boys scored poorly and similarly to diagnosed girls on university attendance, two measures of problems in their work lives, disability from work, all three measures of substance abuse, and seven measures of crime-related experiences. (Diagnosed girls had higher self-reported violence scores than subclinical boys, but the violence measure included assaults against partners and family members, and we have seen in chapter 5 that females exceed males on this type of violence.) Altogether, when the outcome scores of sub-clinical boys were as poor as the outcome scores of diagnosed girls, this happened mainly for outcomes that were masculine sex-typed.

Comment: predictive validity for subclinical symptoms, or just gender-typed outcomes?

We tested whether the predictive validity of girls' subclinical conduct symptoms was as strong as the predictive validity of boys' diagnosed conduct disorder. Initially, this appeared to be at least partially true. However,

Table 15.1. *Mean levels of standardized young-adult outcomes for females with a lifetime diagnosis of mild subclinical conduct problems versus males with diagnosed conduct disorder. If females who have subclinical conduct symptoms experience outcome consequences as poor as males who have diagnosed conduct disorder, then relaxed diagnostic criteria for females are justified*

Young adult outcome[a]	Means of females with subclinical CD n = 156	Means of males with diagnosed CD n = 154	Planned comparison p<0.05
Schooling			
Age left high school	−0.08	−0.56	males worst
Enrolled in college/university	14%	11%	females = males
Work			
Perceived opportunities for future success in life	−0.04	−0.35	males worst
Index of job desirability	0.04	−0.26	males worst
Months of unemployment	−0.02	0.63	males worst
Establishing one's own home			
Age left parents' home	−0.17	−0.51	males worst
Number of residence moves	0.11	0.41	males worst
Number of cohabitations	0.34	0.20	females = males
Parent of a child before age 21	12%	17%	females = males
Sources of welfare support	0.11	0.43	males worst
Relationship with partner			
Satisfaction with partner	−0.09	−0.20	females = males
Relationship quality scale	0.08	−0.33	males worst
Conflicts with partner	0.14	0.20	females = males
Physical abuse perpetration	0.22	0.14	females = males
Physical abuse victimization	0.05	0.36	males worst
Mental health			
Anxiety symptoms	0.09	0.09	females = males
Psychosis symptoms	−0.03	0.48	males worst
Mania symptoms	−0.06	0.56	males worst
Depression symptoms	0.07	0.07	females = males
Suicide attempter	2%	5%	females = males

Table 15.1 (*cont.*)

Young adult outcome[a]	Means of females with subclinical CD n = 156	Means of males with diagnosed CD n = 154	Planned comparison p<0.05
Physical health			
Medical problems	0.24	−0.11	females = males
Subjective poor health	0.04	0.23	females = males
Months disabled	−0.03	0.3	males worst
Substance abuse and dependence			
Variety of drugs used	−0.04	0.67	males worst
Marijuana dependence symptoms	−0.13	0.85	males worst
Alcohol dependence symptoms	−0.27	0.66	males worst
Self-reported attitudes and experiences related to crime			
Peers' delinquency	−0.02	0.62	males worst
Self-concept as an offender	−0.29	0.74	males worst
Perceived risk of detection for crime	0.32	−0.46	males worst
Perceived informal sanctions against crime	0.02	−0.57	males worst
Self-reported offending at 21	−0.26	1.02	males worst
Self-reported violence at 21	−0.13	0.76	males worst
Months with an arrest	−0.14	0.63	males worst
Months with incarceration	−0.14	0.66	males worst
Crime victimization[b]	−0.06	0.1	females = males

Notes:
[a] The continuously distributed adult outcome measures were standardized for the whole sample as z-scores. Note: for the outcome variables, the measurement ages and the numbers of subjects are the same as shown in table 13.1.
[b] Crime victimization was not significantly related to a history of conduct disorder for males or females.

Table 15.2. *Mean levels of standardized young-adult outcomes for males with a lifetime diagnosis of mild subclinical conduct problems versus females with diagnosed conduct disorder. The analysis tests the hypothesis that males who have even subclinical conduct problems will experience outcome consequences similar to females who have diagnosed conduct disorder,* if *the domains measured are relevant to male gender roles*

Young adult outcome[a]	Means of males with subclinical CD n = 176	Means of females with diagnosed CD n = 72	Planned comparison p < 0.05
Schooling			
Age left high school	0.10	−0.67	females worst
Enrolled in college/university	19%	13%	males = females
Work			
Perceived opportunities for future success in life	0.17	−0.41	females worst
Index of job desirability	−0.03	0.01	males = females
Months of unemployment	−0.18	0.08	males = females
Establishing one's own home			
Age left parents' home	0.14	−0.54	females worst
Number of residence moves	−0.12	0.24	females worst
Number of cohabitations	−0.25	0.55	females worst
Parent of a child before age 21	2%	29%	females worst
Sources of welfare support	−0.08	0.57	females worst
Relationship with partner			
Satisfaction with partner	0	−0.51	females worst
Relationship quality scale	−0.03	−0.37	females worst
Conflicts with partner	0.04	0.35	females worst
Physical abuse perpetration	−0.24	0.91	females worst
Physical abuse victimization	−0.05	0.46	females worst
Mental health			
Anxiety symptoms	−0.12	0.28	females worst
Psychosis symptoms	−0.08	0.42	females worst
Mania symptoms	0.03	0.54	females worst
Depression symptoms	−0.15	0.64	females worst
Suicide-attempter	2%	6%	females worst

Table 15.2 (*cont.*)

Young adult outcome[a]	Means of males with subclinical CD n = 176	Means of females with diagnosed CD n = 72	Planned comparison p < 0.05
Physical health			
Medical problems	−0.25	0.76	females worst
Subjective poor health	−0.18	0.74	females worst
Months disabled	−0.07	0.14	males = females
Substance abuse and dependence			
Variety of drugs used	0.08	0.33	males = females
Marijuana dependence symptoms	0.11	0.32	males = females
Alcohol dependence symptoms	0.34	0.17	males = females
Self-reported attitudes and experiences related to crime			
Peers' delinquency	0.04	0.49	females worst
Self-concept as an offender	0.26	0.24	males = females
Perceived risk of detection for crime	−0.35	0.21	males = females
Perceived informal sanctions against crime	−0.24	−0.4	males = females
Self-reported offending at 21	0.26	0.29	males = females
Self-reported violence at 21	0.07	0.46	females worst
Months with an arrest	−0.04	−0.06	males = females
Months with incarceration	−0.09	−0.11	males = females
Crime victimization[b]	0.08	0.04	males = females

Notes:

[a] The continuously distributed adult outcome measures were standardized for the whole sample as z-scores. Note: for the outcome variables, the measurement ages and the numbers of subjects are the same as shown on table 13.1.

[b] Crime victimization was not significantly related to a history of conduct disorder for males or females.

subclinical girls' outcome scores, were as extreme as diagnosed boys' outcome scores primarily on outcome variables for which the whole population of females scores higher than the whole population of males during the developmental period surrounding the transition to young adulthood. This raised the possibility that prior reports of poor outcomes for subclinical females relative to diagnosed males had mistaken mean-level sex differences in the population on the outcomes for evidence of predictive validity for subclinical symptoms. Consistent with this revisionist view, when we reversed the analysis, we found something not anticipated by Zoccolillo's hypothesis: the predictive validity of boys' subclinical conduct symptoms was as strong as the predictive validity of girls' diagnosed conduct disorder, when the outcomes were variables for which the population of adult males scores higher than the population of adult females. According to the logic of Zoccolillo's recommendation to relax diagnostic criteria based on predictive validity, if the criteria were to be relaxed for females they must be relaxed for males as well. The most parsimonious interpretation of this set of findings is that they do not attest to any special predictive utility for subclinical conduct problems for either sex. Rather, the findings simply reflect two facts: (a) there are mean-level sex differences in measures of developmental outcomes in young adulthood, and (b) the more conduct disorder symptoms a young person has, the worse he or she will perform on the developmental outcomes that are relevant to sex.

Take-home messages

- The recommendation to relax the diagnostic criteria for conduct disorder for girls is not supported by our systematic test of the predictive validity of girls' sub-clinical conduct symptoms.
- Increasing numbers of symptoms of conduct disorder predict increasingly poor young adult outcomes, irrespective of gender.

CHAPTER SIXTEEN

Life-course persistent and adolescence-limited antisocial behaviour among males and females

This chapter reports a comparison of Dunedin Study males and females who exhibited childhood-onset versus adolescent-onset antisocial behaviour. We tested whether childhood-onset delinquents had childhoods of inadequate parenting, neurocognitive problems, and temperament and behaviour problems, whereas adolescent-onset delinquents did not have these pathological backgrounds. We also queried whether females as well as males showed this differential pattern of risk, asking whether childhood-onset females had high-risk backgrounds, but adolescent-onset females did not. Finally, we ask whether Dunedin Study members on the life-course persistent antisocial path had more problem outcomes as young adults compared to those on the adolescence-limited delinquent path.

Between 1985 and 1988, when the members of the Dunedin Study grew from age 13 to age 15, we observed that many Study members who had not shown antisocial behaviour problems began to take up delinquent activities as they made the transition from childhood to adolescence. Our first descriptive report of this phenomenon contrasted those adolescent-onset delinquents with their counterparts who had been showing antisocial behaviour problems since early childhood (Moffitt, 1990b). We reported that childhood-onset delinquents were characterized by abnormal levels of individual and contextual risk factors (hyperactivity, low IQ and family adversity, among others) whereas adolescent-onset delinquents were not. The adolescent-onset delinquents' backgrounds were not inordinately healthy, but they were not pathological either; they were simply average. This initial observation prompted us to develop a theoretical taxonomy, in which different aetiologies and different predictions about life-course outcomes were proposed for childhood-onset versus adolescent-onset conduct problems (Moffitt, 1993a; Moffitt, 1994; Caspi and Moffitt, 1995; Moffitt, 1997).

In a nutshell, we suggested that 'life-course persistent' antisocial behaviour begins early in life when the difficult behaviour of a high-risk young child is exacerbated by a high-risk social environment. (How vulnerable children come to coincide with criminogenic home environments was the topic of chapter 14.) The child's risk emerges from inherited or acquired neuro-psychological variation, initially manifested as subtle cognitive deficits, difficult temperament, or hyperactivity. The environment's risk comprises factors such as inadequate parenting, disrupted family bonds, and poverty. The environmental risk domain expands beyond the family, as the child ages, to include poor relations with people such as peers and teachers. Over the first two decades of development, negative transactions between the child and his or her environment accumulate and gradually construct a disordered personality, having hallmark features of physical aggression and antisocial behaviour persisting to midlife.

In contrast, we suggested that 'adolescence-limited' antisocial behaviour emerges alongside puberty, when otherwise healthy youngsters experience dysphoria during the relatively role-less years between their biological maturation and their access to mature privileges and responsibilities, a period we called the maturity gap. While adolescents are in this gap it is virtually normative for them to mimic the life-course-persistent youths' delinquent style as a way to demonstrate autonomy from parents, win affiliation with peers, and hasten social maturation. However, because their pre-delinquent development was healthy, most young people who become adolescence-limited delinquents are able to desist from crime when they age into adult maturity, turning gradually to a more conventional lifestyle. This recovery may be delayed if adolescence-limited delinquents encounter factors we called 'snares', such as a criminal record or addiction. According to the theory, adolescence-limited antisocials are common, relatively temporary, and near normative. Life-course persistent antisocials are few, persistent, and pathological.

This theory has since prompted discussion of its implications (e.g., Brezina, 2000; Howell and Hawkins, 1998; Lahey, Waldman, and McBurnett, 1999; Mazerolle et al., 2000; Osgood, 1998; Scott and Grisso, 1997; Silverthorn and Frick, 1999) and its hypothesis of two types having distinctive correlates has received empirical support from follow-up studies in the Dunedin cohort (Jeglum-Bartusch et al., 1997; Moffitt, Lynam, and Silva, 1994; Moffitt et al., 1996; Moffitt and Caspi, 2001; Moffitt et al., forthcoming), and from tests conducted in several other samples (e.g., Dean,

Brame and Piquero, 1996; Kratzer and Hodgins, 1999; Nagin and Land, 1993; Nagin, Farrington, and Moffitt, 1995; Piquero, forthcoming; Patterson *et al.*, 1998; Taylor, Iacono and McGue, forthcoming; Tibbetts and Piquero, 1999; Raine *et al.*, forthcoming; Roeder, Lynch, and Nagin, 1999). Some studies have reported findings partly consistent with the hypothesis of two types, but have suggested useful alterations to it (e.g., Aguilar *et al.*, 2000; Fergusson, Horwood, and Nagin, 2000; Moffitt *et al.*, forthcoming). Altogether, support for the taxonomy comes from studies in six countries.

Other studies, although not necessarily presented as a test of the two types, have reported findings consonant with predictions from the taxonomy. For example, studies supporting the theory of life-course persistent delinquency have reported that measures of infant nervous-system development interact with poor parenting and social adversity to predict chronic aggression from childhood to adolescence (Arseneault *et al.*, forthcoming), and violent crime (Raine, Brennan and Mednick, 1994; Raine *et al.*, 1996) but not non-violent crime (Arseneault *et al.*, 2000b), and that prenatal malnutrition predicts antisocial personality disorder, presumably by harming neuro-cognitive development (Neugebauer, Hoek, and Susser, 1999). One study within a high-risk sample (Aguilar *et al.*, 2000) did not find significant differences between childhood-onset and adolescent-onset groups for neuro-cognitive measures taken prior to age three, although it did find significant neuro-cognitive differences later in childhood. In contrast, the studies reporting significant relations between infant neuro-cognitive indicators (e.g., birth complications or low birth-weight) and life-course persistent type of offending have used large representative cohorts, and the relation was seen primarily when the interaction between perinatal risk and socioeconomic status was tested (Arseneault *et al.*, 2000b; Arseneault *et al.*, forthcoming; Kratzer and Hodgins, 1999; Tibbetts and Piquero, 1999; Raine *et al.*, 1994). Other reports have shown that aggressive behaviour characteristic of the life-course persistent type is highly stable (Stanger, Achenbach, and Verhulst, 1997) and heritable (Edelbrock *et al.*, 1995), whereas, in contrast, rule-breaking behaviour characteristic of the adolescence-limited type increases between ages 10 and 17 (Stanger *et al.*, 1997) and is less heritable than aggression (Edelbrock *et al.*, 1995).

Reports supporting the theory of adolescence-limited delinquency show that when young people enter adolescence they begin to admire aggressive peers and find good students less attractive (Bukowski, Sippola and Newcomb, 2000; Luthar and McMahon, 1996), adolescents' concerns about appearing immature increase their likelihood of delinquency (Zebrowitz *et al.*, 1998), and delinquent peers directly promote adolescence-onset delinquency, whereas parenting and behaviour problems lead to early-onset delinquents' affiliations with delinquent peers (Simons *et al.*, 1994; Vitaro *et al.*, 1997).

Does the taxonomy apply to females?

Unfortunately, the majority of this research has focused on males, prompting some researchers to wonder whether or not females fit into the taxonomy or require a separate theory of their own (Silverthorn and Frick, 1999). The original statement of the taxonomy asserted that the theory accounts for the behaviour of females as well as it accounts for the behaviour of males. The full text of the theory, which included predictions about females, was published as a book chapter that is not widely available (Moffitt, 1994). Therefore we quote the original statement, written in January 1991:

> The crime rate for females is lower than for males. In this developmental taxonomy, much of the gender difference in crime is attributed to sex differences in the risk factors for life-course persistent antisocial behaviour. Little girls are less likely than little boys to encounter all of the putative initial links in the causal chain for life-course persistent antisocial development. Research has shown that girls have lower rates than boys of symptoms of nervous system dysfunction, difficult temperament, late milestones in verbal and motor development, hyperactivity, learning disabilities, reading failure, and childhood conduct problems. Thus, the consequent processes of cumulative continuity ensue for far fewer girls than boys. Most girls lack the personal diathesis elements of the evocative, reactive, and proactive person/environment interactions that initiate and maintain life-course persistent antisocial behaviour.
>
> Adolescence-limited delinquency, on the other hand, is open to girls as well as to boys. According to the theory advanced here, girls, like boys, should begin delinquency soon after puberty, to the extent that they (1) have access to antisocial models, and (2) perceive the consequences of delinquency as reinforcing . . . However, exclusion from gender-segregated male antisocial groups may cut off opportunities for girls to learn delinquent behaviours . . . Girls are physically more vulnerable than boys to risk of personal victimization (e.g., pregnancy, or injury from dating violence) if they affiliate with life-course persistent antisocial males. Thus, lack of access to antisocial models and perceptions of serious personal risk may dampen the vigour of girls' delinquent involvement somewhat. Nonetheless, girls should engage in adolescence-limited delinquency in significant numbers.
>
> If females are seldom life-course persistent, but often adolescence-limited, then the sex difference in antisocial behavior should be smaller during adolescence than during childhood or adulthood. Further, the sex difference should be larger for crimes against victims, which are the prerogative of life-course persistents, than for crimes which fulfil the aspirations of adolescence-limited youths (drug offences, truancy, vandalism, petty thefts). (Moffitt, 1994, pp. 39–40)

The original theory thus proposed that (a) fewer females than males would become delinquent (and conduct disordered) overall, and that (b) within delinquents the percentage who are life-course persistent would be larger among males than females. Following from this, (c) the majority of delinquent females will be of the adolescence-limited type, and further, (d) their delinquency will have the same causes as adolescence-limited males' delinquency. In contrast, Silverthorn and Frick (1999) suggested that despite the fact that girls' onset of delinquency is delayed until adolescence, there is no analogous pathway in girls to the adolescence-limited pathway in boys. They argued for a female-specific theory in which all delinquent girls will have the same high-risk causal backgrounds as life-course-persistent males.

Several observations that we have reported so far in this book seem generally consistent with the taxonomic theory. With regard to the *origins of the life-course-persistent type*, chapter 9 has shown that males have higher levels than females of the childhood risk factors that contribute to serious and persistent antisocial behaviour. Chapter 8 showed that most risk factors affect males and females in the same way, although a few risk factors, such as hyperactivity and cognitive deficits, affect males somewhat more strongly than females. Chapter 7 showed that more males than females begin their antisocial acts at a young age. With regard to *outcomes* of the life-course-persistent type, chapter 3 showed that more males than females become high-frequency offenders and that more males than females continue antisocial involvement after adolescence and into young adulthood. Chapter 5 showed that more males than females become violent against victims. With regard to *females resembling the adolescence-limited type*, chapters 4 and 6 showed that females' conduct disorder is closely linked to the peri-pubertal period. Chapter 3 showed that females resemble males most on drug and alcohol related offences. Chapters 8 and 14 showed that females' delinquency, like most males' delinquency, is strongly associated with peer influence. These several observations seem supportive of the theory's predictions that few females will fit the life-course-persistent type and most females who become antisocial will fit the adolescence-limited type.

The focus on males in prior empirical tests of the theory has arisen from a pragmatic circumstance. A test of this developmental–epidemiological theory requires an epidemiological (non-clinical) sample that is followed longitudinally with repeated measures of antisocial behaviour. Few such studies have included females in large enough numbers to study the rare phenomenon of the female life-course persistent offender with adequate power for significance testing. This constraint applies to the Dunedin cohort too. In this chapter, we explore how Dunedin females fit into an operational definition of life-course persistent and adolescence-limited groups that we have previously published for Dunedin males (Moffitt *et al.*, 1996).

According to the theory, we anticipated that very few females would meet the operational criteria for the life-course persistent type. However, also according to the theory, we anticipated that the pattern of purported aetiological factors should be the same for males and females. That is, life-course persistent males and females should resemble each other in having extreme scores on risk factors specified by the theory of life-course persistent development (childhood hyperactivity, neuro-cognitive functions, and family adversity). According to the theory, we anticipated that females would predominantly show the late onset that typifies the adolescence-limited type, and that adolescence-limited males and females should resemble each other in having many delinquent peers, but virtually normative scores on other risk factors.

Method

Measures
Antisocial behaviour scales used to define the comparison groups in this section were the Rutter Child Scales, completed by parents and teachers when the children were aged 5, 7, 9, and 11, and the Self-Reported Delinquency interview administered to Study members at ages 15 and 18. These measures were described in detail in chapter 3. Altogether, the complete complement of ten measures we required for classifying behavioural histories was present for 457 males and 445 females (89 per cent of each sex, who closely represented the original sample).

As risk factors we selected from our list twenty-eight variables in the Study that were most closely specified by the theory. We present data for twenty-six measures taken in childhood, selected to represent the three domains of childhood risk specified by the theory: family adversity and inadequate parenting (ten measures), child neurocognitive health (eight measures), and child temperament and behaviour (eight measures). In addition, we present the Study's two measures of peer delinquency, taken at ages 13 and 18. The variables were described earlier in chapters 5 and 8.

Designating the comparison groups of the taxonomy
To operationalize the theory of two types, we designated comparison groups on the basis of individual life histories from age 5 to 18. The procedure for

defining the groups has been described in detail in our earlier report about Dunedin males (Moffitt *et al.*, 1996), and therefore is only briefly summarized here. The first step of the computerized algorithm divided the sample into Study members who had childhood histories of antisocial behaviour problems versus those who did not. Study members were considered to be antisocial children if they had evidence of extreme childhood antisocial behaviour problems that were both stable across time (at least three of the assessment occasions at ages 5, 7, 9, and 11) and pervasive across situations (reported by parents at home and corroborated by teachers at school). The second step divided the sample into Study members who participated in many antisocial acts during mid-adolescence versus those who did not. Study members were considered to be antisocial adolescents if they self-reported extreme delinquency at the age-15 interview or at the age-18 interview. On the third step, the childhood categories were cross-tabulated with the adolescent categories to yield developmental profiles. Our earlier publication (Moffitt *et al.*, 1996) defined groups of males using cut-off criteria that were determined on the distributions of the ten aforementioned measures of antisocial behaviour *within* males. Here, the goal was to provide a comparison of male and female groups defined using a single standard. Therefore, we repeated the group designation exercise using the same computerized algorithm that defined the groups in Moffitt *et al.* (1996), but applying uniform cut-offs calculated on the distributions of the ten antisocial measures for the full sample, regardless of sex.

Study members who met criteria for extreme antisocial behaviour across both childhood and adolescence were designated on the *life-course-persistent path*, hereafter referred to as the LCP path. Study members who met criteria for extreme antisocial behaviour as adolescents, but who had not been extremely antisocial as children, were designated on the *adolescence-limited path*, hereafter called the AL path. We use the term 'path' because until Study members are followed up in their thirties, it is not possible to confirm that those on the life-course-persistent path persisted or that those on the adolescence-limited path desisted, as further specified by the theory.

Data analysis approach

With respect to gender, the theory predicted two central patterns of findings: males and females who were members of the life-course-persistent group should share the *same* childhood risk factors specified by the theory, and males and females who were members of the adolescence-limited group should share the *same lack* of childhood risk factors. The conventional approach to testing would be an ANOVA with group (LCP vs AL paths) and sex (males vs. females) as factors, comparing mean levels on a risk variable. A significant group-by-sex interaction term would attest that there were sex differences on risk factors within a subtype group. By predicting a *lack* of sex differences within types, the theory called for seeking to confirm the null hypothesis via a non-significant sex interaction term. However, statistical power posed a problem for significance testing. We knew from our 1996 publication that few Dunedin sample males met criteria for the life-course persistent path, and our theory predicted that even fewer females would meet the criteria. As a result of these small cell sizes, it was not meaningful to test the significance of sex-difference interaction terms because the null hypotheses could be 'confirmed' falsely as a result of low statistical power. Therefore, we did not attempt tests involving LCP females. Instead, we simply present the males' and females' mean scores on risk factors for visual inspection of effect sizes in figure 16.1 for the LCP path and in figure 16.2 for the AL path.

Table 16.1 gives details of group means and standard deviations, shows group differences that could be tested with adequate power, and notes which measures had mean-level differences between cohort males and females. Because the groups were defined using norms for the full cohort, the figures and the table show risk factors plotted as z scores standardized on the full cohort with a mean of 0 and *SD* of 1. Thus, each group's mean z score indicates how far that group deviates from the mean score for the representative sample (0), a mean which can be interpreted as a normative standard. The distance in *SD* units between the group's mean and the normative zero may be interpreted as the effect size (Cohen, 1988).

Results

How many females were on the life-course persistent path?

Gender-neutral group assignment yielded for the adolescence-limited path: 122 males (26 per cent) and 78 females (18 per cent). On the life-course persistent path were 6 females (1 per cent of females) and 47 males (10 per cent). Thus, consistent with the expectations from the theory, the male-to-female ratio for the LCP path was 10:1, whereas the sex ratio for the AL path was 1.5:1.

Do females and males on the same subtype path share the same risk background?

If the taxonomy applies to females as well as to males, we should observe the following three patterns in figures 16.1 and 16.2: (a) both males and females on the LCP path should deviate from the cohort norm on the risk factors; (b) both males and females on the AL path should score near the norm (z score $= 0$) on the childhood risk factors. (c) Both males and females on the AL path should deviate from the norm on peer delinquency. Visual inspection of figures 16.1 and 16.2 reveals that the data are generally consistent with the three patterns expected by the theory.

Consistent with the aforementioned pattern (a), figure 16.1 shows that the forty-seven males and six females on the LCP path were more similar to each other than different on most risk factors. Notably, the LCP-path girls were almost as extreme on fighting at ages 5 to 11 relative to the full sample as were LCP-path males, confirming that these girls were physically aggressive before adolescence. The pattern of means across measures within the LCP-path females was somewhat less consistent than the pattern within LCP-path males, but some of this inconsistency may be ascribed to the ease with which a variable's mean can be influenced in a group of only six individuals. One pattern seemed consistent enough to be noteworthy: LCP-path females stood apart from LCP-path males by having mothers whose parenting was rated by observers as average, who reported few mental health problems, and who were no more likely to be single than the average Study mother.

Comparison of figure 16.1 with figure 16.2 shows that LCP-path members of both sexes tended to have worse levels of risk than their counterparts on the AL path. LCP-path males scored worse than the average Study member, and worse compared to AL-path males, on every measure excepting the Peabody Picture Vocabulary test at age 3. Effect sizes were at least small, and many were medium. Contrasts of the difference between LCP-path males and AL-path males revealed that LCP-path males scored significantly worse on twenty of the twenty-six risk measures (table 16.1, sixth column, note b). Likewise, LCP-path females scored worse on most of the measures than the average Study member, and worse compared to AL-path females.

Consistent with the aforementioned predicted pattern (b), both girls and boys on the AL path generally showed mean levels of risk that were near-normative for the sample (see figure 16.2). When exceptions to this normative pattern arose for AL-path males, the exceptions reflected unusually low risk, that is, AL-path boys were *less likely* to be rejected by peers than the cohort average. When exceptions to this normative pattern arose for AL-path females, the exceptions also reflected unusually low risk. This generally occurred because there are mean-level sex differences on the risk factor; that is, relative to the sample norm AL-path girls were better readers, less hyperactive, and less likely to fight, because girls in general score better than boys on these variables (table 16.1, note a). Contrasts revealed that AL-path

Table 16.1. *Male and female Dunedin Study members on the life-course-persistent and adolescence-limited paths, compared on risk factors for delinquency*

	Life-course-persistent		Adolescence-limited		Contrast: LCP males vs. AL males	Contrast: AL females vs. AL males	Contrast: LCP males vs. AL females
	Males	Females	Males	Females			
Group N	47	6	122	78			
	Mean Z-score (SD)						
Family Risk factors (age)							
Parents' criminal conviction	0.20±1.1	0.20±1.3	−0.01±1.0	0.15±1.1			
Mother's age at her first birth	−0.47±0.9	−0.20±1.2	0.02±1.1	−0.36±0.9	b	d	
Mother–child observation (3)	0.32±1.1	−0.04±1.0	0.01±0.9	0.05±1.3	b		
Harsh discipline (7–9)[a]	0.41±0.9	0.46±1.2	0.17±1.2	0.01±1.1			e
Inconsistent discipline (7–9)	0.45±1.1	0.58±1.7	0.01±0.9	0.25±1.0	b		
Moos family conflict (7–9)	0.54±1.1	0.42±0.9	0.16±1.0	0.12±1.0	b		e
Mother's mental health (7–11)	0.70±1.2	−0.41±0.7	−0.16±0.8	0.08±1.0	b		e
Care-giver changes (birth–11)	0.47±1.3	0.15±1.2	0.00±1.0	0.09±1.0	b		e
Years single parent (birth–11)	0.37±1.3	0.12±1.0	−0.02±0.8	0.20±1.2	b		e
Family SES (birth–15)	−0.44±0.9	−0.35±1.0	−0.02±1.0	−0.17±1.0	b		
Child neuro-cognitive risk factors							
Neurological abnormality (3)[a]	0.21±1.2	0.43±1.8	−0.01±0.9	−0.09±0.9			e
Bayley motor test (3)	−0.17±1.0	0.26±0.7	0.08±0.8	0.12±0.8			e
Peabody Vocabulary (3)	−0.02±0.9	−0.82±0.8	0.07±1.0	0.02±0.9			
Binet IQ (5)[a]	−0.34±0.8	−0.05±1.2	−0.03±1.0	0.17±0.9	b		
WISC-R VIQ (7, 9, 11)	−0.31±0.9	−0.35±1.0	0.13±1.0	0.02±0.9	b		
Reading (7, 9, 11)[a]	−0.46±1.0	−0.42±0.9	0.01±1.0	0.26±0.9	b	c	e
Neuropsych. memory (13)[a]	−0.48±1.2	0.05±0.9	−0.11±1.0	0.10±1.0	b		e
Heart rate (7, 9, 11)[a]	−0.46±1.0	−0.42±0.9	0.01±1.0	0.26±0.9			e

Child temperament-behaviour risk factors

Difficult to manage (2)	0.41±0.9	0.28±0.0	−0.03±1.0	0.07±0.9	[b] [e]
Undercontrol observed (3)[a]	0.33±1.2	0.83±2.2	−0.03±0.9	−0.07±1.0	[b] [e]
Hyperactive (parent) (5–11)[a]	1.04±1.1	0.65±1.2	−0.08±1.0	−0.15±0.9	[b] [e]
Hyperactive (teacher) (5–11)[a]	1.36±1.1	1.02±1.5	0.06±0.9	−0.31±0.7	[b] [c] [e]
Fighting (parent) (5–11)[a]	1.08±0.9	0.81±0.7	0.05±0.9	−0.01±0.8	[b] [e]
Fighting (teacher) (5–11)[a]	1.34±1.2	1.13±0.9	0.03±0.9	−0.31±0.7	[b] [c] [e]
Peer rejection (parent) (5–11)	0.97±1.3	0.75±1.6	−0.25±0.7	−0.15±0.7	[b] [e]
Peer rejection (teacher) (5–11)	0.93±1.4	0.81±0.8	−0.10±0.8	−0.26±0.7	[b] [e]

Peer delinquency in adolescence

Delinquent peers (13)[a]	0.59±1.3	0.52±1.0	0.50±1.0	0.11±1.0	[c] [e]
Delinquent peers (18)[a]	0.55±1.0	0.44±0.8	0.64±1.0	0.49±1.0	

Delinquency in adolescence Mean variety-score (SD)

Variety of offences (15)	8.3±7.0	7.6±2.1	7.3±7.3	8.4±5.7
Variety of offences (18)[a]	11.7±6.2	5.1±5.1	11.1±5.3	7.3±4.7

Notes: N=922 for every variable except parents' criminal conviction, where N=870 (see Moffitt and Caspi, 2001).

[a] In the full cohort, the boys' mean score showed significantly worse level of risk on this variable than girls' mean score, all planned contrast t (912) > 2.5, all p<0.05.

[b] LCP-path males scored significantly worse than AL-path males on 20 of the 26 childhood risk measures, all planned contrast t (912) > 1.9, all p<0.05.

[c] AL-path females actually scored significantly better than AL-path males on 3 of the 26 childhood risk measures, all planned contrast t (912) > 2.5, all p<0.05.

[d] AL-path females scored significantly worse than AL-path males on only 1 of the 26 childhood risk measures, planned contrast t (912) = 2.17, p<0.05.

[e] LCP-path males scored significantly worse than AL-path females on 19 of the 26 childhood risk measures, all planned contrast t (912) >1.7, all p<0.05.

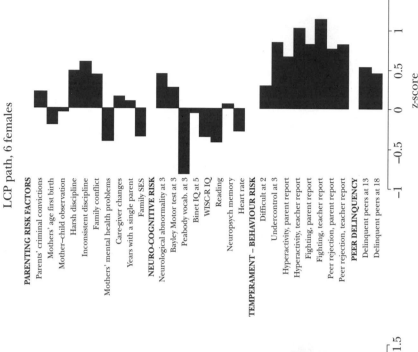
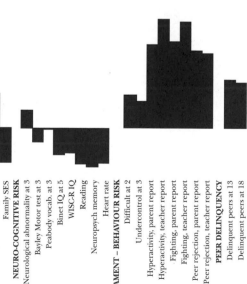

16.1 Risk factors for LCP males and females

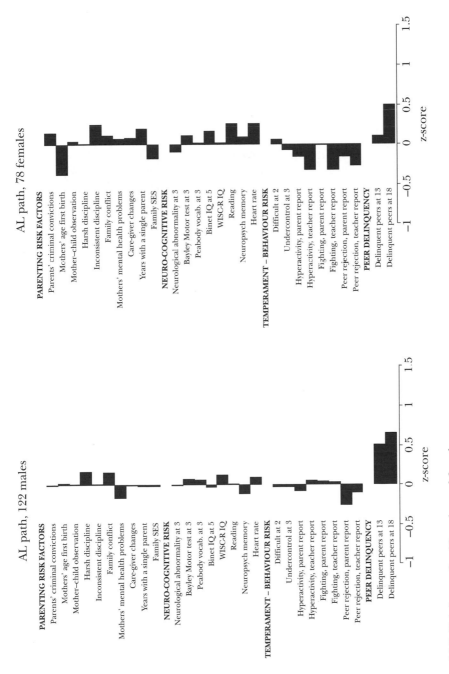

16.2 Risk factors for AL males and females

females did not score significantly worse than AL-path males on any of the twenty-six risk measures excepting one: AL-path females had mothers who were younger the first time they gave birth (table 16.1). However, these adolescent-onset girls' backgrounds did not otherwise resemble the high-risk backgrounds of childhood-onset males. Contrasts of the difference between AL-path females and LCP-path males revealed that AL-path females scored significantly better on nineteen of the twenty-six risk measures (table 16.1, note *e*).

Consistent with the predicted pattern (c), regardless of their sex, AL-path offenders knew a lot more delinquent peers than the average Dunedin cohort member.

There is one final requirement before concluding that the group differences shown in figures 16.1 and 16.2 are consistent with the theory. It is important to establish that the LCP-path and AL-path groups showed similar levels of participation in delinquency as adolescents. This is important because the theory specifies that LCP and AL types have *different* mean levels of risk factors despite exhibiting *similar* elevated levels of delinquent offending. The bottom two rows of table 16.1 reveal that the LCP- and AL-path males were well matched on offending at age 15 and age 18. (The two rows also show the expected increase in offending from age 15 to age 18 among males.) We have previously shown that the two path groups did not differ during adolescence on police arrests or court convictions (Moffitt *et al.*, 1996). The bottom rows of table 16.1 also reveal that the LCP and AL females were well matched on offending. (The two rows also show the oft-reported female pattern of a peak in delinquent involvement at age 15 followed by a decrease by age 18; for a review of studies see chapter 4.) Both female groups matched both male groups at age 15; all four delinquent groups reported approximately 7–8 different offence types then, which was approximately 1 SD more than the normative Study member. Therefore, even though life-course persistent and adolescence-limited offenders were well matched on levels of extreme antisocial involvement as teenagers, both males and females differed on their profiles of background risk factors.

Do young people on the life-course-persistent path have more problematic adult outcomes than young people on the adolescence-limited delinquent path?

We compared the life-course-persistent versus adolescence-limited offenders on an index of adult adjustment that comprised many of the young-adult outcomes already described in chapter 13. Specifically, one point each was summed for a conviction for violent crime, a conviction for non-violent crime, a diagnosis of substance dependence, a diagnosis for a mental disorder, perpetration of partner abuse, no high-school qualification, dependence on government welfare benefits, long-term unemployment of more than six months, and having a child outside marriage. Results are shown in figure 16.3.

The left panel of figure 16.3 shows as a comparison standard the percentage of the full birth cohort having present data (n = 902). Approximately two-thirds of the cohort had no problem outcome or only one problem outcome, and only 4 per cent of the cohort suffered severe impairment with six or more problems. The circumstances of the AL men and women were worse compared to the full cohort; having one to three problem outcomes seemed normative for the adolescence-limited offenders. Compared to the full cohort, twice as many of them (8 per cent) were in the range of severely impaired function with six or more problems.

Only two of the six women who had been on the LCP pathway experienced multiple poor outcomes. Surprised by this, we explored the data archive on a case by case basis for the four women reporting no problems, or one problem, to learn more about them. We found that all four of them had sub-threshold problems (e.g., drink-driving or public intoxication but not substance dependence; financial distress or conflicts with employers but not long-term unemployment; early motherhood but married). All four women reported that religion had become very important in their lives. This group is too small to support conclusions, but instead it suggests hypotheses to test in larger female samples.

The LCP men, shown on the right panel of figure 16.3, had the most troubled outcomes among the groups. Although it is hopeful that one-quarter of these men had no or only one problem outcome, their rate of success was lower than the success rate for their adolescence-limited counterparts. Compared to the full cohort, five times as many LCP men (20 per cent) were in the range of severely impaired function with six or more problems. ANOVA tests of mean group differences on the problem index with planned contrasts revealed that the LCP men, AL men, and AL women all had elevated problems relative to the rest of the cohort, and the LCP men had significantly more problems on average than the AL males (all $p < 0.01$).

Comment: the developmental typology fits both sexes

Findings in this chapter suggest that the taxonomy describes parsimoniously the antisocial development of both males and females. Moreover, as predicted, the sex difference is very large for the life-course-persistent form of antisocial behaviour (10:1 in this sample) whereas the sex difference is negligible for the adolescence-limited form (1.5:1).

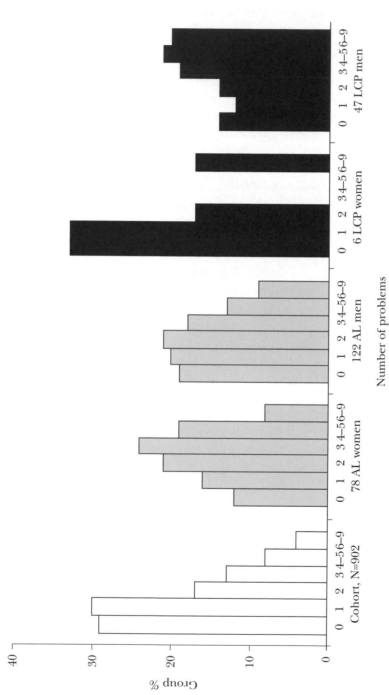

16.3 Young adult problems of AL and LCP delinquents

Only a few studies have tested the taxonomy while including sex comparisons, but it appears that our findings about females are broadly consistent with previous studies. In the Christchurch sample (n = 1,000), a single model described male and female trajectories of antisocial behaviour, and the male to female ratio was 4:1 for early-onset, versus only 2:1 for late-onset subjects (Fergusson, Horwood, and Nagin, 2000; Fergusson and Horwood, forthcoming). Kratzer and Hodgins (1999), studying a Swedish cohort (n = 13,000), found similar childhood risk factors for males and females in the LCP group, and the male to female ratio was 15:1 for early onset, versus only 4:1 for late-onset subjects. Mazerolle *et al.* (2000), studying a Philadelphia cohort (n = 3,655), reported that early onset signalled persistent and diverse offending for males and females alike. Tibbetts and Piquero (1999), studying a Philadelphia cohort (n = 987), found too few females on the LCP path to study their backgrounds with adequate statistical power. The evidence from studies of representative cohorts is fairly consistent in showing that females are seldom childhood-onset or LCP-type.

We suggest that the theories we have articulated about the origins of life-course-persistent and adolescence-limited offending are explanatory across the sexes and apply irrespective of sex. According to one of the theories, life-course-persistent antisocial behaviour emerges when inherited or acquired neuro-developmental vulnerabilities are present in childhood and promote transactions with criminogenic environments. The rarity of female life-course-persistent offenders follows from our observation in chapter 9 that females experience lower levels of neuro-cognitive deficit, undercontrolled temperament, and hyperactivity. According to the other theory, adolescence-limited antisocial behaviour emerges in teenagers who do not have neuro-developmental vulnerabilities, because these young people mimic antisocial peers in an effort to cope with their dysphoria in the maturity gap. The ubiquity of adolescence-limited offenders among females follows from our observations in chapters 4, 5, and 14 that females are most antisocial soon after puberty, and when they are under the influence of relationships with males, who are more antisocial than females on average. In other words, no special female-specific theory is needed.

This chapter focused on childhood characteristics that distinguish life-course persistent from adolescence-limited offenders, but a brief look at the offenders' young-adult adjustment showed the life-course-persistent males to be faring especially poorly, with half of them suffering four or more signs of difficulty, such as a criminal record, long-term unemployment, psychiatric or substance-dependence diagnosis, no educational qualifications or fathering an out-of-wedlock child. Elsewhere we have reported in more detail the characteristics that distinguish the groups during adolescence and young adulthood. Our studies of outcomes in adolescence have shown that the life-course persistent path is differentially associated in males with weak bonds to family, early school leaving, and psychopathic personality traits of alienation, impulsivity, and callousness (Moffitt *et al.*, 1996), and poor scores on neuropsychological tests (Moffitt *et al.*, 1994), as well as conviction for violent crimes (Jeglum-Bartusch *et al.*, 1997; Moffitt *et al.*, 1996). In contrast, we found that the adolescence-limited path is differentially associated in adolescence with delinquent peers (Jeglum-Bartusch *et al.*, 1997), with a tendency to endorse unconventional values, with a personality trait called social potency (Moffitt *et al.*, 1996), and with non-violent delinquent offences (Jeglum-Bartusch *et al.*, 1997). Followed up to adulthood, males on the life-course persistent path scored more extremely than adolescence-limited males on psychopathic personality traits, mental-health problems, substance dependence, numbers of children, financial problems, work problems, and drug-related and violent crimes, including violence against children and women (Moffitt *et al.*, forthcoming). As adults, Dunedin males on the adolescence-limited path scored less extremely, but nonetheless had problems with mental health, substance dependence, financial woes, and property offences (Moffitt *et al.*, forthcoming). More research is needed on the adolescent and adult outcomes of girls on the two pathways.

All of the components of the two developmental theories have not yet been tested, and more evaluation is needed. Here, for the purpose of addressing sex differences, we compared dichotomous groups defined via simple clinical cut-offs. However, the theory does not require dichotomous groups; others have tested aspects of the theory using continuously distributed measures to capture the main features that distinguish the two developmental paths, such as age of onset of antisocial behaviour, persistence across years, or extent of recidivistic violence (Tibbets and Piquero, 1999; Jeglum-Bartusch *et al.*,1997). Our own studies have operationalized the two prototypes of antisocial behaviour using varying statistical models, including clinical comparison groups (Moffitt, 1990b; Moffitt *et al.*, 1996; Moffitt and Caspi, 2001; Moffitt *et al.*, forthcoming), repeated-measures multiple regression (Moffitt, Lynam, and Silva, 1994), confirmatory factor analysis (Jeglum-Bartusch *et al.*, 1997), and trajectory modelling (Nagin, Farrington, and Moffitt, 1995). A variety of data-analysis approaches can and should be used to stretch the theory and reveal its limitations.

Comment: more research is needed about the adolescent-onset path

Most research on the taxonomy to date has focused on testing hypotheses about the aetiology of life-course persistent offenders. Findings that this group can be distinguished in the early years of life have garnered much attention, contributing to the current enthusiasm for early-childhood interventions. Unfortunately, adolescence-limited offenders have been relegated to the status of a contrast group and the original hypothesis about the distinct aetiology of adolescent-onset offending has not captured the research imagination (but see Brezina, 2000; Bukowski *et al.*, 2000; Zebrowitz *et al.*, 1998). This is unfortunate, because adolescent-onset offenders are quite common (one-quarter of both males and females, as defined in this study), and they are not benign.

Aguilar *et al.* (2000) discovered that adolescent-onset youths experienced elevated internalizing symptoms and perceptions of stress at age 16, bringing a fresh emphasis to the taxonomy's assertion that these adolescents experience dysphoria. Fergusson *et al.* (2000) pointed out that a normative developmental history is not necessarily a salutary developmental history, and that the normative, moderate levels of risk in the backgrounds of adolescence-limited youngsters may leave them without protection against delinquent peer influence. Kratzer and Hodgins (1999) drew attention to the risk of criminal conviction in adulthood for people with late-onset offending. We have shown that the antisocial behaviour of adolescence-limited offenders is not inconsequential; in fact, it exposes them to numerous snares during the adolescent years, for example, leaving school without credentials, becoming a teen parent, developing dependency on tobacco, drugs or alcohol, serious injury, sexually transmitted diseases, a criminal record, and incarceration (Moffitt *et al.*, 1996). Such snares can compromise their ability to make a successful transition to adulthood, impair their health, and set in motion a snowball of cumulative disadvantage (Moffitt, 1993a; Moffitt *et al.*, forthcoming; see also chapters 13 and 14). This chapter showed that young adult men and women on the adolescence-limited path were not as severely impaired as life-course persistent males, but nevertheless most of them entered young adulthood with one to three significant life difficulties. Almost all females who engage in antisocial behaviour fit the adolescence-limited path, and their adult outcomes can be very poor (chapter 13; Robins, 1986).

The theory of adolescence-limited antisocial behaviour regards it as an adaptation response to modern teenagers' social context, not as the product of a cumulative history of pathological mal-development. Nonetheless, it specifies that adolescence-limited behaviour often attracts harmful consequences, and it does not presume that the problems of adolescence-limited offenders will remit spontaneously without remediation efforts (Moffitt *et al.*, 1996). Legal scholars point out that harsh sentencing applied to adolescence-limited delinquents incurs societal costs, including damaged future employment prospects and delayed desistence from crime. These scholars call for juvenile justice policy that gives adolescence-limited delinquents 'room to reform' (Scott and Grisso, 1997, p. 180). This book and our previous report (Moffitt *et al.*, 1996) have shown that young people on the adolescent-onset path do not have a pathological history, problem personalities, low IQ, reading failure, inadequate parents, or broken attachment relationships, suggesting that they should be ideal candidates for intervention. Therefore, we hope this book will stimulate more research to improve knowledge about the adolescence-limited developmental path.

Take-home messages

- The female life-course-persistent antisocial individual is extremely rare. Approximately 1 in 100 females in a birth cohort appear to be on the life-course-persistent path. The sex ratio is 10 males to 1 female.
- Females and males on the life-course-persistent path share similar risk factors of poor discipline, family adversity, cognitive deficit, undercontrolled temperament, hyperactivity, and rejection by peers.
- Almost all females who engage in antisocial behaviour best fit the adolescence-limited type. The sex ratio is 1.5 males to 1 female.
- Males on the life-course-persistent path suffer from multiple poor outcomes as young adults, and young people on the adolescence-limited path have some poor outcomes as well.

Unanswered questions

- Why do fewer females than males suffer the primary individual-level risk factors for life-course-persistent antisocial behaviour?
- What causal processes explain adolescent-onset antisocial behaviour among both boys and girls?

CHAPTER SEVENTEEN

Priorities for a research agenda

This final chapter integrates the findings in this book. Tables 17.1 to 17.4 summarize the 'take-home' messages from the various studies conducted for this book, and in the following paragraphs we extract unifying themes from these findings to develop recommendations for future research. Based on the findings in this report, two high-priority areas for future research suggest themselves. These priorities are: (a) research into a set of critical individual-level neuro-developmental factors, and (b) research into a set of influential social contexts. These two priority areas map at least partly on to the typology of life-course persistent and adolescence-limited antisocial behaviour that was presented in chapter 16. On the one hand, a consequential few male offenders (and the rare female) exhibit the life-course persistent pattern. When the objective is to understand the origins of this persistent serious form of antisocial behaviour, this chapter will direct scientific attention toward the neuro-developmental factors that account for the male excess of antisocial behaviour. On the other hand, the majority of male offenders and virtually all female offenders appear to share the adolescence-limited pattern. When the objective is to understand the origins of this situational form of antisocial participation, this chapter will direct scientific attention toward social-context factors that can make females act antisocially along with males. In both cases, the chapter may be read as a template for harnessing sex differences to articulate hypotheses about the origins of problem behaviour.

Drawing this book to its close, we found it useful to reflect on why we first embarked on this study of sex differences in antisocial behaviour. We knew that the sex difference was the most robust fact known about antisocial behaviour, suggesting to us that it must be an important topic of enquiry. As

Table 17.1. *What have we learned about sex differences? a summary of the major findings*

That males fare worse than females:

On diagnosed conduct disorder . . .
- The sex ratio for the lifetime prevalence of antisocial disorder appears to be about 2.4 males to one female, across studies using different methods and different samples.
- More males than females have diagnosed conduct disorder at every age.
- Although antisocial girls retain their rank across time relative to their sex, just as boys do, girls are less likely than boys to sustain behaviour extreme enough to warrant a diagnosis. Males show much more continuity of diagnosed disorder than females.

On serious and violent behaviours . . .
- Males exhibit more physical aggression and violence than females at every age.
- At every age, more males than females are beginning the onset of theft and violence.
- High-rate offending is concentrated among a few members of the population for females as it is for males, but even the most active females offend at a rate much lower than the most active males.
- Males' antisocial behaviour is more often officially sanctioned, probably because it is more frequent and more serious.

On exposure to risk factors . . .
- Males have higher rates than females of the most important risk factors for antisocial behaviours, including more compromised neuro-cognitive status, more hyperactivity, and more peer problems.
- Males have more Negative Emotionality and less Constraint on average than females, and these are the very personality traits that are associated with antisocial behaviour.
- The findings support the hypothesis that males are more likely to be antisocial than females because they are exposed to greater levels of individual and social risk for antisocial behaviour.

On developmental pathways . . .
- The female life-course-persistent antisocial individual is extremely rare. When males and females are held to the same criteria, fewer than 1 in 100 females in a cohort are on the life-course persistent path. The male:female ratio is 10:1. This rarity follows naturally from the low base rates of risk factors for persistent antisocial behaviour among females.
- Almost all females who engage in antisocial behaviour best fit the adolescence-limited type. The male:female ratio is 1.5:1.

Table 17.1. (*cont.*)

That males fare worse than females (*cont.*):
• Males on the life-course-persistent path suffer from multiple poor outcomes as young adults, and young people on the adolescence-limited path have some poor outcomes as well.
That females fare worse than males:
On adult depression . . .   • For females, major depression frequently follows conduct problems. The depression of females with an antisocial history grows more severe as they enter adulthood.

Table 17.2. *What have we learned about sex similarities? A summary of the major findings*

That the sexes resemble each other:

During the peri-pubertal period . . .
- Males and females are most alike in their antisocial behaviour during middle adolescence, at around age 15.
- During the peri-pubertal period for females, their prevalence and incidence of conduct disorder rises to produce the narrowest gap between the sexes (and smallest sex ratio) seen at any time in the life course.

On two particular kinds of antisocial behaviour . . .
- Males and females are similar in their drug- and alcohol-related offences, and, at every age, males and females tend to begin in approximately the same numbers to engage in drug- and alcohol-related offences.
- On measures of partner abuse, the physically violent behaviour of males is matched or exceeded by that of females.
- The sex similarity on partner violence appears to be robust, applies to clinically significant couples whose abuse is injurious, treated, and/or adjudicated, and cannot be explained by the hypothesis that women's aggression is self-defense.

On age of onset . . .
- Among young people who do begin antisocial behaviour before adulthood, age of onset is markedly similar between the sexes. Antisocial males and females onset within six months of each other.

On stability of individual differences in antisocial behaviour . . .
- Parent-, teacher-, and self-ratings reveal positive and moderate cross-time correlations for both sexes, suggesting that the antisocial behaviour of males and females is predictable across time.
- Over the first two decades of life, *relative to their same-sex peers*, antisocial males and females are equally likely to retain their standing in the distribution of individual differences in antisocial behaviour. Both sexes show at least moderate stability.

On which risk factors explain antisocial behaviour . . .
- The same risk factors predict antisocial behaviour in both males and females: we did not detect any replicable sex-specific risk factors for antisocial behaviour.
- Family adversity, compromised intelligence, difficult temperament and hyperactivity have somewhat stronger effects on males' than on females' antisocial behaviour, but these sex differences in association are relatively small and, at best, offer only weak support to the hypothesis that males are more vulnerable than females to risk factors for antisocial behaviour.

Table 17.2. (*cont.*)

That the sexes resemble each other (*cont.*):

- The personality trait correlates of antisocial behaviour are the same for males and females.
- Females and males on the life-course persistent path share similar risk factors of family adversity, poor discipline, cognitive deficit, rejection by peers, and hyperactivity.

On comorbid conditions . . .
- The sexes are more similar than different in their comorbidity patterns across disorders and ages.
- Comorbid disorders commonly appear alongside conduct disorder, for both males and females; only 10 per cent of lifetime conduct disorder cases are 'pure.'
- The disorders most often found co-occurring with conduct disorder among both males and females are anxiety, depression, substance dependence, ADHD, and reading retardation.

On the adult consequences of antisocial behaviour . . .
- The data provide no support for the hypothesis that a history of antisocial behaviour has fewer consequences for females than for males. Antisocial behaviour has disruptive effects on both females and males as they make the transition from adolescence to adulthood.
- Increasing numbers of symptoms of conduct disorder predict increasingly poor young adult outcomes, irrespective of gender.
- Both males and females who were antisocial adolescents are likely as adults to form intimate unions with members of the opposite sex who are involved in crime and who hold attitudes that encourage antisocial behaviour.

Table 17.3. *What have we learned about measurement? A summary of the major findings*

Lessons for measurement:

On measuring age at onset of antisocial behaviour . . .

• Estimates of the age at which antisocial behaviour begins will vary widely when different sources of data are consulted. For both males and females, onset measured via conviction data will lag three to five years behind onset measured via self-report interviews. Official data may be used to study individual differences in age of onset, but official data give an inaccurate picture of actual onset and they should not be used for this purpose.

• Self-report data reveal that adult onset of antisocial behaviour de novo after adolescence is extremely rare among both men and women.

On diagnosing conduct disorder . . .

• DSM criteria cut-offs for a diagnosis of conduct disorder appear to be somewhat arbitrary points along a continuum of severity.

• The best number of symptoms for making a diagnosis may vary by setting. It is important to take into account features of clinical or research settings that make it easy or difficult to ascertain symptoms.

• Most of the analyses in this book were repeated using two ways of measuring antisocial behaviour: continuously distributed scales and categorical diagnoses. Overall, the findings were the same regardless of which measure was used, and there was no indication here of an incremental validity for the diagnostic approach to measurement. (Diagnostic categories did give the impression that the conduct problems of girls are not stable, but this finding emerged from a population shift rather than a lack of stable individual differences: the severity of conduct problems did shift for girls as a group which changed the number of girls who passed the diagnostic cutoff, but nevertheless each girl retained her rank in the distribution of conduct problems within the sample of girls.)

On a syndrome of related disorders . . .

• Two thirds of young people who develop ADHD, marijuana dependence, and schizophreniform symptoms also experience conduct disorder, making these four disorders virtually part and parcel of an antisocial syndrome in adolescence/young adulthood.

Table 17.4. *What have we learned about theory and research? A summary of the major findings*

Lessons for theory and research:

On accounting for the sex difference in antisocial behaviour . . .
- The selection of risk measures available in the Dunedin archive were able to account for most of the reliable variation in the antisocial behaviour of both males and females.
- Sex differences in early-emerging undercontrolled temperament and hyperactivity problems can account for over one-third of the sex difference in antisocial behaviour.
- Sex differences in peer relationships can account for one-quarter of the sex difference in antisocial behaviour.
- Sex differences in personality traits can account for almost all of the sex differences observed in antisocial behaviour.
- Family adversity risk factors affect boys and girls alike, and therefore cannot account for the more serious antisocial behaviour of males.

On the importance of developmental contexts . . .
- *Puberty as a context:* During the peri-pubertal period for females, the prevalence and incidence of conduct problems rises to the highest level for females at any time in the life course.
- *Older peers as a context:* Females behave most like males in their drug- and alcohol-related offenses, which may emerge because girls have opportunities to obtain substances via older peers.
- *Intimate relationships as a context:* Unless a young woman pairs off with an antisocial man, her own antisocial behaviour is unlikely to persist into adulthood, but young women who pair off with antisocial men remain engaged in criminal activities as adults. In the specific case when violence happens inside the intimate relationship, the violent behaviour of females matches that of males.
- *Gender roles as contexts:* We observed gender-stereotyped outcomes during the transition to young adulthood. In particular, antisocial behaviour among young men is significantly more likely to be associated with subsequent problems in work, substance abuse, and legal arenas whereas antisocial behaviour among young women is significantly more likely to be associated with relationship problems, depression, suicidality, and poor physical health.

Table 17.4. (*cont.*)

Lessons for theory and research (*cont.*):

On hypotheses that female antisocial behaviour warrants special status . . .

- The threshold/gender paradox hypothesis finds no support in this sample. When compared to males, females with conduct disorder do not have more comorbid disorders, worse family backgrounds, more severe neuro-cognitive problems, more extreme hyperactivity, or more antisocial, unemotional, or callous personalities.
- Although fewer females than males indeed become antisocial, females do not pass a higher threshold that requires a stronger aetiological press. Rather, fewer females become antisocial, despite having the same threshold as males, because they experience lower levels of risk factors exerting the same or weaker aetiological press.
- The recommendation to relax the diagnostic criteria for conduct disorder for females is not supported by our systematic test of the predictive validity of subclinical symptoms.
- Although all of the components of our taxonomic theory of life-course persistent and adolescent-limited antisocial behaviour have not yet been tested, so far it appears that the theory, as originally formulated, can parsimoniously describe the antisocial development of both males and females.

On the inter-generational transmission of antisocial behaviour . . .

- Adolescent antisocial males and females form intimate relationships with partners who engage in crime, have less education, are poorer readers, and who abuse them physically. Such cross-trait assortative mating promotes socioeconomic problems for young families and endangers the physical health of women in them.
- Antisocial males and females selectively reproduce at a young age, with an antisocial mate. Conduct disordered study members were one fifth of the sample, but they produced two-thirds of the offspring born to Dunedin cohort members as teen parents.
- The twin roles of assortative mating and selective reproduction must be taken into account when investigating the persistence of antisocial behaviour across the life course and across generations, and females should be included in developmental studies to build knowledge about the aetiology of antisocial behaviour.

expected, the research in this book confirmed that, in general, females are less antisocial than males. Like all others before us, we found that fewer females exhibit antisocial behaviour, those who do exhibit it do so less frequently, and females' antisocial behaviour is less serious (chapters 3, 4, and 5). However, the sex difference was less universal than we had assumed. At least three remarkable and robust exceptions to the sex difference emerged: females' antisocial behaviour resembles males' (1) when alcohol and drugs are involved (chapter 3), (2) near the time of female puberty (chapter 4), and (3) in intimate relationships with men (chapters 5 and 14). The findings persuaded us that future research can safely turn away from producing more reports of differences between the sexes' levels of antisocial behaviour, because such studies have become commonplace. Instead, research can turn more profitably toward examining the contextual circumstances that promote the exceptional sex similarity in antisocial behaviours associated with puberty, substance use, and heterosexual intimacy.

Beyond the basic fact that there is a sex difference in antisocial behaviour, our research uncovered few sex differences in the causes, correlates, and consequences of antisocial behaviour. For example, the same risk factors promote antisocial behaviour in both males and females; we unearthed no sex-specific risk factors (chapter 8). Moreover, males and females who do participate in antisocial behaviour take it up within months of each other (chapter 7), and thereafter individual differences in participation remain moderately stable for both sexes (chapter 6). In addition, comorbid mental disorders beset most of the people with antisocial behaviour, irrespective of their gender (chapter 11). Finally, both men and women as young adults tend to experience maladjustment that is commensurate with the extent of their past adolescent antisocial involvement (chapter 13), with life-course-persistent males having the poorest adult adjustment (chapter 16). The research in this book did indicate that it is advisable to measure antisocial involvement in studies of female development, as antisocial conduct is a heretofore unappreciated determinant of adult adjustment in three domains that are especially relevant to women: family formation, health, and depression (chapter 13). The nexus of assortative mating for antisocial involvement, early parenthood, and family violence (chapter 14) also requires more study. However, provocative claims in the past about sex differences in the processes causing antisocial behaviour probably arose from studies with limited samples and incomplete statistical testing (Cohen *et al.*, 1995), and continued scientific focus on the search for sex-specific processes causing antisocial behaviour is unlikely to be profitable.

We learned lessons of parsimony from this research. There was certainly no evidence in the data that warrants continued efforts to portray females' antisocial behaviour as somehow obeying different laws from those that apply to males. We join others calling for scientific approaches that transcend sex to search for the most parsimonious explanation for the causes of antisocial behaviour (Giordano and Cernkovitch, 1997; Fergusson, Woodward, and Horwood, forthcoming; Zahn-Waxler, 1993). In this respect the findings suggested that there is no need for continued investigation of the threshold paradox with respect to antisocial behaviour, as conduct-disorder girls do not earn their diagnosis by surmounting a higher threshold of risk (chapter 12). Instead of a paradox in which the least afflicted sex suffers the worst aetiology, our data fit a straightforward notion that the more afflicted sex suffers the worst aetiology. Moreover, further efforts to develop special relaxed diagnostic criteria for females would probably be misplaced, as girls' subclinical conduct disorder symptoms have no special predictive significance that is unshared by boys' (chapter 15). Although both of these hypotheses have proved to be appealing to many scientists and practitioners, our empirical tests turned up no evidence to support them (and our literature review revealed that they were never based on very solid empirical ground). Also with parsimony, we found that the same typology of life-course-persistent and adolescence-limited antisocial behaviour can safely be applied to describe both males and females (chapter 16).

When we began the study, we shared the field's tacit belief that if research could only answer the mystery of why females are antisocial so seldom, the answer would also reveal the magic key to the mystery of why males are antisocial so often. Analyses following this logic did reveal one 'magic key'. The key to understanding the origins of persistent and severe antisocial behaviour that warrants inclusion among mental disorders (i.e., early-onset conduct disorder or antisocial personality disorder), and is found primarily among males, is likely to be the neuro-developmental problems that more often afflict males than females (chapters 8, 9, 10, 16). This link between neuro-developmental risk and persistent, severe male antisocial behaviour has been reported from at least nine studies from six countries (see chapter 16). These findings persuade us that future research into persistent and serious antisocial disorders can safely turn away from a focus on females as a special group, and turn more profitably toward a focus on neuro-developmental problems.

Research priority 1: individual-level neuro-developmental factors

The data showed it is imperative for scientific effort to concentrate on building more basic knowledge about certain key individual-level risk factors for the life-course persistent pattern of antisocial behaviour that selectively afflicts males. One finding that leads us to this conclusion was that in our analyses of different types of antisocial measures the effect size for the sex difference changed in a lawful way. The sex difference was small when we analysed single snapshot ratings of antisocial behaviour, and it widened to moderate when we analysed diagnoses of conduct disorder (which incorporated severity) or a composite of adolescent rating scales (which incorporated pervasiveness across settings and persistence across ages). The sex difference widened to huge when we counted how many males and females were on a path of life-course persistent antisocial behaviour (which incorporated severity, pervasiveness, and persistence from childhood to adulthood); the sex ratio was 10 males per female. In marked contrast, the sex ratio for the adolescence-limited path was only 1.5 males per female. This exercise reminds us that it is specifically the persistent, serious type of antisocial behaviour on which males and females differ; the sexes do not differ as much on lesser forms of antisocial behaviour. This reminder pointed our search for the cause of this sex difference toward the neuro-developmental factors hypothesized to cause the life-course persistent antisocial type.

The Dunedin Study contained a wide variety of risk factors for study, but only a few were shown to have three key features: (a) they predict antisocial behaviour in both sexes, but (b) males are more likely to experience them, and as a result (c) these factors explain the sex difference (chapters 9 and 10). Empirical focus can be narrowed further by adding a fourth key feature: (d) the risk factor predicts antisocial outcomes more strongly among males than females, which suggests greater male vulnerability (chapters 8 and 10). Narrowing the focus in this way promotes just four of the many risk factors we studied to the top of the antisocial research agenda: neuro-cognitive deficits, undercontrolled temperament, a personality trait called weak constraint, and hyperactivity. These neurodevelopmental risk factors that best accounted for the difference between the sexes were also as a rule the same factors that explained the most variation in antisocial behaviour within each sex. This is the case because males suffer greater exposure to the very risk factors that are also the strongest predictors of antisocial behaviour (chapters 8, 9 and 10). We use the term 'neuro-developmental problems' as short-hand to describe the four risk factors (as they doubtless originate both in the brain and in developmental experience), but it is important to note that much more research is needed to understand whether and how these factors might be interrelated at the level of the nervous system.

Among the risk factors that did not emerge in our conceptual analysis as priorities for a research agenda were the numerous parental and family characteristics we studied. This requires comment. We do not imply that families are irrelevant or trivial in the origins of antisocial behaviour. On the contrary, the factors from these domains accounted for a substantial portion of the variation in antisocial outcomes within each sex (chapter 8). However, *what family risk factors cannot do is explain the greater antisocial behaviour of males.* The data showed that family factors predict antisocial behaviour in both sexes (i.e., both sexes are vulnerable) and both sexes are equally exposed to most family risks, and therefore family factors cannot account for the features that distinguish the nature of life-course persistent male antisocial behaviour: (1) the greater prevalence of males who exhibit antisocial behaviour, (2) the higher frequency and broader variety of criminal offending among males who do participate, and (3) the greater seriousness and violence of antisocial behaviours committed by males. Moreover, whereas chapter 9 showed that hyperactive children in adverse homes were at greater risk for later antisocial behaviour than hyperactive children in other homes, this was equally true for both sexes. As such, the antisocial sex difference is not the product of a potentiating effect of family adversity on at-risk boys or a protective effect of healthy families on at-risk girls. Instead, our research demonstrated that girls are exposed to just as much family risks as boys are, but they are less antisocial because they are less likely to suffer from neuro-cognitive deficits, undercontrolled temperament, weak constraint, and hyperactivity (chapters 9 and 10). Research efforts should turn to building a basic understanding of these key neuro-developmental factors.

Obviously, the priority list should remain open to factors we did not study, and we look to other longitudinal studies to check the replicability of the neuro-developmental priority list that has emerged from the Dunedin Study. Nonetheless, it is clear that the four problems of neuro-cognitive deficits, undercontrolled temperament, weak constraint, and attention-deficit hyperactivity constitute a core aetiological risk for the most persistent, severe forms of antisocial behaviour. Much literature already indicates that these four problems are present very early in life and often coincide in the same individuals who have problem behaviours. Our findings suggest further that they are priority keys to understanding the root causes of persistent and serious antisocial behaviour. If low exposure to these risk factors, and less vulnerability to them, explains why females are seldom seriously antisocial, more basic knowledge about these four factors should open doors to preventing antisocial development, especially among males. Science needs to understand exactly how this constellation of factors engenders life-course persistent antisocial behaviour.

We need research to uncover how these four problems are related to each other. We need to understand the root sources of these neuro-developmental problems, and whether they unfold in the course of development in a sequential way. We need to understand why these four problems afflict males so much more than females. We need to look beyond antisocial disorders to ask whether the male excess of other disorders such as reading disabilities, attention-deficit hyperactive disorder, mental retardation, and autism shares the same neuro-developmental explanations. A major research question is whether the relatively rare early-onset, persistent form of antisocial behaviour should be grouped with developmental neuropsychiatric disorders rather than with common social maladaptations of adolescence.

Of course, many research designs will feed into this work, from traditional child-development observations to tools now emerging from neuroscience and genetics. Studies are needed that measure neuro-cognitive functions, undercontrolled temperament, constraint, attention-deficit hyperactivity, reading problems, autism-related traits, and childhood-onset antisocial behaviours in the same samples. The samples should be epidemiological, because a sample must faithfully represent the full population distribution to yield accurate assessments of the interrelatedness of these problems (Berk, 1983). If these epidemiological studies sample twins, they can also yield estimates of how the problems interrelate via genetic as well as environmental processes (Kendler, 1993; Rutter *et al.*, 1997). Extending data collection to the molecular genetic level may further elucidate the male excess of the problem constellation (Plomin and Rutter, 1998), as might incorporating measures of neural development in infancy and childhood (Nelson and Bloom, 1997). The samples should be followed longitudinally. The strong comorbidity among antisocial disorders, schizophreniform symptoms, and substance dependence (observed in chapter 11) suggests that samples should be followed long enough to examine how this constellation emerges. Long-term commitment to life-course longitudinal studies will be required to observe the cumulative construction of a persistent serious anti-social style, as neuro-developmental vulnerabilities are shaped by social experiences (Moffitt, 1993a).

Research priority 2: social contexts as aetiological factors

When 'social contexts' and 'sex differences in antisocial behaviour' are spoken of in the same breath, we almost automatically think of how sex-stereotyped socialization practices generate sex differences in children's behaviour. The commonly understood effect of social context is to make males and females *different* from each other; boys and girls would be similarly aggressive if it were not for parental social contexts in which little girls' aggression is discouraged or even punished, while little boys' aggression is encouraged or at least condoned. In contrast, the research for this book reveals quite an opposite circumstance. We found three special instances where males and females are similar to each other in their antisocial behaviour, instances that are almost certainly attributable to the influences of peer social contexts. Females' antisocial behaviour resembles males' near the time of female puberty, when alcohol and drugs are involved, and in intimate partner relationships with men. These three instances of sex similarity are the only exceptions to the otherwise robust rule that males are always and everywhere more antisocial than females. The three instances are remarkable because the very omnipresence of the sex difference in antisocial behaviour suggests that any factor that can nullify it must be a powerful influence on behaviour indeed. As we discuss next, all three of these social-context effects may constitute instances of the influence of male models on females in the crucibles of mixed-sex groups and heterosexual relationships during adolescence and young adulthood. More generally, these instances illustrate the remarkable power of associations with antisocial others to generate antisocial behaviour.

The first instance in which females' antisocial behaviour resembles males' is during the period immediately following the completion of female puberty. This phenomenon has now been observed in at least ten large-scale studies from six countries (see chapter 4). The female peri-pubertal period takes its contextual importance from the fact that in a school class (or a research sample) containing boys and girls who are all the same chronological age, for a year or two almost all the girls are more developed than almost all the boys. This period occurs between ages 12 and 16, the exact timing depending on factors such as societal modernity and historical period. The social-stimulus value of girls' older appearance seems to exert a powerful press toward antisocial behaviour, perhaps by signalling to older peers or to the girl herself that she looks old enough to join in prohibited activities. We interpret this peri-pubertal similarity as a social-stimulus effect (rather than a direct activating effect of hormones on behaviour) because hormonal activation should affect any child who experiences puberty, whereas research has shown that the effect on antisocial participation is virtually limited to girls, to girls whose pubertal development is unusually early relative to their social maturation, and to girls whose social context provides ample opportunity to interact with male peers (Caspi *et al.*, 1993). This peri-pubertal similarity is temporary, as all studies show that the familiar antisocial sex difference emerges again by age 18, though the reason for this is unknown.

The second instance in which females' antisocial behaviour resembles males' is in drug- and alcohol-related offences, comprised of illicit use, but also in drug-trafficking and offences arising from substance use, such as public drunkenness and disorderly conduct, under-age purchase of alcohol, and driving under the influence of drink. This phenomenon has now been observed in more than fifty large-scale studies from more than fifteen countries (see chapter 3). The drug and alcohol participation of females takes some of its contextual importance from the aforementioned social-stimulus effect of girls' older appearance during adolescence. Perhaps adolescent girls have more opportunities to obtain alcohol and drugs; older peers provide them with illicit intoxicants, males may ply them with intoxicants to smooth the way into romance, and certainly girls deceive licit sellers about their age. On average more constrained and less assertive than typical boys, girls may seek intoxicants for the courage these impart as girls leave their parents' shelter to cope with new social challenges in peer groups and intimate relationships. Perhaps drug- and alcohol-related activities are equal-opportunity offences, accessible to females because, unlike housebreaking, assault, or robbery, substance offences do not require physical size, strength, or intimidation. Ethnographic studies confirm that drug use and trafficking go hand in hand with sex trafficking (Fagan, 1994), the only crime having more female than male participants, and incidentally both substance-related and sex-related offences are special in being 'victimless' crimes. Although some studies show that male–female similarity for substance offending is greatest in the peri-pubertal period, Dunedin data revealed that males and females initiated substance-related offending at the same rate at every age from 13 to 21 (see chapter 7). The phenomenon of sex similarity in substance offences remains unexplained and virtually unexplored.

The third instance in which females' antisocial behaviour resembles males' is in the intimate context of a relationship with a partner. This phenomenon has now been observed in at least twenty large-scale studies from five countries, is robust across reporting sources, and applies to clinically severe cases of abuse (see chapter 5). Until recently the majority of scientific energy has gone into the struggle either to document or discredit the notion that women are aggressive toward their partners, but now that the fact is inescapable that women are aggressive in the context of intimate relationships, attention can turn to uncovering why this is so. Self-defence has been the prominent hypothesis. Although it is certainly true that some women strike men in self-defence, current research shows that female perpetrators' abuse is prospectively predicted by the same behaviour-problem history that predicts male perpetrators' abuse, even after statistical controls for their experience as victims (see chapter 5). This fact renders self-defence inadequate as an explanation for the majority of abusive women (Giordano et al. 1999; Moffitt et al., 2000). Clearly, female domestic violence is a rich and almost unmined topic in need of further investigation.

One hypothesis for why women are aggressive in intimate relationships is a simple extension of the now-classical differential association theory of peer influence on antisocial behaviour (Sutherland and Cressy, 1978). The intimate relationship is one in which a woman becomes tightly yoked to the influence of a male peer 'pacer' and his masculine norms for allowable behaviour. Consistent with a peer-influence effect is the evidence that risk for domestic violence escalates as couples' relationships increase in duration, intimacy and cohesion, and as they move from dating to cohabitation (Magdol et al., 1998). Generally, when criminologists think about the effects of intimate bonds on antisocial behaviour, they envisage that liaisons with women lower men's antisocial behaviour downward toward the female mean (Laub, Nagin, and Sampson, 1998), but there is no inherent reason why liaisons with men should not simultaneously raise women's antisocial behaviour upwards towards the male mean. Indeed, one key finding was that young women's delinquency is strongly exacerbated when they partner with an antisocial mate (chapter 14). Moreover, Dunedin data show that females and males who have an antisocial history are quite likely to pair off selectively, suggesting that partners already share beliefs and experiences about violating the rights and safety of others when they meet. This assortative mating promotes women's crime, but also their partner abuse (chapter 5).

Another hypothesis for why women are aggressive in intimate relationships is an extension of the now-classical rational choice theory of antisocial behaviour (Cornish and Clarke, 1986). The rule not to hit smaller, weaker and younger people is inculcated early and often, but when women feel angry toward a partner the potential target is generally bigger, stronger and older. Therefore, rational considerations of rules that normally deter aggression need not apply. Consistent with this view, in childhood and adolescence both girls and boys are most likely to hit other boys (Cairns and Cairns, 1994). In adulthood both Dunedin women and men expressed the belief that female-to-male physical aggression is unlikely to have the same serious consequences that male-to-female aggression has. Study members were asked what would happen if they hit their partners as hard as they could; 98 per cent of men but only 38 per cent of women thought they could injure their partner, 56 per cent of men but only 4 per cent of women thought their partner would call the police, and 51 per cent of men but only 24 per cent of women thought their partner would hit back. Thus, perhaps aggression is a 'rational choice' for an angry young woman if she believes that she can hit a bigger, stronger, older male with impunity, simultaneously wagering that he will not retaliate because she is smaller, weaker, and younger (Magdol *et al.*, 1997). Young women who encounter men who retaliate may grow wiser as they grow older. This hypothesis that victimization experience produces a within-individual decrease in women's abuse needs to be tested with longitudinal research.

Our observation that females can be made to act as antisocially as males in certain circumstances, even though females generally are not at neurodevelopmental risk, shifts scientific focus away from male–female comparisons on antisocial behaviour as such, and instead focuses on uncovering the secrets behind the power of interpersonal contexts to elicit antisocial behaviour. We use the term 'interpersonal contexts' here as a shorthand way to describe the three situations (as they doubtless involve processes of peer affiliation, emerging sexuality, and male–female intimacy), but it is important to note that much more research is needed to understand whether and how they might be interrelated by common psychological features. All three situations appear on the face of it to involve greater exposure of females to male peer influence, as young people shift from the same-sex peer groups of childhood to mixed-sex peer groups in adolescence (Bukowski, Sippola, and Newcomb, 2000) and thence to the heterosexual intimate dyads of young adulthood, but this hypothesis of male peer influence on females needs more research. The three circumstances associated with elevated female antisocial behaviour are consistent with our contention that virtually all female antisocial involvement is adolescence-limited antisocial behaviour in type, and thus is attributable to effects of a gap between biological and social maturity, and to delinquent peers.

Research that takes as its target the three powerful contextual effects we have identified here will be well situated to identify essential features shared by criminogenic situations, features that promote antisocial behaviour among males as well as females, of all ages. The research designs should be longitudinal, to follow subjects through the processes of initiating antisocial behaviour, but also to find out why they desist. Rather than the traditional design that follows single children, or mother–child dyads, we recommend a sample of opposite-sex siblings in high-risk homes (Tonry, Ohlin, and Farrington, 1991). A sib-pair study would allow the research to take family risk into account, while acknowledging and exploiting the fact that family factors do not account for sex differences in antisocial behaviour. The schedule and timing of assessments should be developmentally informed, with dense data collection around the times of relevant interpersonal transitions (e.g., transition into secondary school), and with the capacity to accommodate individual differences in transitions (pubertal timing, first cohabiting relationship). The measurement ought to be guided by knowledge about the ethology and psychology of adolescent development, going far beyond the usual perfunctory question about 'how many of your friends' engage in delinquency, to measure adolescents' points of view: dreams and fears, attractions and repulsions, opportunities and limitations, beliefs and myths. The ages, sexes, sexuality, and levels of intimacy and commitment in key peer relationships should be ascertained. The enormous power of interpersonal relationships to elicit antisocial acts will not be uncovered by merely counting delinquent peers.

To summarize, we recommend redoubled efforts to understand both individual differences and social contexts. The social-stimulus consequences of females' puberty for their peer relationships, the opportunities and contextual motivations that promote illicit activities surrounding drugs and alcohol, and the special situations of abusive intimate relationships and assortatively mated offender relationships are of key importance, because this constellation of interpersonal circumstances exerts a powerful influence to make the antisocial behaviour of males and females the same.

Neuro-cognitive deficits, undercontrolled temperament, weak constraint, and hyperactivity are of key importance because this constellation of individual differences exerts powerful influences to make the antisocial behaviour of males and females different. Research should investigate why the sexes are neuro-developmentally different and the extent to which neuro-developmental factors influence all disorders that have a male preponderance. More generally, we recommend that researchers investigate the implications of sex differences for understanding disorders beyond antisocial behaviour.

References

Agnew, R. (1985). A revised strain theory of delinquency. *Social Forces, 64,* 151–67.

Aguilar, B., Sroufe, L. A., Egeland, B., and Carlson, E. (2000). Distinguishing the early-onset-persistent and adolescent-onset antisocial behaviour types: From birth to 16 years. *Development and Psychopathology, 12,* 109–32.

American Psychiatric Association (1980). *Diagnostic and Statistical Manual of Mental Disorders,* third edition. Washington, DC: APA.

American Psychiatric Association (1987). *Diagnostic and Statistical Manual of Mental Disorders,* third edition, revised. Washington, DC: APA.

Anderson, J. C., Williams, S. M., McGee, R. O., and Silva, P. A. (1987). DSM-III disorders in preadolescent children – prevalence in a large sample from the general population. *Archives of General Psychiatry, 44,* 69–76.

Angold, A., Costello, E. J., and Erkanli, A. (1999). Comorbidity. *Journal of Child Psychology and Psychiatry, 40,* 57–87.

Archer, D., and McDaniel, P. (1995). Violence and gender: Differences and similarities across societies. In R. B. Ruback and N. A. Weiner (Eds.), *Interpersonal violent behaviours* (pp. 63–87). New York: Springer Publishing Company, Inc.

Archer, J. (2000). Sex differences in aggression between heterosexual partners: A meta-analytic review. *Psychological Bulletin 126,* 651–680.

Armsden, G. C., and Greenberg, M. T. (1987). The inventory of parent and peer attachment: Individual differences and their relationship to psychological well-being in adolescence. *Journal of Youth and Adolescence, 16,* 427–454.

Arnett, J. J. (2000). Emerging adulthood: A theory of development from the late teens through the twenties. *American Psychologist, 55,* 469–480.

Arseneault, L., Moffitt, T. E., Caspi, A., Taylor, P., and Silva, P. A. (2000). Mental disorders and violence in a total birth cohort: Assessing the strength and nature of the association. *Archives of General Psychiatry, 57,* 979–86.

Arseneault, L., Tremblay, R. E., Boulerice, B. and Saucier, J-F. (forthcoming). 'The pathway from birth complications to adolescent violent behaviour'. Unpublished manuscript.

Arseneault, L., Tremblay, R. E., Boulerice, B, Seguin, J. R., and Saucier, J-F. (2000b).

Minor physical anomalies and family adversity as risk factors for adolescent violent delinquency. *American Journal of Psychiatry, 157*, 917–23.

Bachman, R., and Saltzman, L. E. (1995). *Violence against women: Estimates from the redesigned survey.* Washington, DC: US Department of Justice.

Baker, L. A., Mack, W., Moffitt, T. E., and Mednick, S. A. (1989). Etiology of sex differences in property crime in a Danish adoption cohort. *Behavior Genetics, 19,* 355–370.

Bank, L., Dishion, T. J., Skinner, M. L., and Patterson, G. R. (1990). Method variance in structural equation modeling: Living with 'glop'. In G. R. Patterson (ed.), *Depression and aggression in family interaction* (pp. 247–79). Hillsdale, NJ: Lawrence Erlbaum Associates.

Bardone, A. M., Moffitt, T. E., Caspi, A., Dickson, N., and Silva, P. A. (1996). Adult mental health and social outcomes of adolescent girls with depression and conduct disorder. *Development and Psychopathology, 8,* 811–29.

Bardone, A. M., Moffitt, T. E., Caspi, A., Dickson, N., Stanton, W. R., and Silva, P. A. (1998). Adult physical health outcomes of adolescent girls with conduct disorder, depression, and anxiety. *Journal of the American Academy of Child and Adolescent Psychiatry, 37,* 594–601.

Bayley, N. (1969). *The Bayley scale of infant development.* New York: The Psychological Corporation.

Bebbington, P. (1996). The origins of sex differences in depressive disorder: Bridging the gap. *International Review of Psychiatry, 8,* 295–332.

Bell, R. Q., and Chapman, M. (1986). Child effects in studies using experimental or brief longitudinal approaches to socialization. *Developmental Psychology, 22,* 595–603.

Benjamin, J., Ebstein, R., and Belmaker, R. H. (eds.), (forthcoming) *Molecular genetics and the human personality.* Washington, DC: American Psychiatric Press, Inc.

Berk, R. A. (1983). An introduction to sample selection bias in sociological data. *American Sociological Review, 48,* 386–98.

Berkowitz, L. (1989). Frustration-aggression hypothesis: Examination and reformulation. *Psychological Bulletin, 106,* 59–73.

Berman, M. E., Kavoussi, R. J., and Coccaro, E. F. (1997). Neurotransmitter correlates of antisocial personality disorder. In D. Stoff, J. Breiling, and J. Maser (eds.), *Handbook of antisocial behaviour* (pp. 305–13). New York: Wiley.

Bettencourt, B. A., and Miller, N. (1996). Gender differences in aggression as a function of provocation: A meta-analysis. *Psychological Bulletin, 119,* 422–47.

Bilchik, S. (1998). *Serious and violent juvenile offenders.* Washington, DC: US Department of Justice.

Bird, H. R., Gould, M. S., and Staghezza, B. (1992). Aggregating data from multiple informants in child psychiatry epidemiological research. *Journal of the American Academy of Child and Adolescent Psychiatry, 31,* 78–85.

Bjerregaard, B., and Smith, C. (1993). Gender differences in gang participation, delinquency, and substance use. *Journal of Quantitative Criminology, 9,* 329–355.

Block, J. H. (1983). Differential premises arising from differential socialization of the sexes: Some conjectures. *Child Development, 54,* 1335–54.

Blumstein, A., Cohen, J., and Farrington, D. F. (1988). Criminal career research: Its value for criminology. *Criminology, 26,* 1–35.

Blumstein, A., Cohen, J., Roth, J., and Visher, C. (1986). *Criminal careers and career criminals*. Washington, DC: National Academy Press.

Bohman, M., Cloninger, R., von Knorring, A., and Sigvardsson, S. (1984). An adoption study of somatoform disorders. III. *Archives of General Psychiatry, 41*, 872–878.

Bouchard, T. J., Jr. (1994). Genes, environment, and personality. *Science, 264*, 1,700–1.

Brezina, T. (2000). Delinquent problem-solving: An interpretive framework for criminological theory and research. *Journal of Research in Crime and Delinquency, 37*, 3–30.

Brooks-Gunn, J., and Duncan, G. J. (1997). The effects of poverty on children. *Future of Children, 7*, 55–71.

Brown, T. A., and Barlow, D. H. (1992). Comorbidity among anxiety disorders: Implications for treatment and DSM-IV. *Journal of Consulting and Clinical Psychology, 60*, 835–44.

Buchanan, C. M., Becker, J. B., and Eccles, J. S. (1992). Are adolescents the victims of raging hormones: Evidence for activational effects of hormones on moods and behaviour at adolescence. *Psychological Bulletin, 111*, 62–107.

Bukowski, W. M., Sippola, L. K., and Newcomb, A. F. (2000). Variations in patterns of attraction to same-and other-sex peers during early adolescence. *Developmental Psychology. 36*, 147–54.

Burton, V. S., Cullen, F. T., Evans, T. D., Alardi, L. F., and Dunaway, R. G. (1998). Gender, self-control and crime. *Journal of Research in Crime and Delinquency, 35*, 123–47.

Cadoret, R. J., and Cain, C. (1980). Sex differences in predictors of antisocial behaviour in adoptees. *Archives of General Psychiatry, 37*, 1,171–75.

Cadoret, R. J., Yates, W. R., Troughton, E., Woodworth, G., and Stewart, M. A. (1995). Genetic-environmental interaction in the genesis of aggressivity and conduct disorders. *Archives of General Psychiatry, 52*, 916–24.

Cairns, R. B. and Cairns, B. D. (1984). Predicting aggressive patterns in girls and boys: a developmental study. *Aggressive Behaviour, 10*, 227–42.

Cairns, R. B., and Cairns, B. D. (1994). *Lifelines and risks: pathways of youth in our time.* Cambridge University Press.

Campbell, S. B. (1995). Behaviour problems in preschool children: a review of recent research. *Journal of Child Psychology and Psychiatry, 36*, 113–49.

CAN and Council of Europe. (1997). *The 1995 European School Project on Alcohol and Drugs Report.* Strasbourg: Council of Europe Publishing.

Canter, R. J. (1982). Sex differences in self-report delinquency. *Criminology, 20*, 373–93.

Capaldi, D. M., and Clark, S. (1998). Prospective family predictors of aggression toward female partners for young at-risk young men. *Developmental Psychology, 34*, 1175–88.

Caron, C., and Rutter, M. (1991). Comorbidity in child psychopathology: Concepts, issues and research strategies. *Journal of Child Psychology and Psychiatry, 32*, 1063–80.

Caspi, A. (1998). Personality development across the life course. In W. Damon and N. Eisenberg (eds.), *Handbook of child psychology: Vol. 3. Social, emotional, and personality development* (pp. 311–88). New York: Wiley.

Caspi, A. (2000). The child is father of the man: Personality continuities from childhood to adulthood. *Journal of Personality and Social Psychology, 78,* 158–72.

Caspi, A., Begg, D., Dickson, N., Harrington, H., Langley, J. D., Moffitt, T. E., and Silva, P. A. (1997). Personality differences predict health-risk behaviours in young adulthood: Evidence from a longitudinal study. *Journal of Personality and Social Psychology, 73,* 1,052–63.

Caspi, A, Harrington H. L., Milne, B, Amell, J. W., Theodore, R. F., and Moffitt, T. E.. (forthcoming). The human personality shows stability from age 3 to age 26. Unpublished manuscript.

Caspi, A., Henry, B., McGee, R. O., Moffitt, T. E., and Silva, P. A. (1995). Temperamental origins of child and adolescent behaviour problems: From age 3 to age 15. *Child Development, 66,* 55–68.

Caspi, A., and Herbener, E. S. (1990). Continuity and change: Assortative marriage and the consistency of personality in adulthood. *Journal of Personality and Social Psychology, 58,* 250–8.

Caspi, A., Lynam, D., Moffitt, T. E., and Silva, P. A. (1993). Unraveling girls' delinquency: Biological, dispositional, and contextual contributions to adolescent misbehaviour. *Developmental Psychology, 29,* 19–30.

Caspi, A., and Moffitt, T. E. (1991). Individual differences are accentuated during periods of social change: The sample case of girls at puberty. *Journal of Personality and Social Psychology, 61,* 157–68.

Caspi, A., and Moffitt, T. E. (1995). The continuity of maladaptive behaviour: From description to explanation in the study of antisocial behaviour. In D. Cicchetti and D. Cohen (eds.), *Developmental psychopathology* (vol II; pp. 472–511) New York: Wiley.

Caspi, A., Moffitt, T. E., Newman, D. L., and Silva, P. A. (1996). Behavioural observations at age 3 predict adult psychiatric disorders. Longitudinal evidence from a birth cohort. *Archives of General Psychiatry, 53,* 1033–9.

Caspi, A., Moffitt, T. E., Silva, P. A., Stouthamer-Loeber, M., Schmutte, P. S., and Krueger, R. (1994). Are some people crime prone? Replications of the personality-crime relation across nation, gender, race and method. *Criminology, 32,* 301–33.

Caspi, A., Moffitt, T. E., Thorton, A., Freedman, D., Amell, J. W., Harrington, H. L., Smeijers, J., and Silva, P. A. (1996). The Life History Calendar: A research and clinical assessment method for collecting retrospective event-history data. *International Journal of Methods in Psychiatric Research, 6,* 101–14.

Caspi, A., and Roberts, B. W. (1999). Personality continuity and change across the life course. In L. A. Pervin and O. P. John (eds.), *Handbook of personality theory and research* New York: Guilford Press.

Caspi, A., and Silva, P. A. (1995). Temperamental qualities at age 3 predict personality traits in young adulthood: Longitudinal evidence from a birth cohort. *Child Development, 66,* 486–98.

Caspi, A., Wright, B. R., Moffitt, T. E., and Silva, P. A. (1998). Early failure in the labour market: Childhood and adolescent predictors of unemployment in the transition to adulthood. *American Sociological Review, 63,* 424–51.

Cattell, R. B. (1973). *Personality and mood by questionnaire.* San Francisco: Jossey-Bass.

Christiansen, K. O. (1977). A review of studies of criminality among twins. In S. A.

Mednick and K. O. Christiansen (eds.), *Biosocial bases of criminal behaviour* (pp. 45–88). New York: Gardner Press.

Church, T. A., and Burke, P. J. (1994). Exploratory and confirmatory tests of the Big Five and Tellegen's three- and four-dimensional models. *Journal of Personality and Social Psychology, 66,* 93–114.

Clark, L. A., Watson, D., and Reynolds, S. (1995). Diagnosis and classification of psychopathology: Challenges to the current system and future directions. *Annual Review of Psychology, 46,* 121–53.

Clarkin, J. F., and Kendall, P. C. (1992). Comorbidity and treatment planning: Summary and future directions. *Journal of Consulting and Clinical Psychology, 60,* 904–8.

Cloninger, C. R. (1998). The genetics and psychobiology of the seven-factor model of personality. In K. R. Silk (ed.), *Biology of personality disorders* (pp. 63–92). Washington, DC: American Psychiatry Press, Inc.

Cloninger, C. R., Svrakic, D. M. and Przybeck, T. R. (1993). A psychobiological model of temperament and character. *Archives of General Psychiatry, 50,* 975–90.

Cohen, J. (1992). A power primer. *Psychological Bulletin, 112,* 155–9.

Cohen, M. A., Miller, T. R., and Rossman, S. B. (1994). The costs and consequences of violent behavior in the Unites States. In A. J. Reiss, Jr. and J. A. Roth (eds.), *Understanding and preventing violence: Vol. 4. Consequences and Control* (pp. 67–166). Washington, DC: National Academy Press.

Cohen, P., Cohen, J., and Brook, J. S. (1995). Bringing in the sheaves, or just gleaning? A methodological warning. *International Journal of Methods in Psychiatric Research, 5,* 263–6.

Cohen, P., Cohen, J., Kasen, S., Velez, C. N., Hartmark, C., Johnson, J., Rojas, M., Brook, J., and Streuning, E. L. (1993). An epidemiological study of disorders in late childhood and adolescence – I. Age- and gender-specific prevalence. *Journal of Child Psychology and Psychiatry, 34,* 851–67.

Cohen, P., Slomkowski, C., Robins, L. N. (eds.). (1999). *Historical and geographical influences on psychopathology.* Mahwah, NJ: Lawrence Erlbaum Associates, Inc.

Coie, J. D., Dodge, K. A., and Kupersmidt, J. B. (1990). Peer group behavior and social status. In S. R. Asher and J. D. Coie (Eds.), *Peer rejection in childhood* (pp. 17–59). New York: Cambridge University Press.

Compas, B. E., Hinden, B., R., and Gerhardt, C. A. (1995). Adolescent development: pathways and processes of risk and resilience. *Annual Review of Psychology, 46,* 265–93.

Cook, P. J., and Laub, J. H. (1998). The unprecedented epidemic in youth violence. In M. Tonry and M. H. Moore (eds.), *Crime and Justice: A review of research* (vol. 24; pp. 27–64). University of Chicago Press.

Cornish, D., and Clarke, R. V. (1986). *The reasoning criminal: Rational choice perspectives on offending.* New York: Springer-Verlag.

Costello, A., Edelbrock, C., Kalas, R., Kessler, M., and Klaric, S. A. (1982). *Diagnostic Interview Schedule for Children (DISC).* Bethesda, MD: National Institute of Mental Health.

Costello, E. J. (1989). Developments in child psychiatric epidemiology. *Journal of the American Academy of Child and Adolescent Psychiatry, 28,* 836–41.

Costello, E. J., Angold, A., Burns, B. J., Stangl, D. K., Tweed, D. L., Erkanli, A., Worthman, C. M. (1996). The Great Smoky Mountains Study of Youth – Goals, design, methods and the prevalence of DSM–111–R disorders. *Archives of General Psychiatry*, 53, 1129–1136.

Costello, E. J., Farmer, E. M. Z., Angold, A., Burns, B. J., and Erkanli, A. (1997). Psychiatric disorders among American Indian and white youth in Appalachia: The great Smoky Mountains study. *American Journal of Public Health*, 87, 827–32.

Crick, N. R., and Dodge, K. A. (1994). A review and reformulation of social information-processing mechanisms in children's social adjustment. *Psychological Bulletin*, 115, 74–101.

Crijnen, A. A. M., Achenbach, T. M., and Verhulst, F. C. (1997). Comparisons of problems reported by parents of children in 12 cultures: Total problems, externalizing, and internalizing. *Journal of the American Academy of Child and Adolescent Psychiatry*, 36, 1269–77.

Dabbs, J. M., and Morris, R. (1990). Testosterone, social class, and antisocial behaviour in a sample of 4,462 men. *Psychological Science*, 1, 209–11.

Danielson, K. K., Moffitt, T. E., Caspi, A., and Silva, P. A. (1998). Comorbidity between abuse of an adult and DSM-III-R mental disorders: Evidence from an epidemiological study. *American Journal of Psychiatry*, 155, 131–3.

Davidson, R. J. and Irwin, W. (1999). The functional neuroanatomy of emotion and affective style. *Trends in Cognitive Science*, 3, 11–21.

Dean, C. W., Brame, R., and Piquero, A. R. (1996). Criminal propensities, discrete groups of offenders, and persistence in crime. *Criminology*, 34, 547–74.

Denno, D. W. (1990). *Biology and violence: From birth to adulthood.* Cambridge University Press.

Dick, D., Rose, R. J., Viken, R. J., and Kaprio, J. (2000). Pubertal timing and substance use: Associations between and within families across late adolescence. *Developmental Psychology*, 36, 180–9.

Dishion, T. J., Andrews, D. W., and Crosby, L. (1995). Antisocial boys and their friends in early adolescence: Relationship characteristics, quality, and interactional process. *Child Development*, 66, 139–51.

Dishion, T. J., and McMahon, R. J. (1998). Parental monitoring and the prevention of child and adolescent problem behaviour: A conceptual and empirical formulation. *Clinical Child and Family Psychology Review*, 1, 61–75.

Dishion, T. J., and Patterson, G. R. (1997). The timing of severity of antisocial behaviour: Three hypotheses within an ecological framework. In D. M. Stoff and J. Breiling (Eds.), *Handbook of antisocial behavior* (pp. 205–17). New York: John Wiley and Sons, Inc.

Dishion, T. J., Patterson, G. R., Stoolmiller, M., and Skinner, M. L. (1991). Family, school, and behavioural antecedents to early adolescent involvement with antisocial peers. *Developmental Psychology*, 27, 172–80.

Dodge, K. A., Bates, J. E., and Pettit, G. S. (1990). Mechanisms in the cycle of violence. *Science*, 250, 1678–83.

Downey, G., and Coyne, J. C. (1990). Children of depressed parents: an integrative review. *Psychological Bulletin*, 108, 50–76.

Dugan, L., Nagin, D. S., and Rosenfeld, R. (1999). 'Explaining the decline in the intimate partner homicide rate: The effects of changing domesticity, women's status, and domestic violence resources.' Unpublished manuscript.

Dunn, L. M. (1965). *Peabody Picture Vocabulary Tests.* Circle Pines, MN: American Guidance Service.

Eagly, A. H., and Steffen, V. J. (1986). Gender and aggressive behaviour: A meta-analytic review of the social psychological literature. *Psychological Bulletin, 100,* 309–30.

Earls, F. (1987). Sex differences in psychiatric disorders: Origins and developmental influences. *Psychiatric Developments, 1,* 1–23.

Eaves, L., Rutter, M., Silberg, J., Shillady, L., Maes, H. H., and Pickles A. (2000). Genetic and environmental causes of variation in interview assessments of disruptive behaviour in adolescent twins. *Behaviour Genetics, 30,* 321–334.

Ebstein, R. P. (1997). Saga of an adventure gene: Novelty seeking, substance abuse and the dopamine D4 receptor (D4DR) exon III repeat polymorphism. *Molecular Psychiatry, 2,* 381–4.

Edelbrock, C., Rende, R., Plomin, R., and Thompson, L. A. (1995). A twin study of competence and problem behaviour in childhood and early adolescence. *Journal of Child Psychology and Psychiatry, 36,* 775–85.

Eisenberg, N., and Lennon, R. (1983). Sex differences in empathy and related capacities. *Psychological Bulletin, 94,* 100–31.

Elander, J., and Rutter, M. (1996). Use and development of the Rutter parents' and teachers' scale. *International Journal of Methods in Psychiatric Research, 6,* 63–78.

Elder, G. H., Jr. (1998). The life course and human development. In W. Damon and R. M. Lerner (Eds.), *Handbook of child psychology: Vol. 1. Theoretical models of human development* (5th edn., pp. 939–91). New York: Wiley.

Eley, T. C., Lichtenstein, P., and Stevenson, J. (1999). Sex differences in the aetiology of aggressive and non-aggressive antisocial behaviour: Results from two twin studies. *Child Development, 70,* 155–68.

Elkins, I. J., Ianoco, W. G., Doyle, A. E., and McGue, M. (1997). Characteristics associated with the persistence of antisocial behaviour: Results from recent longitudinal research. *Aggression and Violent Behavior, 2,* 101–24.

Elley, W. B., and Irving, J. C. (1976). Revised socio-economic index for New Zealand. *New Zealand Journal of Educational Studies, 11,* 25–36.

Ellickson, P., Saner, H., and McGuigan, K. A. (1997). Profiles of violent youth: substance use and other concurrent problems. *American Journal of Public Health, 87,* 985–91.

Elliott, D. S. (1994). Serious violent offenders: onset, developmental course, and termination. *Criminology, 32,* 1–22.

Elliott, D. S., Ageton, S. S., Huizinga, D., Knowles, B. A., and Canter, R. J. (1983). The prevalence and incidence of delinquent behaviour. *The National Youth Survey Report No. 26.* Boulder, CO: Behavioural Research Institute.

Elliott, D. S., and Huizinga, D. (1989). Improving self-reported measures of delinquency. In M. W. Klein (Ed.), *Cross-national research in self-reported crime and delinquency* (pp. 155–86). Dordrecht: Kluwer Academic Publisher.

Elliott, D. S., Huizinga, D., and Menard, S. (1989). *Multiple problem youth: Delinquency, substance use, and mental health problems.* New York: Springer-Verlag.

Eme, R. F. (1979). Sex differences in childhood psychopathology: A review. *Psychological Bulletin, 86,* 574–95.

Eme, R. F. (1992). Selective female affliction in the developmental disorders of childhood: A literature review. *Journal of Clinical Child Psychology, 21,* 354–64.

Eme, R. F., and Kavanaugh, L. (1995). Sex differences in conduct disorder. *Journal of Clinical Child Psychology, 24,* 406–26.

Emslie, C., Hunt, K., and MacIntyre, S. (1999). Gender differences in minor morbidity among full time employees of a British university. *Journal of Epidemiology and Community Health, 53,* 465–75.

Engfer, A., Walper, S., and Rutter, M. (1994). Individual characteristics as a force in development. In M. Rutter and D. Hay (eds.), *Development through life: A handbook for clinicians* (pp. 79–111). Oxford: Blackwell Scientific Publications.

Ennett, S. T., and Bauman, K. E. (1994). The contribution of influence and selection to adolescent peer group homogeneity: The case of adolescent cigarette smoking. *Journal of Personality and Social Psychology, 67,* 653–63.

Esbensen, F-A, Deschenes, E. P., and Winfree, L. T., Jr. (1999). Differences between gang girls and gang boys. *Youth and Society, 31,* 27–53.

Espiritu, R. C. (1998). 'Are girls different?: An examination of developmental gender differences in pathways to delinquency.' Unpublished manuscript. University of Colorado at Boulder.

Eysenck, H. J. (1964). *Crime and personality.* Boston, MA: Houghton Mifflin Co.

Fagan, J. (1994). Women and drugs revisited: Female participation in the cocaine economy. *The Journal of Drug Issues, 24,* 179–225.

Fagan, J. and Browne, A. (1994). Violence between spouses and intimates: Physical aggression between women and men in intimate relationships. In A. J. Reiss, Jr. and J. A. Roth (Eds.), *Understanding and preventing violence: Vol. 3. Social influences* (pp. 115–292). Washington, DC: National Academy Press.

Fagot, B. I., and Leve, L. D. (1998). Teacher ratings of externalizing behaviour at school entry for boys and girls: similar early predictors and different correlates. *Journal of Child Psychology and Psychiatry, 39,* 555–66.

Fantuzzo, J., Boruch, R., Beriama, A., Atkins, M. and Marcus, S. (1997). Domestic violence and children: Prevalence and risk in five major US cities. *Journal of the American Academy of Child and Adolescent Psychiatry, 36,* 116–22.

Faraone, S. V., Biederman,J., Weiffenbach, B., Keith, T., Chu, M. P., Weaver, A., Spencer, T. J., Wilens, T. E., Frazier, J., Cleves, M., and Sakai, J. (1999). Dopamine D4 gene 7-repeat allele and attention deficit hyperactivity disorder. *American Journal of Psychiatry, 156,* 768–70.

Farrington, D. P. (1986). Age and crime. In M. Tonry and N. Morris (Eds.), *Crime and justice: An annual review of research* (Vol.7; pp. 189–250). University of Chicago Press.

Farrington, D. P. (1994). Childhood, adolescent, and adult features of violent males. In L. R. Huesmann (Ed.), *Aggressive behaviour: Current perspectives* (pp. 215–40). New York: Plenum Press.

Farrington, D. P. (1995). The development of offending and antisocial behaviour from childhood. *Journal of Child Psychology and Psychiatry, 36,* 929–64.

Farrington, D. P. (1998). Predictors, causes, and correlates of male youth violence.

In M. Tonry and M. H. Moore (Eds.), *Crime and Justice: A review of research* (vol. 24; pp. 421–75). University of Chicago Press.

Farrington, D. P., Barnes, G. C., and Lambert, S. (1996). The concentration of offending families. *Legal and Criminological Psychology, 1*, 47–63.

Farrington, D. P., and Junger, M. (Eds.). (1995). Crime and physical health. *Criminal Behaviour and Mental Health, 5* (4).

Farrington, D. P., Loeber, R., Elliott, D. S., Hawkins, D. J., Kandel, D. B., Klein, M. W., McCord, J., Rowe, D., and Tremblay, R. (1990). Advancing knowledge about the onset of delinquency and crime. In B. Lahey and A. Kazdin (eds.), *Advances in clinical child psychology* (vol.13; pp. 231–342). New York: Plenum Press.

Farrington, D. P., Ohlin, L., and Wilson, J. Q. (1986). *Understanding and controlling crime.* New York: Springer-Verlag.

Feehan, M., McGee, R., Nada Raja, S., and Williams, S. M. (1994). DSM-III-R disorders in New Zealand 18-year-olds. *Australian and New Zealand Journal of Psychiatry, 28*, 87–99.

Feingold, A. (1994). Gender differences in personality: A meta-analysis. *Psychological Bulletin, 116*, 429–56.

Felson, R. B. (1996). Big people hit little people: Sex differences in physical power and interpersonal violence. *Criminology, 34*, 433–52.

Fergusson, D. M., and Horwood, L. J. (1993). The structure, stability and correlations of the trait components of conduct disorder, attention deficit and anxiety/withdrawal reports. *Journal of Child Psychology and Psychiatry, 34*, 749–66.

Fergusson, D. M., and Horwood, L. J. (1998). Exposure to interparental violence in childhood and psychosocial adjustment in young adulthood. *Child Abuse and Neglect, 22*, 339–57.

Fergusson, D. M. and Horwood, L. J. (forthcoming). Male and female offending trajectories. *Development and Psychopathology.*

Fergusson, D. M., Horwood, L. J., Caspi, A., Moffitt, T. E., and Silva, P. A. (1996). The (artefactual) remission of reading disability: psychometric lessons in the study of stability and change in behavioural development. *Developmental Psychology, 32*, 1–9.

Fergusson, D. M., Horwood, L. J., and Lynskey, M. (1992). Family change, parental discord, and early offending. *Journal of Child Psychology and Psychiatry, 33*, 1059–75.

Fergusson, D. M., Horwood, L. J., and Nagin, D. S. (2000). Offending trajectories in a New Zealand birth cohort. *Criminology, 38*, 525–52.

Fergusson, D. M., Woodward, L. J., and Horwood, L. J. (forthcoming). Gender differences in the relation between early conduct problems and later criminality and substance abuse. *International Journal of Methods in Psychiatric Research.*

Fiebert, M. S. (1997). References examining assaults by women on their spouses/partners. *Sexuality and Culture, 1*, 273–86.

Fletcher, G. J. O. (1993). The scientific credibility of commonsense psychology. In K. H. Craik and R. Hogan (eds.), *Fifty years of personality psychology. Perspectives in individual differences* (pp. 251–68). New York: Plenum Press.

Frick, P. J., Lahey, B. B., Applegate, B., Kerdyk, L., Ollendick, T., Hynd, G. W., Garfinkel, B., Greenhill, L., Biederman, J., Barkley, R. A., McBurnett, K., Newcorn, J., and Waldman, I. (1994). DSM-IV field trials for the disruptive behaviour disorders: Symptom utility estimates. *Journal of the American Academy of Child and Adolescent Psychiatry, 33*, 529–38.

Frost, L. A., Moffitt, T. E., and McGee, R. (1989). Neuropsychological function and psychopathology in an unselected cohort of young adolescents. *Journal of Abnormal Psychology, 98*, 307–13.

Gaub, M., and Carlson, C. L. (1997). Gender differences in ADHD: A meta-analysis and critical review. *Journal of the American Academy of Child and Adolescent Psychiatry, 36*, 1036–45.

Ge, X., Conger, R. D., and Elder, G. H., Jr. (1996). Coming of age too early: Pubertal influences on girls' vulnerability to psychological distress. *Child Development, 67*, 3,386–400.

Gilmore, A., Croft, C., and Reid, N. (1981). *Burt Word Reading Test – New Zealand revision. Teacher's manual.* Wellington: New Zealand Council for Educational Research.

Giordano, P. C. (1978). Girls, guys, and gangs: The changing social context of female delinquency. *Journal of Criminal Law and Criminology, 69*, 126–32.

Giordano, P. C., and Cernkovich, S. A. (1997). Gender and antisocial behaviour. In D. M. Stoff, J. Breiling, and J. D. Maser (Eds.), *Handbook of antisocial behavior* (pp. 496–510). New York: Wiley.

Giordano, P. C., Cernkovich, S. A., and Pugh, M. D. (1986). Friendship and delinquency. *American Journal of Sociology, 91*, 1,170–202.

Giordano, P. C., Millhollin, T. J., Cernkovich, S. A., Pugh, M. D., and Rudolph, J. L. (1999). Delinquency, identity, and women's involvement in relationship violence. *Criminology, 37*, 17–40.

Gjone, H., Stevenson, J., and Sundet, J. M. (1996). Genetic influence on parent-reported attention-related problems in a Norwegian general population twin sample. *Journal of the American Academy of Child and Adolescent Psychiatry, 35*, 588–98.

Gjone, H., Stevenson, J., and Sundet, J. M., and Eilertsen, D. E. (1996). Changes in heritability across increasing levels of behaviour problems in young twins. *Behaviour Genetics, 26*, 419–26.

Gottesman, I. I., Goldsmith, H. H., and Carey, G. (1997). A developmental and a genetic perspective on aggression. In N. L. Segal, G. E. Weisfeld, and C. C. Weisfeld (eds.), *Uniting psychology and biology* (pp. 107–30). Washington, DC: American Psychological Association.

Gottfredson, M., and Hirschi, T. (1990). *A general theory of crime.* Stanford, CA: Stanford University Press.

Graber, J., Lewinsohn, P. M., Seeley, J., and Brooks-Gunn, J. (1997). Is psychopathology associated with the timing of pubertal development? *Journal of the American Academy of Child and Adolescent Psychiatry, 36*, 1,768–76.

Greenfield, L. A. and Snell, T. L. (1999). *Women Offenders. Bureau of Justice Statistics Special Report NCJ175688*, Washington, DC: US Dept of Justice.

Grych, J. H., and Fincham, F. D. (1990). Marital conflict and children's adjustment: A cognitive-context framework. *Psychological Bulletin, 108*, 267–90.

Haddock, C. K., Rindskopf, D., and Shadish, W. R. (1998). Using odds ratios as effect sizes for meta-analysis of dichotomous data: A primer on methods and issues. *Psychological Methods, 3*, 339–53.

Hagan, J., Simpson, J., and Gillis, A. R. (1987). Class in the household: A power-control theory of gender and delinquency. *American Journal of Sociology, 93*, 788–816.

Hankin, B. L., Abramson, L. Y., Moffitt, T. E., Silva, P. A., McGee, R., and Angell, K. E. (1998). Development of depression from preadolescence to young adulthood: Emerging gender differences in a 10-year longitudinal study. *Journal of Abnormal Psychology*, *107*, 128–40.

Hart, E. L., Lahey, B., Loeber, R., and Hanson, K. S. (1994). Criterion validity of informants in the diagnosis of disruptive behaviour disorders in children: A preliminary study. *Journal of Consulting and Clinical Psychology*, *62*, 410–14.

Hartung, C. and Widiger, T. (1998). Gender differences in the diagnosis of mental disorders: Conclusions and controversies of the DSM-IV. *Psychological Bulletin*, *123*, 260–78.

Hawkins, J. D., Catalano, R. F., and Miller, J. Y. (1992). Risk and protective factors for alcohol and other drug problems in adolescence and early adulthood: Implications for substance abuse prevention. *Psychological Bulletin*, *112*, 64–105.

Hawkins, J. D., Herrenkohl, T., Farrington, D. P., Brewer, D., Catalano, R. F., and Harachi, T. W. (1998). A review of predictors of youth violence. In R. Loeber and D. P. Farrington (eds.), *Serious and violent juvenile offenders: Risk factors and successful interventions* (pp. 106–46). Thousand Oaks, CA: Sage.

Henry, B., Caspi, A., Moffitt, T. E., and Silva, P. A. (1996). Temperamental and familial predictors of violent and non-violent criminal convictions: From age 3 to age 18. *Developmental Psychology*, *32*, 614–23.

Henry, B., Moffitt, T. E., Robins, L. N., Earls, F., and Silva, P. A. (1993). Early family predictors of child and adolescent antisocial behaviour: Who are the mothers of antisocial boys? *Criminal Behaviour and Mental Health*, *3*, 97–118.

Henton, J., Cate, R., Koval, J., Lloyd, S., and Christopher, S. (1993). Romance and violence in dating relationships. *Journal of Family Issues*, *4*, 467–82.

Hill, G. D., and Atkinson, M. P. (1988). Gender, familial control, and delinquency. *Criminology*, *26*, 127–49.

Hindelang, M. J., Hirschi, T., and Weis, J. G. (1979). Correlates of delinquency: The illusion of discrepancy between self-report and official measures. *American Sociological Review*, *44*, 995–1014.

Hinshaw, S., Lahey, B., and Hart, E. (1993). Issues of taxonomy and comorbidity in the development of conduct disorder. *Development and Psychopathology*, *5*, 31–50.

Hirschi, T., and Gottfredson, M. R. (1995). Control theory and the life-course perspective. *Studies on Crime and Crime Prevention*, *4*, 131–42.

Hirschi, T., and Hindelang, M. J. (1977). Intelligence and delinquency: A revisionist review. *American Sociological Review*, *42*, 571–87.

Hodgins, S., Mednick, S. A., Brennan, P. A., Schulsinger, F., and Engberg, M. (1996). Mental disorder and crime: Evidence from a Danish birth cohort. *Archives of General Psychiatry*, *53*, 489–96.

Howell, J. C., and Hawkins, J. D. (1998). Prevention of youth violence. In M. Tonry and M. H. Moore (eds.), *Crime and justice: A review of research* (vol. 24; pp. 263–316). University of Chicago Press.

Huesmann, L. R., Eron, L. D., Lefkowitz, M. M., and Walder, L. O. (1984). Stability of aggression over time and generations. *Developmental Psychology*, *20*, 1120–134.

Huizinga, D., Loeber, R., and Thornberry, T. P. (1993). Longitudinal study of delinquency, drug use, sexual activity, and pregnancy among children and youth in three cities. *Public Health Reports, 108*, 90–96.

Hyde, J. S. (1984). How large are gender differences in aggression? A developmental meta-analysis. *Developmental Psychology, 20*, 722–36.

Jaffe, P. G., Wolfe, D. A., and Wilson, S. K. (1990). *Children of battered women*. Newbury Park, CA: Sage Publications.

Jaffee, S. R. (forthcoming). *Why do young mothers experience adverse outcomes in adulthood?: Factors accounting for the poor adult outcomes of early childbearers.*

Jaffee, S. R., Caspi, A., Moffitt, T. E., Belsky, J. and Silva, P. A. (2001). Why are children born to teen mothers at risk for adverse outcomes in young adulthood? Results from a 20-year longitudinal study. *Development and Psychopathology, 13*, 377–397.

Jaffee, S. R., Caspi, A., Moffitt, T. E., Taylor, A., and Dickson, N. (forthcoming). Predicting early fatherhood and whether young fathers live with their children: Prospective findings and policy reconsiderations. *Journal of Child Psychology and Psychiatry.*

Jang, S. J., and Krohn, M. D. (1995). Developmental patterns of sex differences in delinquency among African American adolescents: A test of the sex-invariance hypothesis. *Journal of Quantitative Criminology, 11*, 195–222.

Jeglum-Bartusch, D., Lynam, D., Moffitt, T. E., and Silva, P. A. (1997). Is age important: testing general versus developmental theories of antisocial behaviour. *Criminology, 35*, 13–47.

Jencks, C. S., Perman, L., and Rainwater, L. (1988). What is a good job? A new measure of labour market success. *American Journal of Sociology, 93*, 1322–57.

Jensen, A. R. (1999). *The g factor: The science of mental ability*. London: Praeger.

Johnson, D. R., and Scheuble, L. K. (1991). Gender bias in the disposition of juvenile court referrals: The effects of time and location. *Criminology, 29*, 677–99.

Johnson, M. P. (1995). Patriarchal terrorism and common couple violence: Two forms of violence against women. *Journal of Marriage and the Family, 57*, 283–94.

Junger-Tas, J. (1993). Policy evaluation research in criminal justice. *Studies on Crime and Crime Prevention, 2*, 7–20.

Junger-Tas, J., Terlouw, G., and Klein, M. (1994). *Delinquent behaviour among young people in the western world*. Amsterdam: Kugler Publications.

Kagan, J. (1969). The three faces of continuity in human development. In D. A. Goslin (Ed.), *Handbook of socialization theory and research* (pp. 983–1,002). Chicago, IL: Rand McNally.

Kagan, J., and Moss, H. A. (1962). *Birth to maturity*. New York: Wiley.

Kandel, D., Simcha-Fagan, O., and Davies, M. (1986). Risk factors for delinquency and illicit drug use from adolescence to young adulthood. *Journal of Drug Issues, 16*, 67–90.

Kandel, D. B., Davies, M., and Baydar, N. (1990). The creation of interpersonal contexts: Homophily in dyadic relationships in adolescence and young adulthood. In L. N. Robins and M. R. Rutter (Eds.), *Straight and devious pathways to adulthood* (pp. 221–41). New York: Cambridge University Press.

Keenan, K., Loeber, R., and Green, S. (2000). Conduct disorder in girls: A review of the literature. *Clinical and Child Family Psychology Review, 2*, 3–19.

Keenan, K., and Shaw, D. (1997). Developmental and social influences on young girls' early problem behaviour. *Psychological Bulletin, 121*, 95–113.

Kellam, S. G., Brown, C. H., and Ensminger, M. E. (1983). Antecedents in first grade of teenage substance use and psychological well-being: A ten-year community-wide prospective study. In D. F. Ricks and B. S. Dohrenwend (eds.), *Origins of psychopathology* (pp. 17–42). New York: Cambridge University Press.

Kendler, K. S. (1993). Twin studies of psychiatric illness. *Archives of General Psychiatry, 50*, 905–15.

Kendler, K. S., Gallagher, T. J., Abelson, J. M., and Kessler, R. C. (1996). Lifetime prevalence, demographic risk factors, and diagnostic validity of nonaffective psychosis as assessed in a community sample. *Archives of General Psychiatry, 53*, 1022–31.

Kenny, D. A. (1998). Couples, gender, and time: Comments on method. In T. N. Bradbury (ed.), *The developmental course of marital dysfunction* (pp. 410–22). New York: Cambridge University Press.

Kerr, M. and Stattin, H. (2000). What parents know, how they know it, and several forms of adolescent adjustment: Further support for a reinterpretation of monitoring. *Developmental Psychology, 36*, 366–80.

Kerr, M., Tremblay, R. E., Pagani, L., and Vitaro, F. (1997). Boys' behavioural inhibition and the risk of later delinquency. *Archives of General Psychiatry, 54*, 809–816.

Kessler, R. C., McGonagle, K. A., Zhao, S., Nelson, C. B., Hughes, M., Eshleman, S., Wittchen, H. U., and Kendler, K. S. (1994). Lifetime and 12-month prevalence of DSM-III-R psychiatric disorders in the United States: Results from the National Comorbidity Study. *Archives of General Psychiatry, 51*, 8–19.

King, A., Wold, B., Tudor-Smith, C., and Harel, Y. (1996). *The health of youth: a cross-national survey*. Bergen: World Health Organisation.

Knight, G. P., Fabes, R. A., and Higgins, D. A. (1996). Concerns about drawing causal inferences from meta-analyses: an example in the study of gender differences in aggression. *Psychological Bulletin, 119*, 410–21.

Kratzer, L., and Hodgins, S. (1999). A typology of offenders: A test of Moffitt's theory among males and females from childhood to age 30. *Criminal Behaviour and Mental Health, 9*, 57–73.

Krueger, R. F., Caspi, A., Moffitt, T. E., and Silva, P. A. (1998). The structure and stability of common mental disorders (DSM-III-R): A longitudinal-epidemiological study. *Journal of Abnormal Psychology, 107*, 216–77.

Krueger, R. F., Moffitt, T. E., Caspi, A., Bleske, A., and Silva, P. A. (1998). Assortative mating for antisocial behaviour: Developmental and methodological implications. *Behavior Genetics, 28*, 173–86.

Krueger, R. F., Schmutte, P. S., Caspi, A., Moffitt, T. E., Campbell, K., and Silva, P. A. (1994). Personality traits are linked to crime among males and females: Evidence from a birth cohort. *Journal of Abnormal Psychology, 103*, 328–38.

Kruttschnitt, C. (1994). Gender and interpersonal violence. In A. J. Reiss, Jr. and J. A. Roth (eds.), *Understanding and preventing violence: Vol. 3. Social influences* (pp. 293–376). Washington, DC: National Academy Press.

Kurz, D. (1993). Physical assaults by husbands: A major social problem. In R. J. Gelles and D. R. Loseke (eds.), *Current controversies on family violence* (pp. 88–103). Newbury Park, CA: Sage.

LaGrange, T. C., and Silverman, R. A. (1999). Low self-control and opportunity:

Testing the general theory of crime as an explanation for gender differences in delinquency. *Criminology, 37*, 41–72.

Lahey, B., Schwab-Stone, M., Goodman, S. H., Waldman, I. D., Canino, G., Rathouz, P. J., Miller, T. L., Dennis, K. D., Bird, H. and Jensen, P. S. (2000). Age and gender differences in oppositional behaviour and conduct problems: A cross-sectional household study of middle childhood and adolescence. *Journal of Abnormal Psychology, 109*, 488–503.

Lahey, B. B., Waldman, I. D., and McBurnett, K. (1999). The development of antisocial behaviour: An integrative casual model. *Journal of Child Psychology and Psychiatry, 40*, 669–82.

Langley, J., Martin, J., and Nada Raja, S. (1997). Physical assault among 21-year-olds by partners. *Journal of Interpersonal Violence, 12*, 675–84.

Laub, J. H., Nagin, D. S., and Sampson, R. J. (1998). Good marriages and trajectories of change in criminal offending. *American Sociological Review, 63*, 225–38.

Laub, J. H., and Sampson, R. J. (forthcoming). Understanding desistance from crime. In M. Tonry (ed.), *Crime and justice: An annual review of research.* University of Chicago Press.

Laub, J. H., and Vaillant, G. E. (2000). Delinquency and mortality: A 50-year follow-up study of 1,000 delinquent and nondelinquent boys. *American Journal of Psychiatry, 157*, 96–102.

Laumann, E. O., Gagnon, J. H., Michael, R. T., and Michaels, S. (1994). *The social organization of sexuality: Sexual practices in the United States.* University of Chicago Press.

Le Blanc, M., and Loeber, R. (1998) Developmental criminology updated. In M. Tonry (ed.), *Crime and justice: A review of research* (Vol. 23; pp. 115–98). University of Chicago Press.

Lewinsohn, P. M., Hops, H., Roberts, R. E., Seeley, J. R., and Andrews, J. A. (1993). Adolescent psychopathology: 1. Prevalence and incidence of depression and other DSM-III-R disorders in high school students. *Journal of Abnormal Psychology, 102*, 133–44.

Lilienfeld, S. O. (1992). The association between antisocial personality and somatization disorders: A review and integration of theoretical models. *Clinical Psychology Review, 12*, 641–62.

Link, B. G., Andrews, H., and Cullen, F. T. (1992). The violent and illegal behaviour of mental patients reconsidered. *American Sociological Review, 57*, 275–92.

Little, R. J. A., and Rubin, D. B. (1987). *Statistical analysis with missing data.* New York: Wiley.

Loeber, R. (1982). The stability of antisocial and delinquent child behaviour: A review. *Child Development, 53*, 1431–46.

Loeber, R., and Farrington, D. P. (eds.). (1998). *Never too early, never too late: Risk factors and successful interventions for serious violent and juvenile offenders.* Thousand Oaks: Sage.

Loeber, R., Green, S., Lahey, B., and Stouthamer-Locber, M. (1990). Optimal informants on childhood disruptive behaviours. *Development and Psychopathology, 1*, 317–37.

Loeber, R., and Hay, D. (1997). Key issues in the development of aggression and violence from childhood to early adulthood. *Annual Review of Psychology, 48,* 371–410.

Loeber, R., and Keenan, K. (1994). Interaction between conduct disorder and its comorbid conditions: Effects of age and gender. *Clinical Psychology Review, 14,* 497–523.

Loeber, R., and LeBlanc, M. (1990). Toward a developmental criminology. In M. Tonry and N. Morris (eds.), *Crime and justice: A review of research* (vol. 12; pp. 375–473). University of Chicago Press.

Loeber, R., and Stouthamer-Loeber, M. (1986). Family factors as correlates and predictors of juvenile conduct problems and delinquency. In M. Tonry and N. Morris (eds.), *Crime and justice: An annual review of research* (Vol. 7; pp. 29–149). University of Chicago Press.

Loseke, D. R. (1992). *The battered woman and shelters: The social construction of wife abuse.* Albany, NY: State University of New York Press.

Luthar, S. S., and McMahon, T. J. (1996). Peer reputation among inner-city adolescents: structure and correlates. *Journal of Research on Adolescence, 6,* 581–603.

Lynam, D. R. (1996). Early identification of chronic offenders: Who is the fledgling psychopath? *Psychological Bulletin, 120,* 209–34.

Lynam, D. R., Caspi, A., Moffitt, T. E., Wikstrom, P. H., and Loeber, R. (2000). The effects of impulsivity on delinquency are stronger in poor neighborhoods. *Journal of Abnormal Psychology, 109,* 563–574.

Lynam, D. R., Moffitt, T. E., and Stouthamer-Loeber, M. (1993). Explaining the relation between IQ and delinquency: Class, race, test motivation, school failure or self-control. *Journal of Abnormal Psychology, 102,* 187–196.

Lytton, H. (1990). Child and parent effects in boys' conduct disorder: A reinterpretation. *Developmental Psychology, 26,* 683–697.

Lytton, H., and Romney, D. M. (1991). Parents' differential socialization of boys and girls: A meta-analysis. *Psychological Bulletin, 109,* 267–96.

McClelland, G. H., and Judd, C. M. (1993). Statistical difficulties of detecting interactions and moderator effects. *Psychological Bulletin, 114,* 376–90.

McCord, J and Ensminger, M. E. (1997). Multiple risks and comorbidity in an African-American population. *Criminal Behaviour and Mental Health, 7,* 339–352.

McFadyen-Ketchum, S. A., Bates, J. E., Dodge, K. A., and Pettit, G. S. (1996). Patterns of change in early childhood aggressive-disruptive behaviour: Gender differences in predictions from early coercive and affectionate mother-child interactions. *Child Development, 67,* 2417–2433.

McGee, R., Clarkson, J. E., Silva, P. A., and Williams, S. M. (1982). Neurological dysfunction in a large sample of three year old children. *New Zealand Medical Journal, 95,* 693–696.

McGee, R., Feehan, M., Williams, S., Partridge, F., Silva, P. A., and Kelly, J. (1990). DSM-III disorders in a large sample of adolescents. *Journal of the American Academy of Child and Adolescent Psychiatry, 29,* 611–619.

McGee, R., Williams, S. M., Bradshaw, J., Chapel, J. L., Robins, A. J., and Silva, P. A. (1985). The Rutter Scale for completion by teachers: Factor structure and relationship with cognitive abilities and family adversity for a sample of New Zealand children. *Journal of Child Psychology and Psychiatry, 26,* 727–739.

McGee, R., Williams, S. M., and Silva, P. A. (1985a). Factor structure and correlates of ratings of inattention, hyperactivity, and antisocial behaviour in a large sample of 9 year old children from the general population. *Journal of Consulting and Clinical Psychology, 53*, 480–490.

McGee, R., Williams, S. M., and Silva, P. A. (1985b). An evaluation of the Malaise Inventory. *Journal of Psychosomatic Research, 30*, 47–152.

McGue, M., Bacon, S., and Lykken, D. T. (1993). Personality stability and change in early adulthood: A behavioural genetic analysis. *Developmental Psychology, 29*, 96–109.

McKerracher, D. W., McGee, R., and Silva, P. A. (1984). Eysenck Personality Inventory scores from 1011 New Zealand women: A report from the Dunedin Multidisciplinary Child Development Study. *New Zealand Journal of Educational Studies, 19*, 82

McLanahan, S., and Sandfeur, G. (1994). *Growing up with a single parent.* Cambridge, MA: Harvard University Press.

McMillan, R. and Gartner, R. (1999). When she brings home the bacon: Labor-force participation and the risk of spousal violence against women. *Journal of Marriage and the Family, 61*, 947–958.

Maccoby, E. E. (1998). *The two sexes: Growing up apart, coming together.* Harvard University Press.

Maccoby, E. E., and Jacklin, C. N. (1980). Sex differences in aggression: A rejoinder and reprise. *Child Development, 51*, 964–980.

Macfarlane, J. W., Allen, L., and Honzik, M. P. (1954). *A developmental study of the behavioural problems of children between twenty one months and fourteen years.* Berkeley, CA: University of California Press.

Magdol, L., Moffitt, T. E., Caspi, A., Newman, D. L., Fagan, J., and Silva, P. A. (1997). Gender differences in partner violence in a birth-cohort of 21-year-olds: Bridging the gap between clinical and epidemiological approaches. *Journal of Consulting and Clinical Psychology, 65*, 68–78.

Magdol, L., Moffitt, T. E., Caspi, A., and Silva, P. A. (1998a). Hitting without a license: Testing explanations of differences in partner abuse between young adult daters and cohabitors. *Journal of Marriage and the Family, 60*, 41–55.

Magdol, L., Moffitt, T. E., Caspi, A., and Silva, P. A. (1998b). Developmental antecedents of partner abuse: A prospective-longitudinal study. *Journal of Abnormal Psychology, 107*, 375–89.

Magnusson, D. (1988). *Individual development from an interactional perspective.* Hillsdale, NJ: Erlbaum.

Magnusson, D., and Bergman, L. (eds.) (1990). *Data quality in longitudinal research.* Cambridge University Press.

Magnusson, D., Stattin, H., and Allen, V. L. (1985). Biological maturation and social development: A longitudinal study of some adjustment processes from mid-adolescence to adulthood. *Journal of Youth and Adolescence, 14*, 267–83.

Malinosky-Rummell, R., and Hansen, D. J. (1993). Long-term consequences of childhood physical abuse. *Psychological Bulletin, 114*, 68–79.

Mandel, H. P. (1997). *Conduct disorder and underachievement.* New York: Wiley.

Matarazzo, J. D. (1972). *Wechsler's measurement and appraisal of adult intelligence.* (5 ed). Baltimore, MD: Williams and Wilkins.

Maynard, R. A. (Ed.). (1997). *Kids having kids: Economic costs and social consequences of teen pregnancy.* Washington, DC: The Urban Institute Press.

Mazerolle, P., Brame, R., Paternoster, R., Piquero, A., and Dean, C. (2000). Onset age, persistence, and offending versatility: Comparisons across gender. *Criminology, 38,* 1143–72.

Mazur, A., and Booth, A. (1998). Testosterone and dominance in men. *Behavioural and Brain Sciences, 21,* 353–397.

Mears, D. P., Ploeger, M., and Warr, M. (1998). Explaining the gender gap in delinquency: Peer influence and moral evaluations of behaviour. *Journal of Research in Crime and Delinquency, 35,* 251–66.

Meltzer, H., Gatward, R., Goodman, R., and Ford, F. (2000). *Mental health of children and adolescents in Great Britain.* London: The Stationery Office.

Miech, R. A., Caspi, A., Moffitt, T. E., Wright, B. R. E., and Silva, P. A. (1999). Low socioeconomic status and mental disorders: a longitudinal study of selection and causation during young adulthood. *American Journal of Sociology, 104,* 1096–1131.

Mihalic, S. W., and Elliott, D. (1997). If violence is domestic, does it really count? *Journal of Family Violence, 12,* 293–311.

Miller, T. R., Cohen, M. A., and Wiersema, B. (1996). *Victims costs and consequences: A new look.* Washington, DC: National Institute of Justice.

Mirlees-Black, C. (1999). *Domestic violence: Findings from a new British Crime Survey self-completion questionnaire, Home Office Research Study 191.* London: Home Office.

Moffitt, T. E. (1989). Accommodating self-report methods to a low-delinquency culture: Experience from New Zealand. In M. W. Klein (ed.), *Cross-national research in self-reported crime and delinquency* (pp. 43–66). Dordrecht: Kluwer Academic Press.

Moffitt, T. E. (1990a). The neuropsychology of juvenile delinquency: A critical review. In M. Tonry and N. Morris (eds.), *Crime and justice: An annual review of research* (vol. 12; pp. 99–169). University of Chicago Press.

Moffitt, T. E. (1990b). Juvenile delinquency and attention-deficit disorder: developmental trajectories from age three to fifteen. *Child Development, 61,* 893–910.

Moffitt, T. E. (1993a). 'Life-course-persistent' and 'adolescence-limited' antisocial behaviour: A developmental taxonomy. *Psychological Review, 100,* 674–701.

Moffitt, T. E. (1993c). The neuropsychology of conduct disorder. *Development and Psychopathology, 5,* 135–51.

Moffitt, T. E. (1994). Natural histories of delinquency. In E. Weitekamp and H. J. Kerner (eds.), *Cross-national longitudinal research on human development and criminal behaviour* (pp. 3–61). Dordrecht: Kluwer Academic Press.

Moffitt, T. E. (1997). Adolescence-limited and life-course-persistent offending: A complementary pair of developmental theories. In T. Thornberry (Ed.), *Advances in criminological theory: Developmental theories of crime and delinquency* (pp. 11–54). London: Transaction Press.

Moffitt, T. E. (1997). Neuropsychology, antisocial behaviour, and neighborhood context. In J. McCord (ed.), *Growing up violent: contributions of inner-city life.* New York: Cambridge University Press.

Moffitt, T. E., and Caspi, A. (1998). Implications of violence between intimate partners for child psychologists and psychiatrists. *Journal of Child Psychology and Psychiatry, 39,* 137–44.

Moffitt, T. E., and Caspi, A. (forthcoming). Preventing the inter-generational continuity of antisocial behaviour: Implications of partner violence. In D. P. Farrington and J. Coid (Eds.), *Primary prevention of antisocial behaviour* New York: Cambridge University Press.

Moffitt, T. E., and Caspi, A. (2001). Childhood predictors differentiate life-course persistent and adolescence-limited antisocial pathways, among males and females. *Development and Psychopathology, 13*, 355–375.

Moffitt, T. E., Caspi, A., Dickson, N., Silva, P. A., and Stanton, W. (1996). Childhood-onset versus adolescent-onset antisocial conduct in males: Natural history from age 3 to 18. *Development and Psychopathology, 8*, 399–424.

Moffitt, T. E., Caspi, A., Harkness, A. R., and Silva, P. A. (1993). The natural history of change in intellectual performance: Who changes? How much? Is it meaningful? *Journal of Child Psychology and Psychiatry, 34*, 455–506.

Moffitt, T. E., Caspi, A., Harrington, H. L., and Milne, B. J. (forthcoming). Males on the life-course persistent and adolescence-limited antisocial pathways: Follow-up at age 26. *Development and psychopathology*.

Moffitt, T. E., Caspi, A., Krueger, R. F., Magdol, L., Margolin, G., Silva, P. A., and Sydney, R. (1997). Do partners agree about abuse in their relationship? A psychometric evaluation of interpartner agreement. *Psychological Assessment, 9*, 47–56.

Moffitt, T. E., Caspi, A., Silva, P. A., and Stouthamer-Loeber, M. (1995). Individual differences in personality and intelligence are linked to crime: Cross-context evidence from nations, neighborhoods, genders, races and age-cohorts. In J. Hagan (ed.), *Current perspectives on aging and the life cycle: Vol. 4. Delinquency and disrepute in the life course: Contextual and dynamic analyses* (pp. 1–34). Greenwich, CT: JAI Press.

Moffitt, T. E., Gabrielli, W. F., and Mednick, S. A. (1981). Socioeconomic status, IQ, and delinquency. *Journal of Abnormal Psychology, 90*, 152–6.

Moffitt, T. E., Krueger, R. F., Caspi, A, and Fagan, J. (2000) Partner abuse and general crime: How are they the same? How are they different? *Criminology, 38*, 199–232.

Moffitt, T. E., Lynam, D., and Silva, P. A. (1994). Neuropsychological tests predict persistent male delinquency. *Criminology, 32*, 101–24.

Moffitt, T. E., Robins, R. W. and Caspi, A. (forthcoming). A couples analysis of partner abuse with implications for abuse prevention. *Criminology and Public Policy*.

Moffitt, T. E., and Silva, P. A. (1988a). Self-reported delinquency: Results from an instrument for New Zealand. *Australian and New Zealand Journal of Criminology, 21*, 227–40.

Moffitt, T. E., and Silva, P. A. (1988b). IQ and delinquency: A direct test of the differential detection hypothesis. *Journal of Abnormal Psychology, 97*, 330–3.

Moffitt, T. E., Silva, P. A., Lynam, D., and Henry, B. (1994). Self-reported delinquency at age 18: New Zealand's Dunedin Multidisciplinary Health and Development Study. In J. Junger-Tas, G. J. Terlouw and M. W. Klein (eds.), *Delinquent behavior amond young people in the western world* (pp. 354–369). Amsterdam: Kugler Publications.

Moos, R., and Moos, B. (1981). *Family Environment Scale Manual*. Palo Alto, CA: Consulting Psychologists Press.

Morse, B. J. (1995). Beyond the Conflict Tactics Scale: Assessing gender differences in partner violence. *Violence and Victims, 10*, 251–72.

Moskowitz, D. S., and Schwartzman, A. E. (1989). Painting group portraits: Assessing life outcomes for aggressive and withdrawn children. *Journal of Personality, 57,* 723–46.

Moss, H. A., and Susman, E. J. (1980). Longitudinal study of personality development. In O. G. Brim, Jr. and J. Kagan (eds.), *Constancy and change in human development* (pp. 530–95). Cambridge, MA: Harvard University Press.

Nada Raja, S., McGee, R., and Stanton, W. R. (1992). Perceived attachments to parents and peers and psychological well-being in adolescence. *Journal of Youth and Adolescence, 21,* 471–85.

Nagel, H. H., and Hagan, J. (1983). Gender and crime: offense patterns and criminal court sanctions. In M. Tonry and N. Morris (eds.), *Crime and justice: An annual review of research* (vol. 4; pp. 91–144). University of Chicago Press.

Nagin, D. S., Farrington, D. P., and Moffitt, T. E. (1995). Life-course trajectories of different types of offenders. *Criminology, 33,* 111–39.

Nagin, D. S., and Land, K. C. (1993). Age, criminal careers, and population heterogeneity: specification and estimation of a nonparametric, mixed poison model. *Criminology, 31,* 327–62.

Nagin, D. S., and Waldfogel, J. (1995). The effects of criminality and conviction on the labour market status of young British offenders. *International Review of Law and Economics, 15,* 109–26.

Nelson, C. A., and Bloom, F. E. (1997). Child development and neuroscience. *Child Development, 68,* 970–87.

Neugebauer, R., Hoek, H. W., and Susser, E. (1999). Prenatal exposure to wartime famine and development of antisocial personality disorder in early adulthood. *Journal of the American Medical Association. 282,* 455–62.

Newman, D. L., Moffitt, T. E., Caspi, A., Magdol, L., Silva, P. A., and Stanton, W. (1996). Psychiatric disorder in a birth cohort of young adults: prevalence, comorbidity, clinical significance, and new cases incidence from age 11 to 21. *Journal of Consulting and Clinical Psychology, 64,* 552–62.

Newman, D. L., Moffitt, T. E., Caspi, A., and Silva, P. A. (1998). Comorbid mental disorders: implications for treatment and sample selection. *Journal of Abnormal Psychology, 107,* 305–11.

Nunnaly, J. C. (1978). *Introduction to psychological measurement.* New York: Mcgraw-Hill.

O'Connor, T. G., McGuire, S., Reiss, D., Hetherington, E. M., and Plomin, R. (1998). Co-occurrence of depressive symptoms and antisocial behaviour in adolescence: a common genetic liability. *Journal of Abnormal Psychology, 107,* 27–37.

O'Leary, K. D., Barling, J., Arias, I., Rosenbaum, A., Malone, J., and Tyree, A. (1989). Prevalence and stability of physical aggression between spouses: A longitudinal analysis. *Journal of Consulting and Clinical Psychology, 57,* 263–8.

O'Leary, K. D., Malone, J., and Tyree, A. (1994). Physical aggression in early marriage: Prerelationship and relationship effects. *Journal of Consulting and Clinical Psychology, 62,* 594–602.

Office of Juvenile Justice and Delinquency Prevention. (1998). *Serious and violent juvenile offenders.* Washington, DC: US Department of Justice.

Offord, D. R., Alder, R. J., and Boyle, M. H. (1986). Prevalence and sociodemographic correlates of conduct disorder. *American Journal of Social Psychiatry, 6,* 272–8.

Offord, D. R., Boyle, M., Campbell, D., Goering, P., Lin, E., Wong, M., and Racine, Y. A. (1996). One-year prevalence of psychiatric disorder in Ontarians 15 to 64 years of age. *Canadian Journal of Psychiatry, 41,* 559–63.

Olson, S. L., and Hoza, B. (1993). Preschool developmental antecendents of conduct problems in children beginning school. *Journal of Clinical Child Psychology, 22,* 60–7.

Olweus, D. (1979). Stability of aggressive reaction patterns in males: A review. *Psychological Bulletin, 86,* 852–75.

Osgood, D. W. (1998). Interdisciplinary integration: Building criminology by stealing from our friends. *The Criminologist, 23,* 1–4.

Ounstead, C., and Taylor, D. C. (1972). *Gender differences: Their ontogeny and significance.* London: Churchill Livingstone.

Ozer, D. (1985). Correlation and the coefficient of determination. *Psychological Bulletin, 97,* 307–15.

Pajer, K. (1998). What happens to 'bad' girls? A review of adult outcomes of antisocial adolescent girls. *American Journal of Psychiatry, 155,* 862–70.

Pan, H. S., Neidig, P. H., and O'Leary, K. D. (1994). Predicting mild and severe husband-to-wife physical aggression. *Journal of Consulting and Clinical Psychology, 62,* 975–81.

Parker, J. G., and Asher, S. R. (1987). Peer relations and later personal adjustment: Are low-accepted children at risk? *Psychological Bulletin, 102,* 357–89.

Parnicky, J. J., Williams, S., and Silva, P. A. (1985). Family environment scale: A Dunedin (New Zealand) pilot study. *Australian Psychologist, 20,* 195–204.

Patterson, G. R. (1982). *Coercive family process.* Eugene, OR: Castalia.

Patterson, G. R., DeBaryshe, B. D., and Ramsey, E. (1989). A developmental perspective on antisocial behaviour. *American Psychologist, 44,* 329–35.

Patterson, G. R., Forgatch, M. S., Yoerger, K. L., and Stoolmiller, M. (1998). Variables that initiate and maintain an early-onset trajectory for juvenile offending. *Development and Psychopathology, 10,* 531–47.

Patterson, G. R., Reid, J. B., and Dishion, T. J. (1992). *A social learning approach: Vol. 4. Antisocial boys.* Eugene, OR: Castalia.

Patterson, G. R., and Yoerger, K. (1993). Developmental models for delinquent behaviour. In S. Hodgins (ed.), *Crime and mental disorders* (pp. 140–72). Newbury Park, CA: Sage Publications.

Paul, C., Fitzjohn, J., Herbison, P., and Dickson, N. (2000). The determinants of sexual intercourse before age 16 in a birth cohort. *Journal of Adolescent Health, 27,* 134–47.

Piacentini, J. C., Cohen, P., and Cohen, J. (1992). Combining discrepant diagnostic information from multiple sources: Are complex algorithms better than simple ones? *Journal of Abnormal Child Psychology, 20,* 51–63.

Pine, D. S., Cohen, P., Brook, J., and Coplan, J. D. (1997). Psychiatric symptoms in adolescence as predictors of obesity in early adulthood: A longitudinal study. *American Journal of Public Health, 87,* 1,303–10.

Piquero, A. (forthcoming). Testing Moffitt's neuropsychological variation hypothesis for the prediction of life-course persistent offending. *Psychology, Crime and Law.*

Piquero, A., Paternoster, R., Mazerolle, P., Brame, R., and Dean, C. W. (1999). Onset age and offence specialization. *Journal of Research in Crime and Delinquency, 36,* 275–99.

Plomin, R., and Caspi, A. (1999). Behavioral genetics and personality. In L. A. Pervin, and O. P. John (eds.), *Handbook of personality: Theory and research* (pp. 251–76). New York: Guilford Press.

Plomin, R., DeFries, J. C., and Loehlin, J. C. (1977). Genotype-environment interaction and correlation in the analysis of human behaviour. *Psychological Bulletin, 84,* 309–22.

Plomin, R., and Rutter, M. (1998). Child development and molecular genetics: what do we do with the genes once they are found? *Child Development, 69,* 1,223–42.

Poulton, R. P., Caspi, A., Moffitt, T. E., Cannon, M., Murray, R., Harrington, H. L. (2000). Children's self-reported psychotic symptoms predict adult schizophreniform disorders: A 15-year longitudinal study. *Archives of General Psychiatry, 57,* 1053–8.

Prime Ministerial Task Force on Employment (1994). *Employment: The Issues.* Wellington, New Zealand.

Pulkkinen, L. (1996). Female and male personality styles: A typological and developmental analysis. *Journal of Personality and Social Psychology, 70,* 1288–1306.

Pulkkinen, L., and Pitkanen, T. (1993). Continuities in aggressive behaviour from childhood to adulthood. *Aggressive Behaviour, 19,* 249–63.

Quay, H. C., and Peterson, D. R. (1987). *Manual for the Behaviour Problem Checklist.* Miami, FL: Authors.

Quinton, D. Pickles, A., Maughan, B. and Rutter, M. (1993). Partners, peers and pathways: assortative pairing and continuities in conduct disorder. *Development and Psychopathology, 5,* 763–83.

Raine, A. (1994). *The psychopathology of crime: Criminal behaviour as a clinical disorder.* New York: Academic Press.

Raine, A., Brennan, P., and Mednick, S. A. (1994). Birth complications combined with early maternal rejection at age 1 year predispose to violent crime at age 18 years. *Archives of General Psychiatry, 51,* 984–88.

Raine, A., Brennan, P., Mednick, B., and Mednick, S. A. (1996). High rates of violence, crime, academic problems, and behavioural problems in males with both early neuromotor deficits and unstable family environments. *Archives of General Psychiatry, 51,* 984–8.

Raine, A., Lencz, T., Bihrle, S., La Casse, L., and Coletti, P. (2000). Reduced prefrontal gray matter volume and reduced autonomic activity in antisocial personality disorder. *Archives of General Psychiatry, 57,* 121–27.

Raine, A., Yaralian, P. S., Reynolds, C., Venables, P. H., and Mednick, S. A. (2000). 'Spatial but not verbal cognitive deficits at age 3 years in life-course persistent antisocials: A prospective longitudinal study.' Unpublished manuscript under review.

Ramrakha, S., Caspi, A, Dickson, N, Moffitt, T. E. and Paul, C. (2000). Psychiatric disorders and risky sex in young people. *British Medical Journal, 321,* 263–6.

Rhee, S. H., Waldman, I. D., Hay, D., and Levy, F. (1999). Sex differences in genetic and environmental influences on DSM-III-R Attention-Deficit/Hyperactivity disorder. *Journal of Abnormal Psychology, 108,* 24–41.

Roberts, B. W., Caspi, A., and Moffitt, T. E. (forthcoming). 'Growth and stability in personality development from adolescence to young adulthood.' *Journal of Personality and Social Psychology.*

Robins, L. N. (1966). *Deviant children grown up.* Baltimore, MD: Williams and Wilkins.

Robins, L. N. (1978). Sturdy childhood predictors of antisocial behaviour: Replications from longitudinal studies. *Psychological Medicine, 8,* 611–22.

Robins, L. N. (1986). The consequence of conduct disorder in girls. In D. Olweus, J. Block, and M. Radke-Yarrow (Eds.), *Development of antisocial and prosocial behaviour* (pp. 385–414). Harcourt Brace Jovanovich.

Robins, L. N., Helzer, J. E., Cottler, L., and Goldring, E. (1989). 'Diagnostic Interview Schedule, Version III-R.' Washington University St. Louis.

Robins, L. N., Helzer, J. E., Croughan, J., and Ratcliff, K. S. (1981). National Institute of Mental Health Diagnostic Interview Schedule. *Archives of General Psychiatry, 38,* 381–9.

Robins, L. N., and Price, R. K. (1991). Adult disorders predicted by childhood conduct problems: Results from the NIMH Epidemiologic Catchment Area project. *Psychiatry, 54,* 116–32.

Robins, L. N., and Regier, D. A. (1991). *Psychiatric disorders in America.* New York: The Free Press.

Robins, L. N., and Rutter, M. (Eds.). (1990). *Straight and devious pathways from childhood to adulthood.* Cambridge University Press.

Robins, R. W., Caspi, A., and Moffitt, T. E. (2000). Two personalities, one relationship: Both partners' personality traits shape the quality of their relationship. *Journal of Personality and Social Psychiatry, 79,* 251–9.

Rodgers, B., Pickles, A., Power, C., Collishaw, S., and Maughan, B. (1999). Validity of the malaise inventory in general population samples. *Social Psychiatry and Psychiatric Epidemiology, 34,* 333–41.

Roeder, K., Lynch, K. G., and Nagin, D. S. (1999). Modeling uncertainty in latent class membership: A case study in criminology. *Journal of the American Statistical Association, 94,* 766–76.

Ronka, A., Kinnunen, U., and Pulkkinen, L. (2000). The accumulation of problems of social functioning as a long-term process: Women and men compared. *International Journal of Behavioural Development, 24,* 442–50.

Rosenthal, R., and Rubin, D. (1982). A simple, general purpose display of magnitude of experimental effect. *Journal of Educational Psychology, 74,* 166–9.

Rothbaum, F., and Weisz, J. R. (1994). Parental caregiving and child externalizing behaviour in nonclinical samples: A meta-analysis. *Psychological Bulletin, 116,* 55–74.

Rowe, D. C., and Farrington, D. P. (1997). The familial transmission of criminal convictions. *Criminology, 35,* 177–201.

Rowe, D. C., Vazsonyi, A. T., and Flannery, D. J. (1994). No more than skin deep: Ethnic and racial similarity in developmental process. *Psychological Review, 101,* 396–413.

Rowe, D. C., Vazsonyi, A. T., and Flannery, D. J. (1995). Sex difference in crime: Do means and within-sex variation have similiar causes? *Journal of Research in Crime and Delinquency, 32,* 84–101.

Rushton, J. P., Brainerd, C. J., and Pressley, M. (1983). Behavioural development and construct validity: The principle of aggregation. *Psychological Bulletin, 94,* 18–38.

Rutter, M. (1990). Commentary: Some focus and process considerations regarding effects of parental depression on children. *Developmental Psychology, 26,* 60–7.

Rutter, M. (1997). Comorbidity: Concepts, claims and choices. *Criminal Behaviour and Mental Health, 7,* 265–85.

Rutter, M., Giller, H., and Hagell, A. (1998). *Antisocial behaviour by young people.* Cambridge University Press.

Rutter, M., Maughan, B., Meyer, J., Pickles, A., Silberg, J. L., Simonoff, E., and Taylor, E. (1997). Heterogeneity of antisocial behaviour: Causes, continuities, and consequences. In R. Dienstbier and D. W. Osgood (eds.), *Nebraska symposium on motivation: Vol.44. Motivation and delinquency* (pp. 45–118). Lincoln, NE: University of Nebraska Press.

Rutter, M., Silberg, J., O'Connor, T., and Simonoff, E. (1999). Genetics and child psychiatry: II. Empirical research findings. *Journal of Child Psychology and Psychiatry, 40,* 19–55.

Rutter, M., and Smith, D. J. (eds.). (1995). *Psychosocial disturbances in young people: Challenges for prevention.* New York: Cambridge University Press.

Rutter, M., Tizard, J., and Whitmore, K. (1970). *Education, health, and behaviour.* New York: John Wiley and Sons.

Sampson, R. J., and Laub, J. H. (1993). *Crime in the making.* Cambridge, MA: Harvard University Press.

Sampson, R. J., and Lauritsen, K. (1994). Violent victimization and offending: Individual-, situational-, and community-level risk factors. In A. J. Reiss, Jr. and J. Roth (eds.), *Understanding and preventing violence: Vol. 3. Social influences* (pp. 1–114). Washington, DC: National Academy Press.

Scarr, S., and McCartney, K. (1983). How people make their own environments: A theory of genotype to environment effects. *Child Development, 54,* 424–35.

Scott, E. S., and Grisso, T. (1997). The evolution of adolescence: A developmental perspective on juvenile justice reform. *The Journal of Criminal Law and Criminology, 88,* 137–89.

Scottish Council for Research in Education. (1976). *The Burt Word Reading Test, 1974 revision.* London: Hodder and Stoughton.

Sellin, T. (1938). Culture conflict and crime. *American Journal of Sociology, 44,* 97–103.

Serbin, L. A., Peters, P. L., McAffer, V. J., and Schwartzman, A. E. (1991). Childhood aggression and withdrawal as predictors of adolescent pregnancy, early parenthood, and environmental risk for the next generation. *Canadian Journal of Behavioural Sciences, 23,* 331–81.

Shea, M. T., Widiger, T., and Klein, M. (1992). Comorbidity of personality disorders and depression: Implications for treatment. *Journal of Consulting and Clinical Psychology, 60,* 857–68.

Sher, K., and Trull, T. (1996). Methodological issues in psychopathology research. *Annual Review of Psychology, 47,* 371–400.

Sickmund, M., Stahl, A. L., Finnegan, T. A., Snyder, H. N., Poole, R. S., and Butts, J. A. (1998). *Juvenile Court Statistics 1995.* Washington DC: National Center for Juvenile Justice.

Silberg, J. L., Erickson, M. T., Meyer, J. M., Eaves, L. J., Rutter, M., and Hewitt, J. K. (1994). The application of structural equation modelling to maternal ratings of twins' behavioural and emotional problems. *Journal of Consulting and Clinical Psychology, 62*, 510–21.

Silva, P. A. (1978). SRA verbal test scores from 1011 women. *New Zealand Psychologist, 7*, 47–8.

Silva, P. A., and Stanton, W. R. (eds.). (1996). *From child to adult: The Dunedin Multidisciplinary Health and Development Study*. Auckland: Oxford University Press.

Silverthorn, P., and Frick, P. J. (1999). Developmental pathways to antisocial behaviour: The delayed-onset pathway in girls. *Development and Psychopathology, 11*, 101–26.

Simmons, R. G., and Blyth, D. (1987). *Moving into adolescence: The impact of pubertal change and school context*. New York: Aldine De Gruyter.

Simonoff, E., Pickles, A., Meyer, J., Silberg, J. L., Maes, H. H., Loeber, R., Rutter, M., Hewitt, J. K., and Eaves, L. (1997). The Virginia twin study of adolescent behavioural development. *Archives of General Psychiatry, 54*, 801–8.

Simons, R. L., Lin, K. H., and Gordon, L. C. (1998). Socialization in the family of origin and male dating violence: A prospective study. *Journal of Marriage and the Family, 60*, 467–478.

Simons, R. L., Miller, M. G., and Aigner, S. M. (1980). Contemporary theories of deviance and female delinquency: An empirical test. *Journal of Research in Crime and Delinquency, 17*, 42–53.

Simons, R. L., Wu, C. I., Conger, R., and Lorenz, F. O. (1994). Two routes to delinquency: Differences between early and late starters in the impact of parenting and deviant peers. *Criminology, 32*, 247–75.

Slutske, W. S., Heath, A. C., Dinwiddie, S. H., Madden, P. A. F., Bucholz, K. K., Dunne, M. P., Statham, D. J., Martin, N. G. (1997). Modeling genetic and environmental influences in the aetiology of conduct disorder: A study of 2,682 adult twin pairs. *Journal of Abnormal Psychology, 106*, 266–79.

Smith, C., and Thornberry, T. P. (1995). The relationship between childhood maltreatment and adolescent involvement in delinquency. *Criminology, 86*, 37–58.

Smith, D. A., and Visher, C. A. (1980). Sex and involvement in deviance/crime: A quantitative review of the empirical literature. *American Sociological Review, 45*, 691–701.

Smith, D. J. (1995). Youth crime and conduct disorders: Trends, patterns, and causal explanations. In M. Rutter and D. Smith (eds.), *Psychosocial disorders in young people* (pp. 299–489). Chichester: Wiley.

Stanger, C., Achenbach, T., and Verhulst, F. C. (1997). Accelerated longitudinal comparisons of aggressive versus delinquent syndromes. *Development and Psychopathology, 9*, 43–58.

Statistics New Zealand. (1994). *Labour market 1993*. Wellington, New Zealand: NZ Department of Statistics.

Stattin, H., and Magnusson, D. (1991a). *Pubertal maturation in female development*. Hillsdale, NJ: Erlbaum.

Stattin, H., and Magnusson, D. (1991b). Stability and change in criminal behaviour up to age 30. *British Journal of Criminology, 31*, 327–346.

Stattin, H., Magnusson, D., and Reichel, H. (1989). Criminal activity at different ages: A study based on a Swedish longitudinal research population. *British Journal of Criminology, 29*, 368–85.

Steffensmeier, D. and Allan, E. (1996). Gender and crime. *Annual Review of Sociology*, *22*, 459–87.

Steffensmeier, D., Kramer, J., and Streifel, C. (1993). Gender and imprisonment decisions. *Criminology*, *31*, 411–46.

Stets, J. E., and Straus, M. A. (1990). Gender differences in reporting marital violence and its medical and psychological consequences. In M. A. Straus and R. J. Gelles (Eds.), *Physical violence in American families: Risk factors and adaptions to violence in 8,145 families* (pp. 151–65). New Brunswick, NJ: Transaction.

Straus, M. A. (1990). Injury and frequency of assault and the 'representative sample fallacy' in measuring wife beating and child abuse. In M. A. Straus and R. J. Gelles (Eds.), *Physical violence in American families: Risk factors and adaptations to violence in 8,145 families* (pp. 75–91). New Brunswick, NJ: Transaction Books.

Straus, M. A. (1993). Physical assaults by wives: A major social problem. In R. J. Gelles and D. R. Loseke (Eds.), *Current controversies on family violence* (pp. 67–87). Newbury Park, CA: Sage.

Straus, M. A. (1997). Physical assaults by women partners: A major social problem. In M. R. Walsh (Ed.), *Women, men and gender: Ongoing debates* (pp. 210–21). New Haven, CT: Yale University Press.

Straus, M. A. (1998). The controversy over domestic violence by women: A methodological, theoretical, and sociology of science analysis. In X. B. Arriaga and S. Oskamp (eds.), *Violence in intimate relationships*. Thousand Oaks, CA: Sage.

Straus, M. A., and Gelles, R. J. (1986). Societal change and change in family violence from 1975 to 1985 as revealed by two national surveys. *Journal of Marriage and the Family*, *48*, 465–79.

Straus, M. A., Sugarman, D. B., and Giles-Sims, J. (1997). Spanking by parents and subsequent antisocial behaviour of children. *Archives of Pediatric and Adolescent Medicine*, *151*, 761–7.

Swanson, J., Oosterlaan, J., Murias, M., Schuck, S., Flodman, P., Spence, M. A., Wasdell, M., Ding, Y., Smith, M., Mann, M., Carlson, C., Kennedy, J. L., Sergeant, J. A., Leung, P., Zhang, Y. P., Chen, C., Whalen, C. K., Babb, K. A., Posner, M. I. (2000). Attention deficit/hyperactivity disorder children with a 7-repeat allele of the dopamine receptor D4 gene have extreme behaviour but normal performance on critical neuropsychological tests of attention. *Proceedings of the National Academy of Sciences*, *97*, 4754–9.

Sutherland, E., and Cressey, D. R. (1978). *Criminology*. Philadelphia, PA: Lippincott.

Tanner, J. M. (1978). *Fetus into man*. Cambridge, MA: Harvard University Press.

Taylor, J., Iacono, W. G., and McGue, M. (2000). 'Evidence for a genetic aetiology for early-onset delinquency.' *Journal of Abnormal Psychology*, *109*, 634–43.

Tellegen, A. (1982). *Brief manual for the Multidimensional Personality Questionnaire*. Minneapolis: University of Minnesota.

Tellegen, A. (1985). Structures of mood and personality and their relevance to assessing anxiety, with an emphasis on self-report. In A. H. Tuma and J. Maser (eds.), *Anxiety and anxiety disorders* (pp. 681–706). Hillsdale, NJ: Erlbaum.

Tellegen, A., Lykken, D. T., Bouchard, T. J., Wilcox, K. J., Segal, N. L., and Rich, S. (1988). Personality similarity in twins reared apart and together. *Journal of Personality and Social Psychology*, *6*, 1031–9.

Tellegen, A., and Waller, N. G. (in press). Exploring personality through test construction: Development of the Multidimensional Personality Questionnaire. In S. R. Briggs and J. M. Cheek (eds.), *Personality measures: Development and evaluation.* Greenwich, CT: JAI Press.

Terman, L. M., and Merrill, M. A. (1960). *Stanford-Binet Intelligence Scale.* Boston, MA: Houghton Mifflin.

Thornberry, T. P. (1987). Toward an interactional theory of delinquency. *Criminology, 25,* 863–891.

Thurstone, T. G., and Thurstone, L. L. (1973). *The SRA verbal form.* Chicago, IL: Science Research Associates.

Tibbetts, S., and Piquero, A. (1999). The influence of gender, low birth weight and disadvantaged environment on predicting early onset of offending: A test of Moffitt's interactional hypothesis. *Criminology, 37,* 843–78.

Tieger, T. (1980). On the biological basis of sex differences in aggression. *Child Development, 51,* 943–963.

Tjaden, P., and Thoennes, N. (1998). *Prevalence, incidence, and consequences of violence against women: Findings from the National Violence Against Women Survey.* Washington, DC: US Department of Justice.

Tonry, M., Ohlin, L. E., and Farrington, D. P. (1991). *Human development and criminal behaviour: New ways of advancing knowledge.* New York: Springer-Verlag.

Touwen, B. C., and Prechtl, H. F. R. (1970). *The neurological examination of the child with minor nervous dysfunction.* London: Heinemann.

Tremblay, R. E. (1991). Aggression, prosocial behaviour and gender: Three magic words, but no magic wand. In D. J. Pepler and K. H. Rubin (eds.), *The development and treatment of childhood aggression* (pp. 71–8). Hillsdale, NJ: Erlbaum.

Tremblay, R. E., Masse, B., Perron, D., LeBlanc, M., Schwartzman, A. E., and Ledingham, J. E. (1992). Early disruptive behaviour, poor school achievement, delinquent behaviour. *Journal of Consulting and Clinical Psychology, 60,* 64–72.

Tremblay, R. E., Masse, L. C., Vitaro, F., and Dobkin, P. L. (1995). The impact of friends' deviant behaviour on early onset of delinquency. Longitudinal data from 6 to 13 years of age. *Development and Psychopathology, 7,* 649–67.

van Dijk, J., and Mayhew, P. (1992). *Criminal victimization in the industrialized world.* The Hague: Ministry of Justice.

Verhulst, F. C., and van der Ende, J. (1993). 'Comorbidity' in an epidemiological sample: a longitudinal perspective. *Journal of Child Psychology and Psychiatry, 34,* 767–83.

Verhulst, F. C., van der Ende, J., Ferdinand, R. F., and Kasius, M. C. (1997). The prevalence of DSM-III-R diagnoses in a national sample of Dutch adolescents. *Archives of General Psychiatry, 54,* 329–36.

Vitaro, F., Tremblay, R. E., Kerr, M., Pagani, L., and Bukowski, W. M. (1997). Disruptiveness, friends' characteristics, and delinquency in early adolescence: A test of two competing models of development. *Child Development, 68,* 676–89.

Wachs, T. D. (1992). *The nature of nurture.* Thousand Oaks, CA: Sage.

Wakefield, J. (1989). Levels of explanation in personality theory. In D. M. Buss and N. Cantor (eds.), *Personality psychology: Recent trends and emerging directions* (pp. 333–46). New York: Springer-Verlag.

Warr, M. (1993). Age, peers, and delinquency. *Criminology, 31*, 17–40.

Watson, D., and Clark, L. A. (1984). Negative affectivity: The disposition to experience aversive emotional states. *Psychological Bulletin, 96*, 465–90.

Watson, D., Clark, L. A., and Harkness, A. R. (1994). Structures of personality and their relevance to psychopathology. *Journal of Abnormal Psychology, 103*, 18–31.

Webster-Stratton, D. (1996). Early-onset conduct problems: Does gender make a difference? *Journal of Consulting and Clinical Psychology, 64*, 540–51.

Wechsler, D. (1974). *Manual for the Wechsler Intelligence Scale for Children – Revised.* New York: Psychological Corporation.

Weiner, N. A., and Wolfgang, M. E. (1989). *Violent crime, violent criminals.* Newbury Park: Sage.

Wells, J. E., Bushnell, J. A., Joyce, P. R., Oakley-Browne, M. A., and Hornblow, A. R. (1991). Preventing alcohol problems: The implications of a case-finding study in Christchurch, New Zealand. *Acta Psychiatrica Scandinavica, 83*, 31–40.

White, J., Moffitt, T. E., Earls, F., Robins, L. N., and Silva, P. A. (1990). How early can we tell? Predictors of childhood conduct disorder and adolescent delinquency. *Criminology, 28*, 507–533.

Widom, C. S. (1989a). Does violence beget violence? A critical examination of the literature. *Psychological Bulletin, 106*, 3–28.

Widom, C. S. (1989b). The cycle of violence. *Science, 244*, 160–6.

Wilson, J. Q., and Herrnstein, R. J. (1985). *Crime and human nature.* New York: Simon and Schuster.

Wilson, D., Killen, J., Hayward, C., Robinson, T., Hammer, L., Kraemer, H., Varady, A., and Taylor, C. (1994). Timing and rate of sexual maturation and the onset of cigarette and alcohol use among teenage girls. *Archives of Pediatrics and Adolescent Medicine, 148*, 789–95.

Windle, M. (1990). A longitudinal study of antisocial behaviours in early adolescence as predictors of late adolescent substance use: Gender and ethnic group differences. *Journal of Abnormal Psychology, 99*, 86–91.

Witkin, H. A., Mednick, S. A., Schulsinger, F., Bakkestrom, E., Christiansen, K. O., Goodenough, D. R., Hirschorn, K., Lundsteen, C., Owen, D. R., Philip, J., Rubin, D., and Stocking, M. (1976). Criminality in XYY and XXY men. *Science, 193*, 547–55.

Wittchen, H.-U. (1996). Critical issues in the evaluation of comorbidity of psychiatric disorders. *British Journal of Psychiatry, 168 (suppl. 30)*, 9–16.

Wolfgang, M. E., Figlio, R. M., and Sellin, T. (1972). *Delinquency in a birth cohort.* University of Chicago Press.

Wright, B. R. E., Caspi, A., Moffitt, T. E., Miech, R. A., and Silva, P. A. (1999). Reconsidering the relationship between SES and delinquency: Causation but not correlation. *Criminology, 37*, 175–94.

Wright, B. R. E., Caspi, A., Moffitt, T. E., and Silva, P. A. (1998). Factors associated with doubled-up housing – a common precursor to homelessness. *Social Service Review*, 92–111.

Wright, B. R. E., Caspi, A., Moffitt, T. E., and Silva, P. A. (1999). Low self-control, social bonds, and crime: Social causation, social selection, or both? *Criminology, 37*, 479–514.

Wright, B. R. E., Caspi, A., Moffitt, T. E., and Silva, P. A. (forthcoming). The effects of social ties on crime vary by criminal propensity: A life-course model of interdependence. *Criminology.*

Zahn-Waxler, C. (1993). Warriors and worries: Gender and psychopathology. *Development and Psychopathology, 5*, 79–89.

Zahn-Waxler, C., Cole, P. M., and Barrett, K. C. (1991). Guilt and empathy: Sex differences and implications for the development of depression. In J. Garber and K. A. Dodge (eds.), *The development of emotion regulation and dysregulation* (pp. 243–272). New York: Cambridge University Press.

Zebrowitz, L. A., Andreoletti, C., Collins, M., Lee, S. H., and Blumenthal, J. (1998). Bright, bad, babyfaced boys: Appearance stereotypes do not always yield self-fulfilling prophecy effects. *Journal of Personality and Social Psychology, 75*, 1,300–20.

Zoccolillo, M. (1992). Co-occurrence of conduct disorder and its adult outcomes with depressive and anxiety disorders: A review. *Journal of the American Academy of Child and Adolescent Psychiatry, 31*, 547–56.

Zoccolillo, M. (1993). Gender and the development of conduct disorder. *Development and Psychopathology, 5*, 65–78.

Zoccolillo, M., Tremblay, R., and Vitaro, F. (1996). DSM-III-R and DSM-III criteria for conduct disorder in preadolescent girls: Specific but insensitive. *Journal of the American Academy of Child and Adolescent Psychiatry, 35*, 461–9.

Zuroff, D. C. (1986). Was Gordon Allport a trait theorist? *Journal of Personality and Social Psychology, 51*, 993–1,000.

Index